GENDER DYSPHORIA

GENDER DYSPHORIA
A Therapeutic Model for Working with Children, Adolescents and Young Adults

Susan Evans and Marcus Evans

First published in 2021 by
Phoenix Publishing House Ltd
62 Bucknell Road
Bicester
Oxfordshire OX26 2DS

Copyright © 2021 by Susan Evans and Marcus Evans

The rights of Susan Evans and Marcus Evans to be identified as the authors of this work have been asserted in accordance with §§ 77 and 78 of the Copyright Design and Patents Act 1988.

All rights reserved. No part of this publication may be reproduced, stored in a retrieval system, or transmitted, in any form or by any means, electronic, mechanical, photocopying, recording, or otherwise, without the prior written permission of the publisher.

British Library Cataloguing in Publication Data

A C.I.P. for this book is available from the British Library

ISBN-13: 978-1-912691-78-4

Typeset by Medlar Publishing Solutions Pvt Ltd, India

www.firingthemind.com

*For Laurie, Oliver
and our families,
with love*

Contents

Acknowledgements ix
About the authors xi
Preface *by David Bell* xiii
Foreword *by Stephen B. Levine* xvii

Part I
The social context

1. Why have we written this book? 3

2. The societal, cultural, and political trends and their effects on the clinical environment 13

3. Detransitioners 39

Part II
Development and gender dysphoria

4. Early development in the context of the family 61

5. Separation–individuation and fixed states of mind	77
6. Adolescence	97
7. Excitement as a psychic defence against loss	117

Part III
Gender dysphoria and comorbidity

8. The link between suicidal ideation and gender dysphoria	135
9. Patients with emotionally unstable personality disorder and gender dysphoria in mental health settings	151
10. Comorbid mental health conditions and gender dysphoria	169

Part IV
Psychoanalytic theory, assessment, and technical challenges in therapeutic engagement

11. Psychoanalytic understanding of gender dysphoria	189
12. Assessment and challenges of therapeutic engagement	211
Afterword	235

Addendum

Useful psychoanalytic and clinical terms used in the book	239
References	243
Index	251

Acknowledgements

Firstly, we would like to thank our patients who share their thoughts and feelings and from whom we have learned so much. We are also grateful to those who publicly share their unique experiences of gender dysphoria.

We would also like to thank therapists and colleagues who share their experiences of working in this field, which contribute to the much-needed development of a body of understanding and knowledge.

We are grateful to the following people who have generously given their time and expertise to the development of this book: Annie Pesskin, Ian Williamson, Richard Stephens, Margot Waddell, Frances Grier, and Ema Syrulnik, as well as all our colleagues at the Society for Evidence-Based Gender Medicine.

We are grateful to Kate Pearce at Phoenix for offering to publish this book.

About the authors

Susan Evans is a psychoanalytic psychotherapist. She worked for nearly forty years in a variety of mental health services in the NHS, including the national gender identity service for children. She now has a private practice in South East London. She is a member of the British Psychotherapy Foundation, the London Psychoanalytic Psychotherapy Service, and is registered with the British Psychoanalytic Council.

Marcus Evans is a psychoanalyst with the British Psychoanalytical Society. He worked in mental health services and as an adult psychotherapist in the NHS for forty years. For several years he was clinical lead of the Adult and Adolescent Departments at the Tavistock and Portman NHS Foundation Trust. He was also one of the founding members of the Fitzjohn's Service for the treatment of patients with severe and enduring mental health conditions and/or personality disorder. He is the author of *Making Room for Madness in Mental Health* and *Psychoanalytic Thinking in Mental Health Settings*.

Preface

I am writing this preface just a few weeks after the result of a judicial review which addressed the legality of the prescribing of so-called "puberty blocking" drugs for children and adolescents. The judgement found in favour of the complainants against the Tavistock and Portman NHS Foundation Trust and University College Hospital, that children are highly unlikely to be able to give informed consent to puberty blocking drugs for the treatment of gender dysphoria. The judgement was, necessarily, narrow in its remit but its broader consequences are very considerable. Reading the judgement, even as someone who has been deeply involved in this issue for some years, still has the effects of leaving me shocked as to how a "treatment" that has no evidence, for which no reasonable consent can be given by children (because of their age, and because of the lack of any evidence on which such consent might reasonably be given), and which has such damaging consequences, could possibly have been continued for so long and could have had such success in terms of professional and institutional capture.

James Kirkup, in an article titled "Is Britain FINALLY coming to its senses over transgender madness", in the *Mail on Sunday*, March 3, 2019, wrote:

> During a Westminster career which began as a junior Commons researcher 25 years ago, I have never encountered a movement that has spread so swiftly and successfully, and has so fiercely rejected any challenge to its orthodoxy ... The transgender movement has advanced through Britain's institutions with extraordinary speed. The only thing more extraordinary than the rapid spread of this new orthodoxy is how little scrutiny it has faced and the aggressive intolerance directed towards those who question it.

How this near hegemony was achieved is an extraordinary story and one that will occupy us for a long time.

This book, written before the result of the judicial review was known, is by two professionals who have stood firm against the attempt to silence all debate that has so characterised this area. Susan Evans as long ago as 2005 raised very serious concerns as regards treatment carried out by the Tavistock's Gender Identity Development Service (GIDS). In 2018, a large number of staff working on GIDS sought me out, in my role as staff representative on the council of governors of the Trust. They did so to raise very serious ethical and clinical concerns about the service. On this basis I prepared a report in order to bring these concerns to the urgent attention of the Trust. These concerns included lack of appropriate consent of patients and families, intimidation of staff, inappropriate involvement in the service of highly politicised lobbying organisations, ignoring the concerns of parents, and lack of support for young people who were unable for various reasons (most particularly internalised homophobia) to accept that they were attracted to the same sex (this being misunderstood as being "trans"). All of these problems with the service were bound up with one central issue—the lack of an appropriate clinical stance (the GID service had adopted affirmation instead of neutrality). The Trust dealt with this report by attempting to deny its significance and undermine those who had raised the concerns. This led to the resignation of Marcus Evans from the council of governors, a principled move.

These events need to be set in context. Over the last ten years or so we have witnessed the exponential increase in the number of children and adolescents who present to services with gender dysphoria, but we have very little understanding of the factors that underlie this. Even so, I believe we can say with a considerable degree of confidence that this must result from a peculiar conjunction of an internal propensity and a cultural transformation. We saw something similar many years ago with the sudden rapid increase in individuals suffering from "false memory syndrome".

In the 1980s a girl who expressed a deep loathing of being female, who wore male clothes and cut her hair like a boy, might have been thought a bit odd. If her parents and local community were reasonably liberal, she might have been thought of as a tomboy. Many such girls would later come to recognise themselves as lesbian, some continuing to look more masculine, others not. Yet others would emerge from this phase in their development and become more conventional heterosexual women. But no one would have thought of such a girl as "*really* a boy". Yet, if that same girl were born thirty years later and exhibited similar behaviour in today's world, she would be in danger of being immediately "affirmed" as a man, going on to take opposite-sex hormones and subject herself to major surgery such as mastectomy, removal of sexual organs, and fashioning of an artificial penis.

This book makes a very substantial contribution to our understanding of gender dysphoria. Although over the last few years there have been a number of excellent academic papers, articles, and some books on this subject, this book is unique in bringing a wide and deep understanding to the phenomenon of gender dysphoria married to a psychoanalytic clinical model of work. As well as providing a general account of the phenomenon of gender dysphoria, the authors take us right into the intimacy of the clinical situation. Here they show how an appropriate clinical attitude (one informed by psychoanalytic understanding) can provide a context for accessing and understanding the complex inner worlds of these young people. This attitude is neither affirmation nor opposition but a kind of deeply engaged neutrality that provides the basis for real thoughtful engagement. I am reminded of a patient of mine whose friend asked what it was like being in analysis. "Well," he responded, "it is like having someone on your side.... But *not* siding with you … that is an entirely different matter." It is this distinction, crucial to the relationship between a mental health worker (be they therapist, nurse, or doctor) that has been so catastrophically dispensed with in most clinical services that deal with young people with these problems. It is of course a great sadness to me that the Tavistock, renowned for the depth of its psychoanalytic engagement both at the level of clinical work and in thinking about broader cultural considerations, has fallen hostage to this "unthinking", causing damage to children and to the reputation of the Trust.

Trying to think through these events at the same time as being caught up in them is no easy task, and this book, fruit of this long labour, is exemplary in its thoroughness. It will provide a rich resource for those working with individuals who express their human suffering through a disturbance in the relation between their mind and their sexual bodies. And, because the authors manage to discuss this complex matter in ways that will be understandable to the non-expert, without compromising or simplifying, it will be of considerable interest to those who, whilst not directly involved in working with people suffering gender dysphoria, seek to understand it in depth.

David Bell, consultant psychiatrist and past president of the British Psychoanalytical Society

Foreword

A new socio-psychological category of gender identity has been firmly established over the last forty years in most cultures. Trans identity, previously an entirely hidden phenomenon, began to evolve in 1948 when Harry Benjamin published a book about his hormonal feminisation of male adults. Five years later, Christine Jorgensen made headlines all over the world when it became known that this American soldier had his genitals removed in Denmark and returned to the United States as a woman. For the next three decades, men and women who wanted to change "sex" were referred to as transsexuals.

Today, transgender communities are far more diverse in their age at presentation, natal sexes, and their aspirations. Cross-gender-identified young people, who used to be known as tomboys and sissies, are being understood in a new way. There has been an explosive increase in the number of never previously recognised as gender-atypical adolescents who identify as trans. An estimated 1–2% of adolescents and adults have modified their bodies with hormones and surgery or are considering it. Some aspire only to use hormones, others want to define their gender differently by combining masculine and feminine attributes in unique ways, still others reject gender categories entirely, and finally there are those who are uncertain about their current and future gender identities. Professionals now separate those who aspire to live in the opposite gender—the gender binary population—from the increasingly prevalent group who want something else—the gender non-binary population. Not only has society shifted, the forms of expression of gender incongruence have as well.

Mental health organisations' views of trans phenomena have evolved from the 1983 *DSM* conception of transsexualism as a psychopathology to current assertions by psychiatric and psychological organisations that no form of gender identity represents an inherent psychological abnormality. Despite this, the American Psychiatric Association's *DSM-5* provides a psychiatric diagnosis of gender dysphoria for those who are distressed by the incongruence of body and gender identity. This within-house contradiction results from the fact that specific organisational policies arise from small psychiatric committees; the same phenomena occur within psychological, paediatric, and endocrine societies. These institutional policies have alarmed family members who consider their offspring's, spouse's, or parent's self-definition as trans to be an indication for psychiatric care rather than for affirmation and transition. They and their clinicians look to science. Many clinicians, informed by institutional policies, assume that science has already established the best approach. They may be surprised to learn that while affirmation, transition, hormones, and surgery have been widely accepted, a definition's scientific basis is uncertain. Hundreds of cross-sectional studies have affirmed the problematic mental health and social patterns at all stages of transition, yet affirmation clinics continue to increase in number. While recent publications acknowledge the uncertain long-term outcomes for young people, adolescents, and adults who have been affirmed, these authors consistently find positive outcomes despite many acknowledged methodological limitations (Branstrom & Pachankis, 2019; Costa et al., 2015). Ironically, the day after writing this last sentence, the *American Journal of Psychiatry* published a reanalysis of the data in Branstrom and Pachankis (2019) after receiving numerous letters to the editor. The authors' major conclusion that gender-confirming surgery improves mental health was retracted (Kalin, 2020).

Clinicians might wonder why after more than a half a century of trans care, the internationally organised field has never agreed upon how to comprehensively assess psychological, social, and medical outcomes. Three specific questions have remained unanswered:

1. How long after an intervention should such an assessment be done?
2. What outcome measures should be used?
3. What constitutes an appropriate control group?

The lack of scientific certainty has enabled other factors to shape the direction of trans care and cultural responses to it.

Positions in the culture war

Modern societies are embroiled in a culture war about this topic. While this battle ebbs and flows with competing news in the media, the dominance of the change-the-body approach is apparent. Transgender phenomena readily elicit intense feelings. Such passion, which is antithetical to objective scientific appraisal, derives from eight overlapping humanistic, clinical, and scientific sources. Their confluence makes it difficult to judge their relative contributions to how individuals or institutions regard trans health care.

1. Fascination with sex change. The intriguing question, "Can 'sex' be changed?" has long been explored in the arts, where men and women have for centuries been presented as the opposite sex in humour, drama, dance, opera, and popular music. Today, it is better understood that in a basic biological sense, sex cannot be changed, but gender presentation can, with or without medical assistance.
2. Political sensibilities. The Right may consider transgenderism morally wrong and dangerous to societal health, and approach studies and clinical services with scepticism. The Left may consider transgenderism the courageous pursuit of self-expression, a civil right, and another praiseworthy social movement to eliminate discrimination, and approach studies and clinical services through a positive lens.
3. Religious sensibilities. They derive from theological assumptions and may resemble either political position. In the United States, vocal religious institutions tend to lean to the political Right.

4. Orientation sensibilities. Membership in the heteronormative or sexual minority communities may influence unease with, or endorsement of, transgender phenomena.
5. Intuitive sensibilities. When people are neither religious nor political, they may have a "gut instinct" that one should be supportive or wary of trans phenomena. Such sensibilities are best reflected through age; younger and older people have different life experiences with which to be intuitive.
6. Personal clinical experience. The writing group of the 7th edition of the *Standards of Care for the Health of Transsexual, Transgender, and Gender Nonconforming People*, by the World Professional Association for Transgender Health (WPATH), downgraded the importance of a comprehensive assessment of psychiatric comorbidities in determining the next step (Coleman et al., 2011). Adult and older adolescents were assumed to know best what should be done, despite their frequent psychiatric comorbidities. This policy diminished the frequency of unpleasant clinical experiences between patients who immediately wanted a transitional service and clinicians, mindful of the ethical guideline of Above All, Do No Harm, who thought it prudent to thoroughly investigate the situation. Depending on patients' attitudes towards these clinicians and the clinicians' knowledge of their patients' outcomes, clinicians may develop a positive or negative attitude.
7. Clinical reports from innovators. Outcome studies of transgender treatments typically consist of retrospective case series without control groups. Encouraged by these pioneering clinicians, others began providing care and formed national and international specialty groups to report on their experiences. Over time, groups that initially existed to share knowledge about how to help these individuals evolved into advocates for their specialty-specific therapy, teaching newer professionals how to care for patients. Once clinicians facilitate transition, they tend to believe they are facilitating happy, successful, productive lives.
8. Scientific studies. Groups of studies demonstrate particular patterns that individual studies do not. The priority of scientific data is assumed to be dominant but at times is ignored. For example, high desistance rates in trans young people have been demonstrated in all

eleven of eleven studies, but a committee of paediatricians created a policy of supporting transition of grade school [UK years 9 to 12] young people (Cantor, 2020). The forces that shape the interpretation of studies and that create policies need to be better understood.

Scientific foundation of medical interventions for transgendered individuals

The principles of evidence-based medicine classify uncontrolled case series and expert opinion as the least trustworthy on its hierarchy of validity. There are many questions in every field that have not been answered by respected scientific processes. The new commitment to quickly providing social affirmation and hormones derives from recipients' observed happiness and hopefulness about the future. A nagging ethical question remains. Is short-term patient happiness a sufficient justification for affirmation given data-based concerns for long-term outcomes? Specifically, do transitional services enable patients to have better social, psychological, economic, vocational, and physical health outcomes? The intensity of ethical concern is greater the younger the patient. Even though to date, the data are not impressively positive, transitional therapies are increasing. There are no international coordinated plans to create a better means of answering the questions.

Science versus advocacy

There are fundamental differences between clinical science and advocacy. Science represents a commitment to ask questions that will be answered with predetermined parameters of measurements to generate objective data. Methods can and should vary in order to establish a fact. Its processes benefit from doubt, scepticism, and the critical appraisal both prior to and after publication. Findings require replication, refinement of next questions, and improvements in methods of measurement. Despite the fact that certainty is rarely achieved in clinical science, such studies ideally precede advocacy.

In contrast, advocacy begins with a social goal in mind. Mental health professionals are ethically called upon to advocate. For instance, we try to destigmatise alcohol-use disorder by emphasising it is a chronic brain-based disease of addiction, or advocate for more funding to help those with serious mental illness. All forms of advocacy marshal facts to advance a goal. Advocacy ignores evidence to the contrary. It does not welcome scepticism; it tends to be certain that the goal is for a greater good. Neither advocacy nor science is free of political influences. While all of medical and behavioural science is philosophically seeking the truth, its various stakeholders weigh evidence differently.

Evidence of continuing maladjustment

Numerous cross-sectional studies have demonstrated that the mental health, physical health, and educational, vocational, social, and economic well-being of trans populations are problematic compared to general populations (Dhejne et al., 2016). The transgendered are commonly described as a vulnerable marginalised group with dramatic health disparities who contend with significant barriers to accessing health care (Ard & Keuroghlian, 2018). Studies in various countries have found elevated prevalence of suicidal ideation, depression, anxiety, substance abuse, eating disorders, domestic violence, and suicide. There have been no consistent distinctions established between trans men, trans women, and the gender non-binary groups. A 2011 national registry study of every Swedish person who had surgery over a thirty-year period documented increased death rates, cancer and cardiovascular disease incidence, criminality, suicide attempts, and completed suicide compared with age-matched controls of both sexes (Dhejne et al., 2011). The shortened life expectancy and high incidence of suicide was demonstrated in Denmark in a thirty-year study (Simonsen et al., 2016) and in a subsequent review of Sweden's experience (Swedish National Board, 2020). Worldwide, the incidence of AIDS among economically poor trans women is dramatically higher than in the general population.

Affirmative treatments have been implemented by assuming that these indications of vulnerability are largely explained by societal prejudice, minority stress, and trans communities' distrust of health professionals. Affirming clinicians hope that as the world is becoming friendlier to trans individuals, the suffering of this cohort will abate.

They prefer to view a trans identity at any age as the unfolding of the true, never-changing self. Two hypotheses are rarely mentioned:

1. A trans identity represents a symptom of an underlying developmental problematic process
2. A trans identity, however established, creates a new worrisome symptomatic relationship to the self, to others, and to the tasks of development.

These hypotheses converge to suggest that the genesis of a trans identity lies within the person but that the actual external obstacles to successful adaptation derive from consequences of the decision to transition. The closest that advocates come to this idea is their notion that trans phenomena are caused by biological embryonic processes, which is an idea still in search of convincing evidence.

Gender dysphoria: a therapeutic model for working with children and young people

This book is a most welcome addition to the professional culture debate about the treatment of trans youth. It provides a powerful argument, particularly for multinational policy debate on treatment for this problem. It suggests scepticism about the clinical and social wisdom of swift hormonal and interpersonal support for young people and adolescents who want to inhabit the gender of the opposite sex. The authors provide guidance for therapists who think it is prudent and ethical to investigate the conscious, socially hidden, and unconscious reasons for patients who repudiate their natal sex. They see a trans identity as a solution and are asking others to consider what problem is being solved by this radical redefinition of the self. They are incisively aware of difficulties that mental health professionals face to suggest a prolonged exploratory process to investigate this significant question. In today's environment, clinicians (or patient, parent, sibling) who respond with alarm about a trans identity are considered to be transphobic. This sounds like a bad thing to be. But a close reading of these chapters will illustrate that such alarm, rather than being deplorable, is reasonable.

Clinicians are permitted to be concerned with the long-term outcomes of these individuals and their families. Trans gender identities have been divorced from the characteristics of the numerous other aspects of identity that are well known to evolve (Levine, 2020). These identities are portrayed as a special case requiring clinical expertise not found among well-trained, experienced, traditional mental health professionals such as the authors. They require professionals with certain ideological beliefs, about which scepticism is not appreciated. Psychological development and its intrapsychic consequences have not changed in the last twenty years, but how these are conceptualised and dealt with has. Today, interfering with the multiple facets of biological, social, psychological, and sexual development with puberty-blocking hormones, cross-sex hormones, and surgery of adolescents is justified by the principle of respect for patient autonomy. These interventions are occurring even when by age, maturation, psychiatric symptomatology, and past egregious disadvantages, patients and their families may be unable to seriously consider the risks being undertaken.

Trans community advocates have a compelling argument. Prior to 1973, society and its agent, the mental health profession, viewed male and female homosexual persons as mentally ill, much to their detriment. It took science to end this view. Advocates argue that sceptical people are merely repeating what society used to promulgate about homosexual persons. The advocates' goal is to similarly make the world safe for trans individuals whether they are binary or non-binary individuals. They see delaying physical interventions for psychotherapy as withholding treatment that has already been proven to be highly effective in relieving the pain of gender dysphoria. In my experience, most clinicians are in favour of civil rights and full opportunities for trans persons despite their alarm over early hormonal interventions.

I suggest keeping ten questions in mind when reading about this psychotherapeutic approach

1. Can one be born into the wrong sex? This is a question of aetiology, which at this point in the history of psychiatry is a bit academic as it is well known that most mental and behavioural phenomena are created by biology, individual psychology, interpersonal relationships, and culture.

2. Is gender identity immutable? A related question is: Is the private understanding and labelling of the self along the masculine–feminine continuum subject to lifelong private evolution? What are we to think when we listen to a professional who asserts that a preschool young person who prefers to play as a member of the opposite sex knows his or her future identity?
3. Are gender identity and orientation separate phenomena that do not influence one another? While trans ideology proclaims that they are, it is readily apparent that there are frequent cross-gender manifestations within sexual minority communities.
4. Where does paraphilia come into the trans clinical picture? Both orientation and gender identity play a role in the shaping of the third component of sexual identity, intention, about which most researchers and clinicians are silent. Intention is how the person imagines or behaves with a sexual partner; the conventional pattern is peaceable mutuality; the stylised and sometimes obligate pattern in order to be aroused is a paraphilic pattern. Paraphilic phantasies and behaviours, particularly sadomasochistic ones, are integral to the adolescent developmental processes of many individuals of any orientation or gender identity. Paraphilic sexuality is relevant because it is a challenge to long-term viability of coupledom, which is one of the adult challenges of the transgendered (Levine, 2016).
5. Is every gender identity a normal variation of gender identity, as trans ideology asserts? If one is not permitted to think of these identities as maladaptive, that is, predisposing to adverse outcomes, another explanation must be found for the presence of more anxiety and mood disorders, substance abuse, suicidal ideation, suicide attempts and completed suicide, eating disorders, other forms of self-abuse, and premature death among trans populations. Trans communities are referred to as vulnerable and marginalised.
6. Does affirmation prevent suicide? The completed suicide rate and the presence of suicidal ideation are higher among trans populations than other sexual minority groups and conventional people. How much so varies from study to study (McNeil, Ellis, & Eccles, 2017). The vast majority of trans people do not kill themselves, although the majority may at times consider it. When a clinician asks parents, "Would you rather have a living daughter than a dead son?" they are not speaking from a knowledge base. In applying the medical ethical

principle of honesty, scientific knowledge—not social or political ideology—is the correct basis of what clinicians share with patients and their families.

7. What have randomised, prospective, controlled studies shown about the efficacy of puberty-blocking hormones for preteens and cross-sex hormones for teenagers or adults? The usual explanation for their absence is that it would be unethical to withhold effective treatment from these suffering individuals who believe interventions will help them. Sophisticated studies are expensive, take years to accomplish, involve a team of professionals, and require a widely perceived relevance and necessity.

8. What is known about the outcome of psychotherapies for trans-identified young people and adolescents? This book's erudite chapters about highly defensive intrapsychic development provide evidence that some psychotherapies can enable some patients to decide to desist from a trans identity. Those of us who have faith in the benefit of such work regardless of the patients' ultimate decisions about their gender expressions do not have compelling data to support our faith. We occupy the same posture of faith as those who support rapid hormonal intervention as to what the appropriate first step should be.

9. Does the psychiatric ideology of the therapist matter in terms of short-term outcome? One must not confuse formal psychoanalysis with what is described here. The authors treat us to descriptions of how they conceptualised the defensive mind and how they have spoken to patients to free them up to be more honest and articulate about what they have thought, felt, and desired. Studies have indicated that therapist ideology is less important in creating a positive short-term outcome than the quality of connection to the patient. Warmth, caring, absence of hostility, and grasp of what the patient is feeling and saying seem to predispose to better outcomes. Insight is vital (Hogland, 2018). The authors' ideology is helpful. It will enable some therapists to refocus their work and deal with their counter-transference more productively. It will help parents to grasp what may be going on in their young person's sessions. The case histories may awaken some patients' memories and give them hope that they can be more equipped to take on their future.

10. Is there a defined standard that must be met before transition, hormones, or surgery is recommended? The value of controlled research is the careful definition of inclusion and exclusion criteria. Clinical work is more subjective and requires trust in the clinicians' judgements about mental health. Given what the authors and others have noted about internet guidance for how to handle the evaluation, we should remain somewhat uncertain about our judgements.

Welcome to the professional aspects of the larger societal culture wars.

Stephen B. Levine, MD, clinical professor of psychiatry at Case Western Reserve University School of Medicine

Part I

The social context

In the first two chapters of this book, we outline our rationale for writing the book before going on to describe the social and political environment surrounding the treatment of gender dysphoria. In Chapter 3 we discuss individuals (detransitioners/desisters) who have been on a treatment path towards transition but who then come to regret their treatment. Detransitioners often express anger and disappointment at the lack of thorough assessment and psychological exploration they received from clinical services prior to their transition.

ONE

Why have we written this book?

Between 2003 and 2007 Susan Evans worked at the Gender Identity Development Service for children at the Tavistock Clinic. During her time there she became concerned about some of the children being referred too quickly for hormone treatments, but when attempting to discuss this with the team, found there was a reluctance to examine things fully. After this she blew the whistle claiming there were ongoing child safeguarding issues. This led to the medical director carrying out an inquiry in 2005–06 and the report made recommendations, amongst other things, that the service should carry out more rigorous investigation and research in the area. Nothing really changed and Susan resigned from the clinic but continued to work elsewhere in the Tavistock Trust.

In the autumn of 2018 Marcus Evans became a governor on the board at the Tavistock Trust. He was aware of two issues that Dr David Bell had been attempting to address before ending his term as a staff governor. The first was a letter from a group of concerned parents regarding the quality of the treatment their children had received at the Gender Identity Clinic. The second was a report authored by David Bell following contact from ten staff who worked in the gender clinic for children.

They had blown the whistle over their concerns for clinical standards and child safeguarding in the GIDS. Marcus quickly became aware there was an attempt to discredit the parents and Dr Bell. The Tavistock board had also asked the medical director of the trust to report on the service.

By February 2019 Marcus had resigned after much intensive discussion with the board members, because he did not believe the Trust intended to take seriously the concerns raised about this controversial treatment approach for children. Several things followed, one of which was an event named "First Do No Harm: the ethics of transgender healthcare" run by Standing for Women and hosted by Dr Lord Lewis Moonie at the House of Lords. Marcus gave a paper there together with Professor Richard Byng, Stephanie Davies-Arai, the Kelsey Coalition, and Dr Michael K. Laidlaw.

Susan was in the audience and after the event, as is often the case, several of the participants reconvened to the local hostelry! Discussions took place on how to tackle the apparent lack of interest (and perhaps lack of courage) from the NHS in the UK to ensure that clinical safeguarding and ethical practice were occurring in the area of gender medicine. It seemed there was a more general reluctance for professionals to publicly speak out on this matter, which was understandable in the attendant political and social environment. Journalists said they had asked many professionals for interviews, but said they couldn't find anybody to go on the record, perhaps fearing for their future careers and any personal backlash. At first we felt the same way, fearful for what we might invite if we persisted. We began to be contacted by many parents, who were extremely thankful and relieved that finally someone had spoken out about this treatment model. It was harrowing to hear some of the upsetting stories from them together with some ex-patients (detransitioners).

After that House of Lords meeting, a group of parents, researchers, doctors, and other clinicians agreed that if the NHS continued to adhere to its clinical stance and was refusing to engage in a more serious evidential review of its practices (despite the serious concerns raised by some of its own staff), then the only route left was the law, because the evidence for this experimental treatment needed to be examined by independent sets of eyes and minds. We all agreed that children, on occasion as young as ten years old, could not adequately understand the risks involved and consent to a treatment which would so affect their future adult lives.

One of the parents was Mrs A, a mother who had a fifteen-year-old daughter who had a diagnosis of autism, and had decided that she was transgender. Her daughter was on the waiting list for the Gender Identity Development Service at the Tavistock and after hearing about Dr Bell's report, Mrs and Mr A were deeply worried that their daughter, due to her age, would be started on hormone treatments without a satisfactory opportunity for thorough assessment and psychological treatments.

Following consultation with a legal team, who believed there were sufficient grounds to represent them, Mrs A and Susan agreed together they should request a judicial review on whether children can indeed give informed consent to this experimental treatment. In October 2019 they applied to the courts for a judicial review and this was accepted. They set about finding expert witnesses in endocrinology, autism, psychiatry, psychology, paediatric neurology, clinical research, and standards of practice, at first, somewhat of a challenge in the UK. Eventually experts were found throughout the world, who generously agreed to contribute to the case, because they all felt strongly about the ethics and safety of this medicalised approach.

In January 2020 the evidence was submitted at the Royal Courts of Justice, London for the judicial review. Then in February 2020 Keira Bell, a twenty-two-year-old woman who had been a patient at the GIDS and subsequently detransitioned, agreed to be a claimant in the case with Mrs A, so Susan stepped aside. Keira believed that at the age of sixteen, her comorbid difficulties had not been sufficiently assessed or psychologically treated before she was started on hormone blockers and cross-sex hormone treatments. She wanted to prevent other children from being mistakenly treated with medication too early in their young lives.

In October 2020 the judicial review took place with three judges at the High Court. On Tuesday December 2 they ruled that a child under sixteen may only consent to the use of medication intended to suppress puberty where he or she is competent to understand the nature of the treatment. The outcome of this is that children under the age of sixteen should only be given hormone blockers after a "best interest" order was made by the court, and this would be granted if the application for the child met the criteria necessary to demonstrate he or she could give an informed consent.

Following this judgement, NHS England immediately changed the NHS website details and said that the GIDS should not begin any more children on hormone treatments without application to the court. They also asked for all the children under sixteen who were currently on hormone treatments to be reviewed as well as undereighteens if there were any aspects of their case where informed consent might have been affected in some way.

Over recent years, there has been an explosion in the numbers of children, adolescents, and young adults presenting as patients in gender clinics who diagnose themselves as gender dysphoric or trans. Many of the gender clinics have adopted the "affirmation model" for care, which is a model that encourages professionals to support the person in their view of themselves and to advocate for them on their path to "transition". (N.B. In the interest of allowing a more fluent text we have used the term "transition" throughout the book—this will variously encompass aspects along a pathway of escalating social and clinical interventions that might culminate in the provision of a lifelong course of cross-sex hormones, sex organ surgeries, mastectomies or breast implants, and other procedures to approximate the appearance of the desired sex, or increasingly, requests to create a non-binary presentation with the individualised mix of feminine and masculine.) Despite this exponential rise in the numbers of gender dysphoric children, there does not appear to be much written about any model for the psychological understanding and treatment of their condition.

Throughout the process of the judicial review, we were acutely aware that the challenge to current medical practices would result in children, their families, and clinical services needing alternative models of treatment. We decided to write a book about this clinical area in the hope that services will develop more appropriate psychological assessments and treatments for this group of children, adolescents, and young adults. We believe a model, such as we provide, is important and will help both professionals and patients.

People with gender dysphoria usually have a preoccupation with their physical body and a wish for concrete physical solutions to their psychological distress. Our aim is to offer professionals working with gender-questioning people a way of trying to think with, and work theoretically with, their patients. Our model is underpinned by a psychoanalytic framework which can deepen empathy and understanding of disturbed states of mind and might be helpful in explaining how defences can be enlisted unconsciously in order to avoid overwhelming psychic pain. Freud described the unconscious as the part of the mind that contains hidden conflicts, impulses, desires, and fantasies (see p. 240 for more information on the unconscious).

Our model

The model is neither "pro" nor "anti" transition. We understand that to transition is, for some adults, the best way to lead their lives and present to the world. Instead, this model concentrates on the individual concerned, to explore and understand what drives and motivates them.

If people decide to transition it is still a challenging world they will face, both internally and externally, where contradictory experiences and emotions about their trans identity are likely to persist throughout their lifespan. Therefore, this model could also be of use for adults as it may be helpful to explore their defences and internal psychic conflicts in order to ameliorate the inevitable emotional hurdles they are asking themselves to face as a trans-identified person. As individuals, we all wrangle and make compromises in our lives. Some of these compromises inevitably result in losses; however, individuals can feel such decisions have provided them with a resolution to the challenges and conflicts that life and relationships might present.

Our hypothesis is that the individual who feels their body or sex is wrong is likely to be defending against psychological traumas from the past: traumas which form part of their psychic structure in the present. It is important to state here that when we use the word trauma, this can refer both to traumas which are apparent in the external world, such as physical abuse and early childhood separation or loss, and to those that are less visible but are experienced internally by the individual as traumatic, such as a developing awareness of limitations or an unfavourable comparison with a sibling.

There is currently much debate around the changing nature of the groups of young people who present with gender dysphoria and we wish to avoid presenting a simplistic causal model of these individuals. One aspect of the discussion is how to categorise and differentiate between a more "traditional" presentation in early childhood and "rapid-onset gender dysphoria" (ROGD) in adolescents who previously did not indicate signs of distress or discomfort with themselves. However, there is no dependable evidence, yet, which can be relied upon and more research into the trends is required. While there are commonalities and shared aspects in presentation, it is important to note that each and every presentation of gender dysphoria is unique, and the individual's personality and choices are driven by many interlocking factors, including genetic inheritance, environmental factors, family dynamics, and peer and social influences.

It is therefore important to keep an open mind about underlying causes and resist simplistic ideas about cause and effect. The model we present reflects this unique nature. Clarification of these conditions might emerge in time, but it is our experience that while psychiatry and psychology will diagnose and describe signs and symptoms at a given moment in a person's life with considerable accuracy, people's mental states and clinical presentations fluctuate. Predictions of prognosis and outcomes based on psychiatric diagnosis in childhood and adolescence are not reliable as the young person will change as they mature. We hold that it is imperative to keep the developmental path open into adulthood and that no long-term social or medical decisions should be made on the basis of a snapshot diagnosis in childhood, even if the presentation appears consistent and persistent.

Individuals can get locked into mental states that aim to defend them against the turbulence caused by physical and psychological development or change. A psychoanalytic model is helpful in understanding these defences and at exploring relationships. Psychoanalytic theory makes much of the experience of the transference and countertransference in the patient/therapist relationship because it helps to access unconscious defences against painful psychic truths (see pp. 207–209 for more information on the transference and countertransference).

There is a risk that by writing this book we open ourselves to accusations of "transphobia". It is probably impossible to avoid as we are attempting to understand unconscious processes and motivations. It is very difficult in the current climate to think about what lies beneath the surface of gender dysphoria and the preoccupation with the physical body and gender identity, without provoking this response. We are committed to the idea that all gender-questioning people should have sufficient opportunity to explore and understand their motives and wish to transition before embarking on any medical interventions which will alter their body's biological development. The therapist should not impose a view of what the ultimate destination should be and what actions the patient should take. In the next chapter we discuss the political environment which forecloses this important psychological exploration.

Language

Words can be felt by some to be weapons and even as violent actions of attack. The words used in psychoanalytic theory are sometimes described as "psychobabble" (perhaps as a way of deflecting from any realities or truth that they might contain?) but our aim in this book is to demystify certain theories which we have found to be particularly relevant in psychodynamic work with our gender dysphoric clients. We hope to explain the concepts without too much jargon, and it might be that parents, teachers, social workers, and other healthcare staff will find some ideas in this book to light their way in this pressured area of work. Language is constantly evolving, as are societal views of what is acceptable at any given time in history. We are particularly aware that any discussions of gender dysphoria and gender identity have areas of linguistic confusion or contention, where it might be easier to focus on or criticise the "correctness" of such terms rather than the meaning behind them. We have observed that words can upset, offend, anger, or be experienced concretely. In discussing this area of work, we have attempted to use terms which seem most appropriate to aid description of the clinical ideas we discuss and have tried to be sensitive but clear in our approach.

Who is this book for?

Primarily, we have written this book for professionals working with gender-questioning children and young people. It is written as an introductory text for those who are interested in developing a psychological approach. We have largely employed theory which we find useful when thinking about our clinical practice and our intention has been to write something accessible. We hope you will find in these chapters an exploration and an explanation of a theoretical model which aims to encourage a serious, multidimensional view of the psychology of gender identity development. Our aim is to encourage a more in-depth, empathetic, and supportive approach to work in this area and encourage adults who encounter any young person with thoughts or feelings of gender confusion to understand this as a symptom to be explored along with other aspects of their life.

What this book is not, is a comprehensive academic review of all of the clinical research done over many years in this area. To date, there is much useful information gathered on the *clinical presentation* of gender dysphoria, but there is no gold standard, randomised control trial to provide an evidence base for best *treatment* models. In 2008, Kenneth Zucker (who had collaborated with Susan Bradley collecting clinical and research data over a period of twenty years) stated that "accordingly the therapist must rely on the 'clinical wisdom' that has accumulated and to utilise the largely untested case formulation conceptual models to inform treatment approaches and decisions". This book is our attempt to utilise our clinical wisdom to present an informed approach to treatment.

Psychodynamic therapists and mental health practitioners who read this book may be helped to process their experience of this work and to understand their gender variant patients better. As a professional environment, it can be fraught at times with anger, sadness, loss, and psychological pressures on all sides. We would like the book to help not only therapists but also other professionals such as health workers, teachers, social workers, counsellors, paediatricians, paediatric psychiatrists, general practitioners, youth workers, charity workers—and perhaps even policymakers.

The problem of defining gender identity work as a "specialism"

In the UK (as elsewhere) at present, there is a growing tendency to refer people on to "specialist gender services" almost as soon as they express any confusion or distress about their biological sex or gender identity. Due to the rapidly rising numbers and various pressures in the system, presenting patients are increasingly likely to be offered the possibility of commencing on life-altering medication and/or surgical treatments, often without a particularly in-depth exploration of their emotional world. Although we know (and have witnessed at first hand), that people in an extremely distressed state of mind are desperate and usually pressuring for some physical action to remove their difficult feelings, we also believe that it is extremely important to explore the environment and circumstances that have led them to this state of mind in the first place. Because as yet so little is known or understood regarding the increase in gender-incongruent patients, it seems precipitous to proceed onto potentially risky and irreversible physical treatments before any of this assessment work has been undertaken. What we do know is that the origins of feeling trans-identified usually develops in the mind of the individual who feels unhappy with, or dislocated from, their natal body. The wish to transition to something/somebody else is symptomatic of them having a mind at odds with the physically sexed body. Many young people presenting as gender dysphoric have complex needs with comorbid problems such as autism, histories of abuse or trauma, social phobias, depression, eating disorders, and other mental health symptoms. Therefore, we are of the view that all aspects of the young person's life deserve a thorough assessment and therapeutic work.

Why a psychoanalytic model of understanding?

The model for psychodynamic and psychoanalytic therapy is that the clinician meets with somebody, without preconceptions or prejudgement, with the aim of learning who the person is and how they feel. The face-to-face work should be about them and their world, and, as much as possible, the political pressures need to be left outside the consulting room. The mindset of the therapist is therefore crucial. The goal of the therapy should be a wish to establish a dialogue with the patient in which underlying anxieties, motivations, beliefs, drives, and conflicts can be explored. Aspects of the patient's internal world and ways of relating emerge in the relationship with the therapist and throw light on the way the patient sees themselves in relation to others; for example, the way they relate to siblings or parental authorities. The setting and structure of the psychodynamic relationship allow these interpersonal dynamics to be examined, thought about, and understood in the therapy. This can allow the individual to develop new ways of thinking about themselves in relation to others as they use the therapeutic relationship to experiment with different aspects of being in relationships. In Chapter 10 we discuss some of the psychoanalytic concepts we have found particularly helpful when considering gender dysphoria. For those who are new to psychoanalytic ideas we have included an addendum of terms referred to throughout the book.

To reiterate, whether or not the person decides to go on to transition, this work is good preparation for their future life. With the case examples provided in this book, things may come across as being more straightforward than they really are; it needs to be made clear that this is a complicated clinical area. There are many confusions and clinical presentations that we do not yet understand. As always in clinical work, some of the best thinking is done in hindsight. In many ways, this book is a study of the ways that all of us, as individuals, try to minimise and sometimes avoid psychic pain. Psychoanalysis has a basic assumption that being involved in life is a painful business and that it helps if the individual can be supported in bearing pain, rather than attempting to eradicate it.

Inevitably, due to the conflicts, pain, and levels of distress that lie behind the gender dysphoric presentation, all parties involved in this work will be subject to forceful emotional states and reactions which can intermittently push thinking and empathy out of the therapeutic encounter. From time to time therapists, patients, and their families may find themselves locked into an impasse in the therapeutic relationship, and at times such as this there is a tendency towards action rather than thought. However, if these negative therapeutic reactions can be weathered, they can often offer an opportunity to deepen the understanding of the forces operating within the psychodynamic relationships.

Any psychological assessment, exploration, or therapy should always be undertaken with an open state of mind. Ideally, the professional needs to aim to create a humane and compassionate atmosphere, sometimes in the face of tremendous pressures, but more importantly there needs to be resilience and an aim to recover from the inevitable ups and downs of the work.

> N.B. We are aware that not all families have a mother and father as parents, but for clarity of purpose, for any discussion of early young person development we have named the primary parent as "mother" or "she" and the young person as "he".
>
> To protect patient confidentiality, the clinical material presented is composite. It is taken from clinical accounts in various settings, but all examples are heavily disguised representations of work in this field.

TWO

The societal, cultural, and political trends and their effects on the clinical environment

> "Truly compassionate, lifesaving care would be to take an individualised approach with each patient and tend fully and as non-ideologically as possible to the mental, health emotional, and physical wellness of the entire human being. Compassionate care would be to help the sufferer comprehend themselves and the root of their distress."
>
> —Helena, 2020

This book will not offer an in-depth socio-political view on the development of transgender culture or the huge increase in the numbers of young people expressing gender incongruence. However, no book on gender dysphoria can ignore the prevailing trends and precipitous clinical changes over the past few decades. It is impossible to ignore the evidence that sociocultural changes have deeply affected the clinical setting and ethical standards in the provision of gender care. The contribution of the worldwide political activism in this area has resulted in highly effective "policy capture" which has had a profound impact. Things have moved quickly and while policies and legislations may change around this issue, the clinical challenges in our opinion remain unchanged.

Gender-questioning youth now frequently appear in various health services, as well as in schools and universities. Many have self-diagnosed as "trans-identified", which is often accompanied by feelings of distress and discomfort, even hatred, towards their body. Current services fall short in the provision of therapeutic care for this patient cohort.

To provide some context regarding our statement of an exponential rise, in 2005 in the UK, there were approximately 100 referrals per year to the only National Health Service Under-18 Gender Clinic. However, in the past five years, this has risen to over 2,500 per annum. The profile of referrals has also undergone a significant transformation: a reversal of the gender ratio from two-thirds male to female to two-thirds female with more females in their teenage years reporting gender-questioning feelings for the first time. The main explanation offered by some of the transgender community for the increase in trans-identified presentations is that people have felt able to "come out". Although this might explain some of the increase, it doesn't explain the exponential rise in gender-questioning young people. In all areas of gender identity services, there is very little understanding of what underlies the changes in numbers and presentation, which is why it is vitally important to examine it from different perspectives.

This is particularly difficult in the current environment, as the necessary debate and discussion is frequently closed down or becomes polarised into "pro-" or "anti-" trans. Individuals interested in examining or researching this area might have new ideas and perhaps develop alternative views to the current affirmative model and research data which WPATH (the World Professional Association for Transgender Health) has utilised as a recommended standard of care. We describe and discuss the affirmative model in more detail later in this chapter. But there are medics, scientists, researchers, and academics, together with journalists, charities, businesses (to name a few) who can recount the challenges and hostility towards any alternative viewpoint. James Kirkup, a journalist, wrote,

> During a Westminster career which began as a junior Commons researcher 25 years ago, I have never encountered a movement that has spread so swiftly and successfully and has so fiercely rejected any challenge to its orthodoxy. The transgender movement has

advanced through Britain's institutions with extraordinary speed. The only thing more extraordinary than the rapid spread of this new orthodoxy is how little scrutiny it has faced, and the aggressive intolerance directed towards those who question it. (2019)

World-renowned and bestselling author J. K. Rowling experienced the difficulty of questioning this orthodoxy when she blogged about her view that the reality of biological sex cannot be denied. She was accused of being transphobic and received extraordinary levels of criticism and verbal abuse, which continues unabated. People and institutions can be prevented from researching or publishing and have received threats of closure or withdrawal of funding. For example, a psychotherapist named James Caspian, who had worked for many years in gender services, was hoping to complete his MA at Bath Spa University by researching trans regret. However, despite this being a subject which has almost no research base, he was not allowed to proceed, because they feared it could attract negative publicity for the university. Also, we have spoken with many professionals in the health, teaching, and social services who confide that due to the hostile environment opposed to enquiry, they self-censor their ideas or views, through fear of the accusation of "transphobia" and the harm it might do to their career and employment.

Progress and learning in any field usually require that the people who work in it continually investigate and challenge the orthodoxy of the moment, which is what has led to so much progress in the medical field. To suddenly find ourselves in a situation where a rapid change has occurred in diagnostic trends of transgender medicine and its recommended experimental treatments, and yet so little of the aetiology is understood, begs the question, "Are we allowed to explore and develop the current treatment models for gender-incongruent individuals or has this become an area of medicine and psychiatry that is untouchable?" For the patients' sake, it should not be. We describe below some of the factors which have powerfully influenced the clinical environment.

The affirmative approach

This is the current clinical approach recommended by most professional bodies in health and education.

One of the problems facing parents and professionals is that the affirmation model is currently promoted almost worldwide in health and social services. It replaced the more conservative and largely less physically harmful model of watchful waiting which had research findings that would strongly suggest most of the cases would eventually desist if left untreated (Steensma et al., 2011). The affirmation model perhaps originally took a valid idea from supportive watchful waiting—to listen to and support young people who expressed gender incongruence without prejudice or judgement—but this came to be interpreted by many involved in this area as a short cut to immediately agreeing (and even colluding) with a young person who expresses any thoughts or doubts in this area.

James Cantor, paediatrician, was critical of the American Academy of Paediatrics' (AAP) policy statement on the issue of affirmation:

> Although almost all clinics and professional associations in the world use what's called the "watchful waiting" approach to helping gender-diverse (GD) young people, the AAP statement instead rejected that consensus, and endorsed gender affirmation as the only acceptable approach. (2017)

The AAP's approach, like that implemented by many clinicians at GIDS, appears to be driven more by political ideology than the clinical needs of presenting young people (Cantor, 2018). Professionals also now seem increasingly propelled to aid the child or young person in pursuing this new identity in a one-dimensional way. This sometimes occurs without the parents' knowledge and the young people are then encouraged along a path of expected social and physical changes, with no, or very little, exploration of the aetiology of the gender dysphoria.

We know this is true because we have spoken with dozens of parents and young people to whom this has happened. It often occurs with a well-intentioned theoretical idea, in this instance "to listen to a person in an accepting, supportive, and non-judgemental way", but the affirmation model becomes a concrete and rigid course of action to "believe and act on what the young person expresses" as if the adults around them have no separate ideas or understanding of what might be affecting the psychology of the person at that particular time in their life.

There have been examples of parents being accused of causing their child's self-harm when they refuse to affirm them in their chosen gender. This simplistic and moralistic approach does little to develop an understanding of the family dynamics or the underlying conflicts within the young person. It can also lead to conflict and splitting between child and other family members when the affirmative therapist appears to side with the child against the parents who are more in favour of a cautious approach towards social or medical transition. It can also place parents against each other or lead to children having "secret" aspects of their lives and identity.

The Memorandum of Understanding on Conversion Therapy (MoU)

In the United Kingdom, we have the *Memorandum of Understanding on Conversion Therapy*, a document that many healthcare providers and other professional associations have signed up to. Its stated aim is to protect the patient from conversion therapy. It says that conversion therapy is an umbrella term for a therapeutic approach, or any model or individual viewpoint that demonstrates an assumption that any one gender identity is inherently preferable to any other and which attempts to bring about a change of gender identity or seeks to suppress an individual's expression of gender identity on that basis. However, this *Memorandum* restricts the clinician's freedom to examine and explore underlying influences in the gender-confused individual. If one reads the document carefully, one can see that there is an underpinning belief that the therapist/clinician/healthcare professional's job is to help the patient discover and come to terms with who they are.

> For people who are unhappy about their sexual orientation or their transgender status, there may be grounds for exploring therapeutic options to help them live more comfortably with it, reduce their distress and reach a greater degree of self-acceptance. (2019)

This *Memorandum* implies there is a fixed category called "transgender" which, like eye colour, is simply a given that need not be thought about or understood. Young people's sexual orientation, gender, and identity are all part of a normal conflictual process that involves an interaction between the body, the mind, and society at large. Sexual attraction and identity are part of a developmental process which can change and fluctuate as the individual goes through different life stages.

In part, this current MoU approach is rooted in the idea that everyone—including young people—has an innate "gender identity", akin to a religious soul, that one may discover and nurture. But as authors William J. Malone, Colin M. Wright, and Julia D. Robertson recently wrote:

> This term commonly is defined to mean the "internal, deeply held" sense of whether one is a man or a woman (or, in the case of children, a boy or a girl), both, or neither. It also has become common to claim that this sense of identity may be reliably articulated by children as young as three years old. While these claims about gender identity did not attract systematic scrutiny at first, they have now become the subject of criticism from a growing number of scientists, philosophers and health workers. Developmental studies show that young children have only a superficial understanding of sex and gender (at best). For instance, up until age 7, many children believe that if a boy puts on a dress, he becomes a girl. This gives us reason to doubt whether a coherent concept of gender identity exists *at all* in young children. To such extent as any such identity may exist, the concept relies on stereotypes that encourage the conflation of gender with sex. (Malone, Wright, & Robertson, 2019)

It is undoubtedly true that therapists should not seek to impose their idea of what is "normal" on a patient who believes he or she is trans. Nor should they engage in any attempt to pressurise the person into changing their mind. However, as in all contexts, the therapist must also resist the temptation to abandon curiosity, or uncritically accept the patient's presentation at face value, and then act as an "affirming" cheerleader for life-changing, irreversible acts of transition. Rather, the goal of exploratory therapy should be to understand the meaning behind a patient's presentation in order to help them develop an understanding of themselves, including the desires and conflicts that drive their identity and choices.

The *Memorandum of Understanding* is one example of the way political agendas have influenced this area of clinical practice. Curiosity and exploration are the central tenets of good mental health practice. As an extreme example, we do not simply accept the anorexic's belief that they are overweight and respect their wish to starve themselves. Instead, we have a duty to try to understand what is driving a belief that does so much damage, while persuading them that they need to eat. If the professional merely "affirmed" their point of view, anorexic patients would die in great numbers. Many anorexics are highly plausible in their arguments that eating will damage them. Their view of themselves is persistent and consistent: "I have to control my food intake and I need to lose weight." We must always listen to our patient's wishes and thoughts, in an attempt to understand their state of mind, but professionals must also be free to think about the underlying meaning of the patient's presentation.

Many clinicians have shared the view that the MoU and affirmation therapy have increased the likelihood that children with ordinary conflicts and questions about their identity and sexuality might be "converted" into a belief that they are "transgender". There is in fact research now emerging that suggests that using affirmation and encouraging a child in social transition means they are in fact more likely to remain gender dysphoric or trans-identifed. This perhaps means that many of the original percentage who might have desisted over time with a supportive, watchful waiting approach could potentially receive unnecessary medicalisation.

The influence of social media

In the past, individuals who might have sought psychiatric or psychological treatments and been diagnosed with, for example, depression or social anxiety disorders, post-traumatic stress disorders, hypochondriasis, or obsessional disorder are now searching for help on the internet where they find trans websites that describe their symptoms. This leads to plenty of "self-diagnosis" often without any professional consultation having taken place. Having found an idea that seems to explain and make sense of their emotional turmoil, especially a sense of not fitting in, such individuals can narrow their research to the trans area exclusively. Many trans websites understandably offer a message of acceptance, inclusivity, and welcome, which can feel very attractive to someone struggling with their relationships or place in the world. Here is an online media community which offers a kind of "one-stop-shop" for reasons a person might feel so at odds with themselves. This leads to a myopic view of the person and their complexity, focusing on one thing only—their self-classification of "trans identity". It is often at this stage that the individual, as well as those around them, can lose sight of the holistic emotional background that has caused the person to feel so distressed or confused at this time in their life. Our concern about this funnelling effect is that the individual narrows the diagnosis of their distress to a single cause—"the wrongly sexed body".

The internet can provide a huge source of reliable information and there are helpful websites offering advice for young people and their families, but it is hard for the novice to know which ones offer a more holistic and evidence-based view. At the current time, most websites for gender-questioning people promote transitioning and some have even been described as providing "online grooming", or appearing cult-like in their message. They advocate for the rights of transgender people, which is important and seems well-intentioned since, of course, people usually need support if they are feeling distressed or disturbed due to their mind/body incongruence. However, the presentation of gender dysphoria and transgender issues is not something which should be viewed simplistically, as there are complications and losses involved which should not be underestimated.

For anybody who expresses gender identity incongruence, there are very few changes, particularly physical ones, that they might make which will not have far-reaching consequences. The physical and chemical treatments used in transgender medicine are mostly irreversible and potentially harmful. The encouragement of young people down this route can be neither sensible nor medically sound. The hormone blockers (GnRH) which are given to children as young as ten years old (sometimes younger), to delay or prevent pubertal development, have been described as "wholly reversible", but the effects on the developing young person are not yet known, mainly due to a lack of any long-term outcome research. What is known is the importance of the effect of the hormonal surge for both physical and mental development in adolescence.

Some transgender websites promote a narrow view of gender conformity and male/female stereotypes, which could lead to the belief that there is only one answer to gender non-conformity. There can be a tendency to ignore the possibility that gender confusion in young people might be connected to their developing sexuality, perhaps with fears about potential homosexuality or a fear of sexual relationships altogether. Transition might then appear to be a solution to this internal conflict about sexual attraction and sexual identity.

The psychological influence of transgender websites is powerful and should not be underestimated for a young person looking to belong somewhere. Some of these websites might be associated with the pull of a potent, and at times seductive, world view; somewhere you can feel more special, where you can have concrete solutions without psychic consequences, which offer only good things and a place to finally belong. They tend to be echo chambers of positivity and do not explore the real and present difficulties of living as a trans-identified person in any society.

The influence of contagious social forces

The internet can spread any message across a worldwide online social network. Young people and young adults are much more involved in social media, often to the ignorance of their less tech-savvy parents. Landing on messages of positivity and acceptance can feel a huge relief for the confused or gender-questioning young person.

Social contagion can have a powerful influence on people's ideas and behaviours and is a well-known and researched psychological phenomenon in mental disorders: mass hysteria, suicide pacts, pro-anorexic websites to name just a few. In her paper "Transgender Children: The Making of a Modern Hysteria" (2019), Lisa Marchiano states, "Social factors that valorize a condition, confer special status on the victim and her family, or link the condition with progressive social movements can create further fertile ground for contagion." Parents of young adults have stated that their children left home for university without any previous doubts or discussion in this area and, within the first term of university, have come out as trans. This could be understood as the first step of independence with the opportunity to come out as trans or as a protest/rebellion against parents, but social influences might also be a consideration. We have observed that some detransitioners or desisters (individuals who have desisted from the belief that they are transgender) will state that becoming trans was like finding a tribe or family to belong to when faced with the huge anxiety of starting at a new school or college, similar to how others will seek out and develop connections in political, sporting, or fashion alliances.

In a pamphlet published in 2019 by Civitas titled "Transgender Children: A Discussion", Stephanie Davies-Arai and Toby Young state:

> We recognise the social contagion factor with other teenage problems such as anorexia, bulimia and self-harm, but adolescents today are growing up with technology which can spread contagion much faster and more widely than anything we have known before.

The power of the transgender identifying groups

The trans community has been likened by some to a cult. While this will be debated, there are detransitioners who have spoken particularly powerfully about their experiences as members/ex-members of these groups. They state that it is easy to get into the community and be accepted, but it is another matter when one questions the orthodoxy, expresses doubts, or attempts to leave. Some of them have experienced rejection, criticism, and been made to feel very unwelcome in the group. Some detransitioners have had their authenticity as "true trans" questioned. This can make discussion and exploration of understandable anxieties extremely difficult.

Political activism and its effects

There is evidence of what is often described as "policy capture" by certain parts of the transgender community who have particular beliefs about gender identity. In many countries they have worked extremely efficiently to ensure that companies, institutions, and organisations are adhering to policies devised around their beliefs. This has occurred despite a wider section of people not fully supporting these beliefs within society as a whole.

It is interesting to consider how this radical change has happened so rapidly and without much widespread challenge, despite the consequences for other protected groups' human rights, particularly women, homosexuals, and young people. The reasons are multifactorial and yet to fully emerge. Perhaps one contributing aspect is to do with how many modern societies, until quite recently, had a dire history of fair treatment for ethnic minorities and homosexuals. Society might wish to avoid a repetition of the horrors and mistakes of racism or homophobia. It is clear to most that trans-identified people should not be victimised or discriminated against and should be entitled to the same human rights as others. An ongoing debate surrounds the rights of the individual to determine their identity when it conflicts with the way others may see them.

Psychological forces in group thinking

The transgender community believes and promotes the idea of a fluid or flexible gender identity, but many others do not, yet are forced to concur in order to avoid conflict. The strength of some of the trans-community's messages and its method of implementation has led to an extraordinary level of groupthink (Asch, 1951) in many institutions and organisations. This leaves many people trying to find a way to accommodate the new ways of thinking about gender identity and biological sex and avoiding the humiliating or frightening aspects of being rejected by the group. An individual might have private thoughts or doubts but is affected by an overriding imperative to remain within the group. It is an anxiety-provoking dynamic where each person has to declare whether they are "for" or "against". This requires a binary choice but leaves many experiencing cognitive dissonance that perhaps originated in the minds of the gender-questioning person.

This has resulted in many individuals, particularly in the workplace, having to close their minds to the reality of the differences in biological sex with all that this entails. It requires a form of mental "double bookkeeping", as the group demands the individuals ignore their own beliefs, doubts, and questions, and proceed as if there is no confusion. The cost in this groupthink is the loss of independence of mind and freedom of thought.

Homosexuality, misogyny, and feminism

To put homosexuality, misogyny, and feminism all in one subheading might appear cursory or flippant about the individual relevance of each and the importance of all three in the discussion of transgender politics. However, we are not writing an academic paper on the subject but attempting to set a scene for the clinical exploration of gender dysphoria, and what we find is that these areas are often inextricably linked within the presentation of this condition.

As previously mentioned, for decades, the more traditional profile of a gender dysphoric patient was male, with long-standing feelings of gender dysphoria in childhood, which persisted into adulthood. There is currently no clear clinical evidence or research for the shift in the profile to a larger proportion of teenage females with no early childhood dysphoria, a change which has been described by Lisa Littman (2018) as rapid-onset gender dysphoria (ROGD). What has been reported is that perhaps 30% or more of these females will have some degree of autism, many with a formal diagnosis. They also have comorbid factors in terms of psychological traumas and social anxieties. One noticeable aspect of many women who detransition is that they come to view themselves as lesbians and not trans men. This is likely to be similarly applicable with young males. There is an acknowledgement among many professionals who work in the gender specialist areas that patients can have an internalised homophobia, which the person is trying to manage by changing their sex by medical means. There might also be parental homophobia, particularly in certain cultures where homosexuality is taboo, but also in families which, either consciously or unconsciously, cannot accept a family member as homosexual. This can lead to some parents actively encouraging their child's transition of gender.

Some females with gender dysphoria describe hatred of their breasts which they disguise or bind. They might find menstruation is a horror to be endured each month and sometimes have eating disorders, perhaps partly as an attempt to prevent their growing female bodies from becoming more overtly sexual. The reasons for the huge rise in the numbers of young women feeling so dislocated from their bodies are complex, but again, one cannot ignore the effects of social media. The online world offers a view of the perfect female form, usually photoshopped to idealise the appearance. Also, the current "ultra-feminine" fashion of highly sexualised celebrities with their augmented lips, cheeks, breasts, and buttocks may be a version of womanhood that many girls fear they cannot achieve or cannot identify with. Perhaps identifying as trans is a way in which they can unconsciously withdraw from the competition or the feeling of not belonging. Interestingly, it is usually this ultra-feminine version of womanhood that many men transitioning to women wish to inhabit.

There is currently a paradox in "queer politics" and gender identity issues whereby society is criticised and expected to abandon its heteronormative view and binary approach to the human race. What seems to have been lost is a tolerance for gender non-conformity in both males and females. The demand from trans people that their beliefs be tolerated and assimilated into wider society seems to have led to a situation in which gender stereotypes have been appropriated for diagnostic categorisations by the trans movement. Some of the features currently used for diagnosing trans-identified kids are that a young person "consistently and persistently" prefers activities or clothing of the opposite sex or wishes/believes they are the other sex, which is simply sexual stereotyping. As recent commentators on this subject confirm, there are many adults who might have been misdiagnosed when younger, because they thought the opposite sex had the more attractive or preferred lifestyles. However, as people age into their mid-twenties, the frontal lobe of the brain matures and we tend to begin to gain a self-acceptance, to feel more certain about who we are, our sense of identity and our sexual orientation.

In the current climate, this is an anxiety-provoking challenge for some. If a young person feels attracted to somebody of the same sex, but believes it is unacceptable, they may find an instant cure for managing their homosexual feelings by becoming trans. If the adults around them collude and immediately affirm this view, it is not going to help them come to terms with their homosexual orientation. We argue that sexual development is a continually changing, developing process as young people move through different stages of same-sex and other-sex attraction. We believe this developmental process needs to play out and unfold. The "affirmation" of this to the developing young person that there is indeed something "wrong" with being lesbian or gay and that the external world is in unquestionable agreement that physical alterations should be pursued, means they can feel their sexual attractions should be ignored.

Rivalry, envy, and difference between the sexes

While Freud's theories about penis envy have been hotly debated, it is undeniable that throughout our lives each of us must come to terms with our physical limitations, as we are born with a body which will be characteristically male or female. Consequently, we grow to be aware of either the lack of a penis and or that we lack the physical creativity to give birth to and feed a baby. Broadly speaking, mothers are powerful figures in most of our early lives and, as adults, men traditionally achieve more power as life proceeds, both physical and societal. Envy and rivalry are part of the human condition that we have to process and incorporate throughout our lives, created variously by the difference in the sexes, by our genetic inheritance of health, our physical attractiveness and abilities, and by the relationships we must endure with parents and siblings. We believe unconscious envy has a part to play in the psychology of some trans-identities.

Clinical environment

It has been argued by some that any in-depth level of assessment and psychological therapy is humiliating or pathologising for people with gender dysphoria. Indeed, some of the trans advocacy groups have successfully managed to argue that being transgender is not a mental illness. However, this ignores several aspects of the understanding of human psychopathology and how mental disturbance can clinically manifest.

Statistically, there is a much higher prevalence of mental illness in the trans community than the general population. It is usually argued that any mental illness presented in this group is due to the discrimination and bullying that trans people experience (Levine, 2020). It is sadly true that a minority of society will always treat any "difference" in a discriminatory manner and there are thankfully laws in most countries against this discrimination. However, one can also quite regularly find trans-identified and particularly detransitioned people who will say their predisposed mental constitution has, perhaps, made them more susceptible to mental illness. Some state that despite their life as a trans person proceeding without too much unkindness and discrimination from the external world, they can experience a continuing depression and suicidality after transitioning. This might be related to the disillusionment following the physical and social transition when the person begins to realise it has not been the required solution they hoped for.

Many can be left dealing with both physical and emotional complications following the transition and, even if all has gone smoothly, a deflated view of post-transition life can emerge. This is often compounded by the paucity of the follow-up care available, both physical and psychological, particularly if they are experiencing doubts about their actions. We believe this is a gap which needs to be urgently addressed in the current clinical environment. In addition to this, services for detransitioners and desisters are virtually non-existent.

It is our opinion that the consideration of mental state should apply to all patients who present requesting transition and body-altering treatments. We think this might help prevent a precipitous move towards a physical treatment model and the concomitant harm this might do. This applies particularly to young people whose brains are not fully developed and are too emotionally immature to give informed consent to the lifelong changes required for transition. In transitioning there is a huge part of the person's unknown future life that could potentially be lost. We contend there will inevitably be a ripple effect from this loss.

Pressure on the professional

The external pressures on the professional can be intense when working with gender dysphoric patients. You will likely be asked or told to refer patients on for medical treatment if requested by the patient and this puts clinicians and the services under enormous duress. This is a strain which can be extremely hard to withstand or resist. It is easier sometimes to "give in" to commencing a medical pathway if there is one readily available. You might be criticised for putting your patients through unnecessary gatekeeping assessments and psychological treatments while they are in such a distressed, possibly suicidal, state. However, it is because a person is in such a disturbed state of mind that this psychological care should be the first imperative step. It is not helpful to fall in with the view that gender identity is something unconnected to the person's mental health.

The current treatment models recommended by WPATH (World Professional Association of Transgender Health) tend to result in a disaggregation of the mind from the body, with the *DSM*-5 stating that the gender dysphoric person does not have any mental illness. The opinion advanced by WPATH, whereby something that so intensely disturbs the mind—believing you are the other sex—is attributed entirely to the physical consequences of having the "wrong body", is unique to the clinical area of transgender health care. It is also unlike any other area of medicine or psychiatry we can think of. In other areas of mental health, such as eating disorders, hypochondriasis, or body dysmorphia, there is a clinical understanding that the manifestation of such feelings about the body originates in the mind. Despite this anomaly, the WPATH guidelines for the affirmative care pathway have been largely adopted throughout the world and currently stand as the preferred model. This is in part because it is extremely difficult in the current climate for professionals to speak out against it or to attempt a longer-term treatment, particularly if they feel vulnerable to accusations of peddling "conversion therapy", or fear being sacked or prosecuted for not, unquestioningly, affirming the person's state of mind.

Having worked with this group of patients, we do understand how pressured this clinical area can feel with emotions and conflicts running high. Young people, often in huge distress, present to professionals hoping for a quick fix for their pain. Their minds can be fixed, and they often believe that they know what their treatment should be because they have usually educated themselves online. It takes mental resilience and good clinical supervision and reflective practice to continue working with a group of patients whose psychological structure is organised around an apparently fixed belief system.

Learning the script

Some clinicians and therapists who work with gender dysphoric patients have commented more recently on how the young person might come into the consulting room with an almost identical script of symptoms and statements. They believe that these young people have been coached online on what to think, how to behave, what to say, and so on in order to proceed down the chemical treatment route. They have learned how to present as "persistent" and "consistent" in their ideas which form their trans self-diagnosis. Of course, some symptoms might continue to persist, but this clinical presentation can be overwhelming for the parents and professionals.

The pressure from the patient, together with the external political pressures applied to the clinical area, can rapidly lead to professionals, such as general practitioners and community mental health teams, believing there is only one course of action—to "affirm" and refer on to specialist gender identity services (GIDS). However, perhaps this is premature and what might be more helpful in the longer term is to encourage the idea that the person needs a more complex understanding of their distress or mental disturbance. People who detransition often say they wish that the professionals had "stood up" to them more and made them wait to see how their minds would develop as adults over time. If we can cultivate a way of thinking together with the patients about their internal emotional worlds and can withstand this clinical pressure, it might aid many gender-confused patients to develop a more complex view of themselves and reduce their demand for physical interventions as the solution to their difficulties.

Ultimately the patient may go on to fully transition, or they may change their mind and decide to live life in their physically unchanged body, but whatever pathway is chosen in the longer term, we maintain a view that all these individuals would benefit from help to think about their internal worlds, and a thorough assessment of their thinking is essential in order to help them make a fully informed decision.

Medical categorisations and the rejection of mental illness

There were changes made in 2015 to the *Diagnostic and Statistical Manual of Mental Disorders, Fifth Edition—DSM-5*, when the diagnostic term "gender identity disorder" was changed to "gender dysphoria" with the aim of reducing stigma for patients.

The *DSM-5*, used mainly in the US, described gender dysphoria as a condition where a person experiences discomfort or distress because there is a mismatch between their biological sex and gender identity.

This differed from the *ICD 10 (International Statistical Classification of Diseases and Related Health Problems, 10th Revision*, used in the UK and Europe), which kept the diagnosis of "childhood identity disorder".

> **ICD 10 F64.2 Gender identity disorder of childhood**
> A disorder, usually first manifest during early childhood (and always well before puberty), characterised by persistent and intense distress about assigned sex, together with a desire to be (or insistence that one is) of the other sex. There is a persistent preoccupation with the dress and activities of the opposite sex and repudiation of the individual's sex. The diagnosis requires a profound disturbance of the normal gender identity; mere tomboyishness in girls or girlish behaviour in boys is not sufficient. (World Health Organization, 2004)

However, this has now been revised in the *ICD 11* (for adoption in 2022) and is described as "gender incongruence".

Throughout the centuries, there have been various terms and descriptions of mental illnesses. While many theories have been rejected (moral degeneracy or lunar lunacy) and practices discontinued (e.g. lobotomies, teeth extraction, unmodified ECT), it is also generally observed that certain early life events, such as traumas, abuse, deprivation, and early parental separation, together with constitutional factors, will make a person more susceptible to developing a mental illness. These factors are frequently found in the histories of people who have been variously diagnosed with schizophrenia, depression, bipolar disorder, and personality disorders. What any study of the history of madness[1] reveals is that psychiatry and mental health work is something of a fashion business and that a new age can be defined by its novel mental disorders. In very recent years, the focus has moved between suicide and suicide pacts, drug and alcohol addictions, and eating disorders to name a few.

---

[1] *Madness in Civilization* (2015) by Andrew Scull gives an excellent account of such trends over three millennia. Published by Thames & Hudson, London.

Although it will no doubt be contested, arguably young people's distress and disturbance is finding expression in gender dysphoria and identity issues. Currently, there is a huge rise in the level of adolescents presenting with these physical manifestations of their distress. The body is often used to act out something that cannot be accepted or processed by the mind. There is sometimes an absence of any anxiety in young people about their beliefs regarding their own gender identity, but it could be a disservice to assume there is no underlying conflict or difficulty which requires support and exploration.

Of course, what the layperson might think of as a "mental illness" is understood within the therapeutic professions as a presentation of a group of signs and symptoms, which are the diagnostic criteria for any disorder. The diagnostic criteria for different diagnoses can be helpful, but should not be slavishly followed, especially in psychiatry and psychological medicine where what a symptom "means" should always be part of the discussion. Diagnoses help us to draw a line between illness and health but we question the value of these diagnostic categories when forming a care plan for a young person. The accuracy of mental-health diagnosis in children is notoriously unreliable prognostically, as children change during the course of their development. Children who are diagnosed with one thing at a particular age may turn out very differently when they reach maturity. Many young people with gender dysphoria appear to be frozen in their current preoccupations, and by the time they present for transition, they typically might have suppressed any of the doubts and anxieties they would naturally entertain, having instead projected them onto those around them. Therefore, our caution is that diagnosis is a limited tool, as it tends to fail to describe the complex nature of the mind and the dynamics that exist between different parts of the personality.

Having spent our working lives in the NHS, firstly as mental health nurses and latterly as psychoanalytic psychotherapists and clinical lecturers, we have been consultants to various mental health services, listening to and working with the professionals who treat patients with challenging behaviours. In this capacity, we have observed, more recently, that patients with a history of serious and enduring mental illness or personality disorder have developed gender dysphoria. A common theme in their presentations is the patients' belief that physical treatments will remove or resolve aspects of themselves that cause them psychic pain. When such medical interventions fail to remove their psychological problems, the disappointment experienced can lead to an escalation of self-harm and suicidal ideation, as the resentment and hatred towards themselves which were acted out in relation to their bodies have not been resolved.

Despite huge strides made this century in the destigmatisation of mental illness, professionals can be made to feel they are making a bigoted, transphobic slur to suggest that people with gender dysphoria might have a disturbed mental state or that their symptoms are connected and influenced by their mental functioning. In fact, the psychological assessment of many young people reveals comorbid histories of trauma, deprivation, and sexual abuse and they frequently report depression and suicidal ideation among their symptoms. Estimates suggest that approximately 30% of referrals to young people's gender identity clinics may also have autism (Van Der Miesen, Hurley, & De Vries, 2016). It is a fact that young people with an ASD/autism diagnosis have particularly rigid aspects in their mental processing. A person's mental health issues and associated anxieties are unlikely to disappear simply by transitioning, as there is a huge amount of psychological work required to go into this course of action. Equally, there are many people who need to have their psychological health attended to in order to help them to work through what is motivating them to believe that they need to change their gender and their physical appearance.

In addition, it could be said that the move to insist that gender dysphoria is not a mental health diagnosis runs the risk of itself perpetuating the stigma that attaches to mental illness.

Gender specialism

Throughout the world, there has rapidly developed a range of so-called specialists or experts on gender identity treatment. While there are many aspects one can learn about presentation, medication, and surgery in this clinical area, what is also apparent, if one examines it a little more closely, is the shallow depth of the research that has been carried out and the disproportionate weight it has given to current treatment models, without any substantial, longer-term evidence based on outcomes. The Dutch protocol, guided by a trans-affirmative approach, was enacted and adopted elsewhere internationally before the ethics of medical transitioning in children had been debated or the efficacy and safety of hormonal and surgical interventions had been established properly (Pilgrim & Entwistle, 2020).

The studies that have been done, on which worldwide treatment recommendations have been made, are usually based on very small numbers of patients. Reliable, longer-term follow-up statistics are patchy, with many patients lost to the recording systems. "Satisfaction surveys" are not worth much if they are only reported on within the first year post treatment, as the patient can still be involved in the excitement of the treatment or surgery and has yet to realise the longer-term implications of their transition choice. This inaccurate conclusion bias in studies has not given a comprehensive picture of the physical and psychological harms that might occur in post-transition patients.

There is also a concerning aspect that despite the clear change in the numbers and clinical picture of the cohort (e.g. increasing numbers of females and increasingly presenting at younger ages) it is common to hear a "gender expert" answer a question about aetiology, changing trends in presentation, or long-term outcomes with the phrase, "We don't really know the answer to that yet." We can think of no other area of medicine where such potentially harmful drug regimens are recommended and implemented, where healthy body tissues are surgically altered or removed, where doctors know the principle of "First do no harm" and yet continue their work with a level of ignorance due to sparse outcome data on which to base their clinical decisions. How have medics been persuaded to pursue this essentially experimental and physically damaging treatment? The answer to that question is a complex one. Concerned medics have an enormous challenge in trying to address the current practices in this climate. In part, this is because professionals can be intimidated out of frank and open discussion, but also there are huge financial interests at play (Bilek, 2018). We are waiting for more answers, as light begins to be shed on the ethical conflicts of interest involved.

The doctor–patient dynamic

Could more unconscious factors behind this rapid change in health service approaches be due to the change in the relationship between patient and doctor? It used to be that the doctor was seen as the expert who would provide the best treatment for the patient who was consulting them. Now there is a way in which the patient has become a client who expects a service. There is currently a societal preoccupation with physical cosmetic appearance, often accompanied by control of the perfect body image through media and surgery. Trans medicine could perhaps be seen as a form of curating service, which will provide the individual with the body they believe will make them happy.

Some medics and surgeons may be drawn to their calling by the feeling of omnipotence (their power to be godlike saving people from illness and misery). Trans medicine might attract a certain kind of doctor or "expert" who is drawn to this area of practice as an unconscious (or conscious) enactment of this phantasy. (Psychoanalysis differentiates between phantasy which is used to describe an unconscious set of beliefs, whereas fantasy is used to describe conscious thoughts and daydreams.) Unconscious phantasy describes the mental activity lying behind conscious thought that structures the individual's relationships with his or her internal objects (see p. 240 for information on the internal object). The influence and consequences of unconscious phantasies are evident when the individual is emotionally upset or disturbed. Phantasies and fantasies can be in operation at the same time at different levels of the mind. Conscious fantasies are often underpinned by unconscious phantasies. A person can be aware of their own fantasies, but unaware of any unconscious phantasies behind them (see p. 240 for more information on fantasy and unconscious phantasy).

It is fascinating to consider how the doctors, who have taken an oath of "Do no harm", square in their minds this particular form of treatment for healthy-bodied young people. Perhaps there is a way they rationalise it as a treatment that relieves the distress of the person. But medicine, as yet, has not offered clear evidence to demonstrate they are not doing irrevocable harm. As always, more research is needed.

Clinical pressures on professional groups?

Since we became publicly involved in the debate about the medicalisation of gender dysphoric young people, we have spoken to media personnel around the world. Some of them have been reporting on transgender issues for several years. They talk of the problem that although many professionals are prepared to talk privately with them about various concerns or criticisms of current gender identity policies, they have struggled to find many prepared to go on the record with their views. We have frequently been informed that we were unusual in our willingness to try to open up the discussion. This is gradually changing in some areas, but largely there has been a silencing of critics or sceptics of the affirmative model in its current guise, particularly for children and young people. In their book, *Inventing Transgender Children and Young People* (2019), Michelle Moore and Heather Brunskell-Evans brought together a mix of experienced clinicians and other academics to critique certain approaches to gender dysphoria. In an extraordinary step, the Tavistock Gender Identity Disorder Service threatened legal action, unsuccessfully, against the publisher and demanded to see the book before publication.

Professionals are afraid to lose their jobs, be litigated against, be labelled as transphobes, speak out against the current prescription for fear of losing sponsorships, and so on. We have lost count of the number of professionals, particularly in health care and education, who have told us "off the record" that they do not agree with the current affirmation model and the social changes and effects this brings about. However, they believe they cannot act in any other way, for fear of transgressing the memorandums of understanding or professional guidelines. This leaves many in a position of mental double bookkeeping, aware that a person might have mental health or other difficulties, but obligated to support them due to the affirmative model in their belief they are "born in the wrong body" and to assist them in curating a new identity.

Workload pressure: financial and ethical conflicts

We are aware that worldwide healthcare systems vary in their operational structure. However, they all have their pressures which manifest in different ways. Many clinicians/professionals operate under a heavy workload, sometimes driven by finances or by contracts and waiting lists. As we have noted previously, health providers are also driven by the wish to remove pain and obtain patient satisfaction. Thus, the clinical environment is affected by external and internal factors. There is perhaps a tendency to receive the wisdom of the "experts" in this area, such as WPATH, who have recommended "best practice" protocols.

Milgram (1963) demonstrated in his research that people obey orders from authority figures. Perhaps staff do not investigate or question too closely as this might lead to conflict with the guidelines and their employers, therefore it is politically and practically easier just to follow them.

There is a worldwide growing question regarding the ethical conflict between medicine, finance, and politics. This is not our primary concern in writing the book, but we are aware that there are currently active groups of people who are making efforts to investigate the potential conflicts of interest of the "influencers" in gender health policy and practice. At the time of writing much of this is speculation, but it is true to say that transgender medicine and surgical treatments are proceeding in the direction of becoming an enormous moneymaking business for pharmaceutical companies and private medical practitioners in the coming years.

Hormone treatments for young people

Throughout most parts of the world, there has been a reduction in the age for prescribing GnRH "hormone blockers" to young people, at Tanner stage 2 usually between nine and twelve years of age, but sometimes younger. (Tanner stage 2 is the second of five stages of observed sexual maturity in adolescence.) These hormone blockers are described in most literature as wholly reversible (although this has changed recently in the UK). However, some endocrinologists and researchers express concerns that a pro-trans medical lobby promotes this view and that again the full outcomes cannot be known due to a lack of long-term follow-up studies, but that there are risks to the developing body and mind. The blockers are usually followed by opposite-sex hormones, which do lead to permanent changes in the body and are known to have some serious side effects and physical risks.

There can be an excitement around "getting onto the hormones" and a lack of any serious discussion that would usually accompany any treatment programme in medicine that is going to affect the body adversely. This phase might then be followed by a renewal of the more distressed state of gender dysphoria, as the person is still left with many of their previous psychological problems which resurface once the excitement of a cure has worn off. Efforts are often renewed, and further physical interventions sought as a way of recreating that initial euphoria when the physical treatments first commenced. What is often lacking is an exploration of why the person dislikes themselves so much in the first place and locates their discomfort in the gender of their natal body.

There have been a few larger, longitudinal studies on gender dysphoria in young people and adolescents in which the gender-incongruent young people and families are psychologically supported, but no affirmative model has been used, and medications have not been implemented. The outcome figures for these studies vary between 70% and 95% of the young people remaining in their natal gender (Steensma et al., 2011). In other words, the vast majority of gender-questioning young people will live their lives in their natal body, without the need for lifelong medication or surgeries. Given this large statistic of desistance, we are advocating that young people are given a chance to learn about themselves and to discover why they feel so uncomfortable about their gender through extensive psychological interventions, before they move down a medical route.

We simply restate our point that in medicine and health care, this dominant political environment is extremely damaging and very likely a medical disaster in the making for many gender-questioning individuals and their families.

THREE

Detransitioners

"The official numbers of detransitioners aren't collected, they aren't known at the moment. But I think we are the tip of the iceberg, there will be many of us to come.

"I wish the psychiatrist at the gender identity clinic had given me a better assessment. Part of me wants to go back to the clinic to look my psychiatrist in the face again, but I know that's driven by anger."

—Sinead, detransitioner, England. https://thetimes.co.uk/article/the-detransitioners-what-happens-when-trans-men-want-to-be-women-again-fd22b7jhs

When doctors always give patients what they want (or think they want), the fallout can be disastrous, as we have seen with the opioid crisis. There is every possibility that the medical treatment of young people with gender dysphoria may follow a similar path. Practitioners understandably want to protect their patients from psychic pain. However, quick fixes based only on self-reporting can have tragic long-term consequences. Already, there are a growing number of people who have desisted from their trans identity, variously known as desisters, detransisitioners, and sometimes regretters. Some are seeking accountability from the medical professionals who affirmed their wish to transition, without adequate assessment. There are an increasing number who are speaking out on social media and at conferences arguing they have also been let down by mental health services which failed to assess their psychological problems before prescribing medical treatments such as puberty blockers, cross-sex hormones, and referring them on for surgeries as a treatment for their gender dysphoria.

Detransitioners, having initially felt welcomed in and encouraged by affirmative groups, often describe being pressurised or ostracised by the same trans-groups when they start to express doubts or questions regarding the treatment. Dagny (2019) writes that she became a different person when she started using the online site Tumblr.

"My online experience, having been affected by that level of groupthink, that level of moral policing and the constant implicit threats of social exposure and ostracisation, made me an intensely internal and anxious person" (https://feministcurrent.com/2019/06/04/dagny-on-social-media-gender-dysphoria-trans-youth-and-detransitioning/).

Case presentation—Bianca

Bianca was a twenty-five-year-old woman who came for an individual psychotherapy consultation, suffering from depression and anxiety. In the initial consultation the therapist asked Bianca to talk about her history. Bianca said that she had had a mastectomy and hysterectomy when she was twenty, after taking puberty blockers aged sixteen then cross-sex hormones aged eighteen. She said she thought the whole thing was a mistake.

Bianca was the middle child of three. According to her, the older brother was clever at school and her younger sister was very pretty and her mother's favourite. She also described her parents having had a fiery relationship; her father gambled and was at times physically abusive. Eventually, he left the family home when Bianca was five years old and her mother became depressed and neglectful of the children. Bianca said that she did not spend much time at home and joined her brother to play football at his local football club.

Bianca was devastated when the teams were divided by sex and she had to join the female team, where she did not get on very well with her teammates. Her school attendance became erratic and following a letter from the school, she had several heated arguments with her mother. Following these arguments, she would go to stay with her father, who by this time had remarried and had young children by his second wife. Bianca said that she did not get on well with her stepmother and would go back to her mother after arguments at her father's home.

Her brother left the maternal home when he was sixteen and Bianca described feeling completely isolated. She missed her brother and her friendships faded with the boys at the football club, because by now they were more interested in girls who appeared more feminine. After eventually telling her mother about her feelings of hating her body and feeling she didn't fit in with the other girls, it was suggested she was trans and that she should go to see her family doctor. The therapist commented on how Bianca did not seem to feel she had a place in her parents' world. Bianca said that she did not have any expectation that her parents would have tried to understand, as they had their own problems to deal with. Bianca started to research trans online and contacted some of the user involvement websites and chat rooms.

First consultation

Bianca: When I started my periods, I felt disgusted and started to hate my body and what I saw as my female sexual development.

Therapist: It sounds like you were trying to distance yourself from your feelings of pain and unhappiness, which seemed to get located in your body.

Bianca: [*Starts to cry*] I started to spend more and more time online, getting into trans websites. I just felt desperately lonely and I would make conversations on these groups about the fact that I did not feel as if I belonged anywhere. Back then they seemed like the only friends I could rely on.

Bianca went on to say that she talked to her doctor about her depression and feelings of anxiety, but when she mentioned the gender dysphoria, the doctor immediately referred her on to the specialist gender service. Her network had been happy when she told them the news. It was as if she had joined a club and others started to share their own experiences with her and reassured her that now she would start to feel much better.

> Therapist: As if they knew the solution to your feelings of unhappiness and detachment.
> Bianca: Yes, it made me feel that I was really loved and belonged somewhere.

In the run-up to the gender clinic appointment, her online friends gave her lots of advice about the appointment: what to say and how to manage questions. "It was like being coached in a football team and I felt they cared about me."

She was seen in the specialist service for two assessment consultations in which she persuaded the worker that she had been gender dysphoric for many years and that she was feeling suicidal and wanting to start taking hormone blockers. Following this, she was placed on puberty blockers.

> Bianca: After an initial feeling of excitement about starting on the blockers, I felt flat, as if all the life had been taken out of me. I spoke to the trans support group, and they said that it was normal and that I would feel better when I progressed onto the cross-sex hormones. Again, the group were incredibly supportive and encouraged me. I also started to experiment with living as a boy and this gave me a feeling of excitement and pleasure. I began to drift away from all my friends, spending more and more time online in my chat group.
> Therapist: You were being given an idea that everything would be OK if only you could stop your development as a girl and transition to be a boy.
> Bianca: [*Angrily*] That was the message throughout the whole process, including some of the professionals who seemed to encourage the idea that transitioning was a solution to my problems.
>
> [*After a pause*] Looking back I can see that the online group was always critical of my previous friends and family, encouraging me to feel that they did not understand me or that they were responsible for my feeling of rejection.

Therapist: As if the group talked directly to that part of you that always felt misunderstood and rejected. But the unhappy little girl who you wanted to be rid of, still needed help and to be understood.

Discussion of the first consultation

It seems that Bianca's parents had long-standing difficulties as a couple, which eventually led to their divorce and it is likely her mother was preoccupied by her husband's gambling and marital arguments. One imagines this may have left Bianca feeling somewhat insecure and unable to match up to her sister's looks or her brother's intelligence. Bianca seemed to have a fraught relationship with her mother from the start and the feeling of rejection was compounded as a teenager when she stayed with her father and his new family. She did not feel she belonged comfortably in either family.

Bianca did feel she discovered a place playing football where she found it easy to identify with the boys and compete with them. This is in marked contrast to her relationship with her sister, with whom she felt rivalrous, perhaps because her sister was close to her mother, while Bianca did not feel close to either of them.

Bianca was devastated when the teams divided into sexes. Her therapist had the impression that she was a very unhappy little girl looking for a place where she could belong. Might the origin of her belief that she was a boy have taken root in the phantasy that she could leave behind this unhappy little girl by transitioning? Her physicality may have helped with her underlying feelings of sadness and increased her self-esteem.

We can see how Bianca feels that she is unlovable and unacceptable. She feels aggrieved towards her parents who were preoccupied with their marital difficulties during her infancy and childhood. It may be that she developed a fantasy that she would have been loved, if only she had been pretty and feminine like her sister; if she cannot compete, she should get rid of any femininity.

The idea of transitioning seems to be connected to a wish to distance herself from underlying feelings of worthlessness and depression. This belief system shifts a further notch when she develops the idea that she would be better off as a boy. The exciting idea is whereas she feels like she is unloved and unlovable as a girl, she would be loved as a boy. The father seems to endorse this through his support for transition.

Second consultation

Bianca started by saying that she was very angry after the first meeting. She said that looking back she probably had doubts during the transition process, but the further she got into it, the more reluctant she was to stop and question what she was doing. She said that she just thought she felt so alone and the support of the online group was so important. Where would she belong if they rejected her?

Therapist: You were desperate to feel you belonged somewhere.

Bianca: I think my brother did question what I was doing. However, I just dismissed him as being interfering, and the group said that he just did not understand. I have never really felt that I have fitted in, but I felt I was joining a group that was different from the rest of the world. A group that could see right through normal people and their narrow view of how things should be.

After about six months, I went back to the clinic, and it was agreed I would start on the cross-sex hormones. When I told the group, they were delighted saying that I was making great progress. Initially, I felt this surge of excitement. I felt powerful and that this was the hit I had been looking for. I increased the frequency and degree of my social transition as I started to feel like I was changing sex. I began to grow facial hair and gradually my voice got lower. Looking back, I can see that I had doubts, which I hid from everyone, including myself.

Therapist: The doubts would threaten to interfere with the powerful feeling of being in control.

Bianca: Yes. I thought, I don't want to give them any space. I had an argument with my brother, who by this time, knew what was going on and started to argue with me asking, "What are you doing to yourself?" He told my mother, and she began to have a go at me. My mum and I had several terrible arguments in which I said to her that it was my body and my decision and that I knew what I wanted. My father, however, was much more accepting. He said that I must do whatever makes me comfortable. I don't think he cared what I was doing, provided I didn't cause any trouble for him and his new family.

    I started to think about going on a dating website and dating some girls. However, I was still looking like a girl and felt very self-conscious. This was when I started to think I needed surgery. I began talking about this in my online group. The group were very encouraging, giving me advice about what to say at the clinic. I became convinced that I had to go through the whole thing—having my breasts removed then having the bottom surgery. I started researching and looking into the next steps. I met up with the trans community at organised events, and they were all so supportive and encouraging. I thought I had finally found somewhere I belonged. Again, I was advised what to say in the interviews. It was like an exciting game.

Therapist: The group supported your belief that you could remove that unwanted girl.

Bianca: I thought with each step I could finally get rid of bad feelings—the cloud that hangs over my head. The rows with my mother increased over this time. She demanded to speak to the mental health professional at the gender clinic. They told her that they couldn't discuss my case with her because of my age and that part of the reason for my distress was that she wouldn't just support me. This made her furious, and she screamed and shouted at me saying I was ruining myself just to get back at her, and my sister joined in saying that I am upsetting everyone in the family. My brother tried to be the go-between, but I accused him of siding with them. All the time, my voice was getting lower and my male characteristics were becoming more obvious. Eventually, the rows got so bad at home that the police were called, and we were referred to social services. The social worker who assessed the family agreed to place me in separate accommodation.

When I turned eighteen, I was transferred from child services to adult services and interviewed by the consultant of that service. I said that I had been living as a male for over a year and yet I still had an uncomfortable feeling of dysphoria. I said I wanted to have a mastectomy, and some bottom surgery as I thought this would make me feel better about who I was. After a brief interview with the consultant, he said he thought the operations would help me in my transition. He said that I should think about it and that I would be seen for a follow-up, in one month. At the second appointment, he agreed to put me on the waiting list for a "top surgery" (mastectomy) first, then once I had recovered from that we would discuss the various bottom surgery options.

I had to wait several months for the first operation, during which time I started to get doubts about what I was doing. I mentioned my doubts to the group, and they said that doubts were normal; they would disappear when I had the mastectomy. They said that I had been unhappy as a girl for many years and that I probably wouldn't be happy until I fully transitioned. They were suspicious of newer members of the group, who expressed serious doubts about the process of transition. In many ways, the group got quite nasty saying that the ones expressing doubts were weak and were selling out on their true selves. I remember feeling anxious about discussing my doubts anymore because I didn't want to get that criticism from the group. By this time, I had left home and I was living on my own in a bedsit, completely separated from my parents and everyone in my family, except for the odd phone conversation with my brother.

I went ahead with the operation and when I came around from the anaesthetic on the ward, I had dressings and drains and was still suffering the effects of the anaesthetic. The surgeon came to see me and said that the surgery was a complete success. A couple of days later, I was discharged, but just before my discharge, a nurse came to change my dressing. When I looked at my scarred body, I collapsed into floods of tears. I got upset about seeing the wounds. Although they were neat, they were ugly cuts into my flesh. I couldn't be discharged that afternoon because I felt so low. Eventually, I went back to my bedsit and still feeling low. I started to think about what I had done to myself.

Therapist: You suddenly felt connected to the wounded body.

Bianca: After some time, I got a message from a friend. He asked what the matter was and said that it was perfectly normal to feel upset immediately after the surgery. He said that the anaesthetic was a depressant and took some time to get over. Then a couple of members of the group came to visit me and brought some drink and we had a bit of a party. After a few days I started to get the dysphoric feelings again, this time mixing in with my doubts about whether I had done the right thing. I talked again to my group online, who all reassured me that this reaction was perfectly normal. They were also very critical of some members who were stalling their transition as if they were letting the side down in some way and being cowardly.

After a couple of months, my mood started to lift again as the wounds healed, and I dressed in boys' clothes. I felt excited about the fact that I was able to pass as a man. I even went on a couple of dates with women but if they wanted to take things further, I realised that I would have to get undressed and then they would see my genitals and would know that I was biologically female. I thought this was an impasse that I couldn't get over. One or two of the older and more vocal members in my online group said that I needed to go for the "bottom surgery" which would help me feel more like a man. At this point, I had serious doubts about going forward, but it was almost as if I had come so far that I couldn't stop now. In a way, there was no way back.

Therapist: To stop would mean losing the excitement of feeling you had found the solution and instead to face what had been done.

Bianca: I felt depressed. I went to my doctor and he gave me some antidepressants. They helped a bit, but I still felt as if I was depressed underneath.

Bianca: I already had a six-monthly follow-up appointment arranged. So, avoiding any discussion of the doubts and the low mood I had experienced, I told the consultant that I was happy with the results of the operation and that I wanted to go ahead with the bottom surgery. Again, I had to wait but there was very little real examination or questioning. The view seemed to be that most people who came through the process went on to be delighted with the results. I don't really think I wanted to know about the negatives at any time.

I had six months of waiting with the usual doubts and feelings of worry about what I'd done to my body. I no longer listened so intently to the voices that said I needed to do more. I heard what they were saying, but I no longer believed them. However, I didn't see any alternative to keeping going—I don't really understand why.

Therapist: Very difficult for you to stop to face all these critical thoughts and feelings. I imagine you were worried you would be rejected by the group and you already felt you had lost connection with your family.

Bianca: Yes, but also, I feel angry now. Why didn't anyone stop me or question me? Why didn't anyone ask me, "Look, what are you doing?" Instead, they all endorsed it, encouraged it even. They all said that it would sort things out—the carelessness. The doctors should have asked more questions, delved a bit deeper.

Therapist: You wanted a professional to see what was driving you. Look behind your certainty, which was masking the hurt and rejection.

Bianca: [*In tears*] I am so angry with that bitch, and my father was useless. I was just under the influence of the group, it's a bit like I was being brainwashed. They believe their nonsense about "everyone adjusts" and "it's part of the journey". Nobody really knows though, because once you've been operated on, no one follows you up. They check the physical wounds but then that's it.

After I'd had the hysterectomy, I had a consultation with the consultant. It was like everything had gone well and was a success and that was it. But there was no follow-up to see me in my depressed state.

Therapist: As if you no longer believed in the physical treatments as a cure for your difficulties, but there is so much to face if you stop—the painful question of what you have allowed to happen.

Bianca: I dropped out of the group. I knew the whole thing had been a mistake. I knew that I would be attacked as others who doubted had been attacked. I just couldn't face it. And far from thinking that I would be able to go out with a woman, I realised that any heterosexual woman would feel cheated by me as a man. I just looked odd, and I couldn't bear to look at myself in the mirror.

A neighbour popped round to see me. He knew I was on my own after the surgery. An elderly man. He was so kind. He looked in and said, "Is everything all right? How did the operation go?"

He had seen me from time to time over the years and I'd thought he must have noticed that I was changing and wondered what he thought of me. I imagined he was one of the normal people that the group looked down on. I burst into tears because I was struck by the fact that he had been watching and realised that I had been going through a difficult time and that I was not well. He was kind and took the trouble to come and see how I was.

Therapist: You felt ashamed and didn't think anyone would take an interest in you, as if you didn't deserve any care. I wonder if you hope that I will be somebody who is interested in you and that you are valued?

Bianca: [*Sobbing*] It was all too much then and I am not sure I can bear to think about it.

Therapist: You feel you need to understand what has gone on and to understand what part both you and others have played in this process.

Bianca: I want to try and understand it all—what's gone wrong? I was just so miserable and didn't feel loved. I didn't listen to my brother and mother; I was just so angry with them and I didn't think my mother had any right to tell me what to do. I just kept going with something so harmful. What a mess.

Discussion of the second consultation

Whenever Bianca expresses her doubts, the support group counters with the idea that full transition would provide a solution to her difficulties. Ordinary doubts and questions about this course of action are attacked and denounced as if thinking around the topic is a weakness; or even downright dangerous. Bianca adopts this position by pushing away conflicts and doubts.

Initially, Bianca describes the excitement involved in medical interventions. This seems to be related to the idea that she can triumph over her feelings of inadequacy and helplessness. However, over time the excitement wears off; she starts to question and doubt the process. The difficulty is that she cannot face the possibility that she has been miserable about herself and the damage being inflicted on her. The doubts, which represent a sane concern that she is taking the wrong path, are dismissed as they threaten to take away the idea of transition as a cure. Giving up the idea of transition would leave Bianca with her underlying feelings of sadness, loneliness, and resentment. Hence, she pushes on to the next stage of treatment despite her misgivings. All the time, the trans group encourage her to go further in pursuing first hormonal, then surgical, interventions. Having felt she "belonged" and was accepted by the group, she cannot risk rejection from it.

We observe the way that the names given to the various interventions are changed so that the descriptions no longer represent a medical intervention with all the serious implications this involves. For example, testosterone is described as "T", mastectomy is described as "top surgery", metoidioplasty, vaginectomy, and hysterectomy as "bottom surgeries". These euphemisms detach the intervention from its medical origins, perhaps in order to prevent painful associations. For example, mastectomies are commonly carried out on women who have a tumour in their breast—as such, it is a treatment designed to save a woman's life. However, this is not the case with "top surgery" as there is nothing physically wrong with the breast. The mastectomy is being undertaken in an attempt to deal with a psychological problem in Bianca's case. It is the psyche's concrete solution to a problem with the inability to tolerate psychological pain through symbolic thinking.

Bianca is angry with the professionals who failed to examine the issues underlying her gender dysphoric presentation. She feels they all took a superficial and narrow gender-focused view of her difficulties. Like the abbreviated terms ("T", "top surgery"), it seems professionals are susceptible to taking an approach that cuts corners and avoids looking at underlying damage and pain. Perhaps the initial assessment of Bianca and her difficulties may have lacked depth and substance, because it failed to understand that a vulnerable part of her, which needed recognition and support, was trapped within a defensive structure in her mind. Any failure by the services to recognise the clinical complexity unwittingly colluded with a phantasy that the vulnerable aspects of the self and the pain of her dysphoria could be removed by physical interventions alone.

We are struck by the nature of the illusion that needed to be maintained by Bianca as she continued to go through the steps of transition. The illusion provided by the process of gender transition promises a way for Bianca to distance herself from being the unhappy and unwanted little girl she feels she carries around inside her. The promise was maintained by her and supported by others in the face of her doubts. For example, when first dating girls, Bianca can appear to be a man, but she can never sexually fully function as a man with a penis. When Bianca goes back to her support group with a doubt, they dismiss this and suggest the remedy is to pursue the transition further. For Bianca at that point in her life, it appears easier to continue along a treatment path that offers her solutions, rather than face her doubts. In order for Bianca to do this alone, so much of the past would have to be faced, including the harm she may have done to herself by asking to transition. It will also require her to confront her own underlying feelings of depression, anger, and disappointment in her family and herself.

Bianca seemed to be looking for someone who could identify the complexities of her clinical situation and who could maintain their own ideas in the face of her persistent beliefs, claims, and rigid certainty. She also needed somebody to help her with her feelings of anger, loneliness, and rejection. Instead, she felt the professionals all succumbed and encouraged her in her thinking that she could change sex. The final breakdown in her mental state occurs when she realises that she still cannot change sex. She realises that she had gone along with a medical belief that she could change from a "woman to a man". Nevertheless, the social position of her gender does not change her biological sex. The doubts she worked so hard to keep out of her mind, with the support of the trans group, did perhaps represent a piece of her reality: "You cannot kill off the sad, little girl who is angry because she feels nobody wants her." Moreover, she can change the way she appears in society, but she cannot change who she really is with all her history.

It appears that many professionals who treated Bianca acted as if they believed it was possible to remove psychological distress by physical interventions. It is as if nobody can help her face her underlying feelings of disappointment, depression, grievance, anger, and despair.

Once Bianca had reached the point of realising no further interventions would help her conquer her underlying feelings, there was a collapse of the concrete defence that transition represented. Bianca was left to face the devastation on her own until the man in the flat next door noticed her pain. He seemed to represent a parental figure, who could see she felt unwell and was in need of care. She burst into tears because his comment touched on the very thing she had tried to keep out of her mind for so long.

In her therapy, Bianca was going to need quite a bit of help mourning the losses, both physical and emotional, and the new identity that she had believed she would become. The mourning process would involve a closer understanding of the patient's feelings about the damage she had allowed to occur, while also acknowledging the damage done by others in their failure to care for her, her body, and her mind.

Emily

Emily was a twenty-two-year-old woman who had detransitioned and requested a psychotherapy consultation because she wanted to understand what had driven her to transition in the first place. She started by telling the therapist about her earlier years. Emily was the eldest child, with two half-brothers on her father's side and four half-brothers and one half-sister on her mother's side. Her father had left home when she was very young, and her mother, who used to binge drink, had had tempestuous relationships with the fathers of her various half-brothers and sister. Emily had helped her mother raise the younger siblings which meant she had grown up quickly. The family moved often, usually due to problems paying rent or arguments with ex-partners and neighbours. The consequence was that Emily went to many different schools which affected her academic work and presented her with problems of fitting in to new peer groups. Her grandmother was the one stable figure in Emily's life and from time to time Emily stayed with her, an arrangement which she said she much preferred. However, her mother needed her to help with childcare so she couldn't stay with her grandmother permanently.

Emily felt the odd one out from the girls at school, who she thought were somehow prettier and cleverer than her, while the boys didn't allow her to join in with their games. She recalled that she had gone through a stage of school refusal and felt very down and lonely when she was about nine years old, and it was during this time there was an assessment of her home conditions and she was put on the social services register. What she never told the services was that the stepfather of her youngest brother would touch her inappropriately when nobody else was looking. She managed the situation by trying to absent herself when he was around.

Emily remembered falling in love with a girl at fourteen years of age and being extremely worried that her grandmother would disapprove, as she was a devout Christian and had strong views on homosexuality. She eventually said something to the friend but was rejected because the girl said that she was "not a les". Emily said that she remembered cutting her arms whenever she spent time thinking about this girl. She remembers feeling unhappy and suicidal, and the family doctor prescribed her antidepressants. During this time, she spent a lot of time online, and she found several LGBT websites where people blogged about being trans. This led her on to watching videos of the journeys of females who were transitioning and she started to believe that she was "one of them". Emily showed an article about female to male transition to her mother, who responded by asking her if she wanted to have her breasts removed. Initially, she thought she did not, as she was not dysphoric about them, but then she thought that it might be a good idea. Her rationale for this was that she remembered thinking that she did not want to have any children in the future, and therefore would have no need of them.

Emily said that she started to tell herself that she did not really like her body, in order to fit in more with the other online friends and their descriptions of gender dysphoria and "being trans". Despite not feeling particularly dysphoric, Emily started to wear a binder for her breasts and eventually reached the stage where she would not leave the house without the binder on. She found it extremely uncomfortable but said that she could remember feeling there was almost something good about being able to withstand the pain as if it was an achievement of some sort. Over time she spent more and more hours on the internet chat rooms where she felt persuaded to go on to transition, and at sixteen she asked her local doctor to refer her to the gender identity clinic. Once referred, she persuaded the clinic that she wanted to transition. She commenced on cross-sex hormones aged seventeen. She explained that she did not really engage with thoughts about why she wanted to transition or what the long-term implications would be. Emily explained to the clinic that she hated herself and hated her love of women which she felt was unacceptable. She described that she used to live in a dream-like state, supported by her trans friends online who encouraged her to believe that she would feel so much better when she had transitioned. At no stage did anyone explain that she could not biologically transition to be a male.

> I was in a state of mind where I always imagined that the solution to my self-hatred and my insecurity as a woman would be cured by my transition in the future. Any obstacle or delay in the process caused me enormous frustration and anxiety. It felt as if people were deliberately making me miserable and refusing to help me.
>
> Any time I felt unhappy, depressed, or anxious about myself I would think it's because I hadn't gone far enough along the process to transition and that I needed to press ahead to the next stage. I was riddled with doubts about my looks and completely preoccupied with how people saw me. It was very difficult to think about anything else. It was as if my whole life was taken over by a preoccupation with whether I passed as a man or not. I was completely self-absorbed.

When I reached 20 years of age, I was having ongoing cross-sex hormones and constantly worried that I would be somehow found out or exposed. I realised that the "T" injections were a reminder that I needed the hormones to continue the changes in my body, but I would never feel confident that I passed as a man. I also realised that I would never actually be a man. Ridiculously I think I had convinced myself that I could change biological sex. I felt ashamed of the fact that I had sustained such a stupid idea for such a long time. It made me feel foolish and I became a bit depressed. Eventually I decided that I didn't want to spend the rest of my life acting a part and constantly feeling like a fraud. It was then that I decided to detransition. Once I had made that decision, I overcame my feeling of embarrassment and anxiety and asked my mum and then my family doctor to help me detransition.

Case discussion

Emily described a chaotic family situation in which she plays the role of a "parentified" child who supported her mother in caring for all the half siblings. She didn't feel like she could measure up against other girls, and the therapist suspected that this was related to problems she had had internalising a good object. (N.B. The object is an internal representation of a significant figure—see p. 198 for more information on triangulation.) Melanie Klein believed that the infant's feeling of confidence about himself in relation to the external world was based on the ability to internalise a good relationship with his primary giver (see p. 201 for more information on the internalisation of the good object). The therapist hypothesised that Emily's mother was likely to have been preoccupied by her father's gambling and the tempestuous nature of their relationship and this might have affected her capacity to bond with her daughter. This in turn would have affected Emily's future confidence in relation to her peers. There is not a straightforward relationship between early traumas and later psychological or relational difficulties. However, studies show that early trauma is a contributing factor in causing ongoing problems in relation to the self and relationships in the external world.

Emily's description of her childhood presented a picture of a rather deprived, unhappy, insecure little girl who did not have a good internal sense of herself. Her grandmother is the one stable influence in her life, and she recognises this relationship's value as she tries to fit in with her grandmother's strict religious values in order to protect and sustain it. This meant that her loving feelings towards other girls are unacceptable to her as they are ego dystonic. The ego integrates perceptions and is aware of the nature of the individual's relationship with the internal and external world (see pp. 239–240 for more information on the ego). The idea of transitioning seems to offer a solution to her dilemma between keeping her grandmother's good opinion and having homosexual phantasy. In fantasy, it might represent the opportunity to get rid of the unhappy, unacceptable little girl inside her and replace her with a happier "male" self. She also likely felt resentful that she did not get the love and attention she needed from her own mother. When she contemplates the removal of her breasts, she is perhaps getting rid of something which represents soft, maternal feelings. It is hard for her to imagine she could become a mother of other children who would need both breastfeeding and loving care when she has felt so deprived of this herself. She has resented having to care for the half siblings who steal her mother's attention, and perhaps cannot envisage herself as an adult who could give generously to another child. We can understand how she might have wanted to get away from the feminine role that she felt leaves her exposed to painful feelings of being unwanted and rejected. Emily also seems to feel that she did not "make the grade" as a woman at school in terms of her attractiveness or in terms of her schoolwork.

The collapse of her belief in transitioning is related to Emily's realisation that she has been seduced by an illusory solution that she could actually change biological sex. The constant persecution of having to "pass" represents a reminder somewhere in her mind that she is not a man. "Passing" as a man allows the illusion that she can change sex to be temporarily maintained. The exhausting nature of the way in which she surveys others' reaction to her, and her own doubts and misgivings about how she is perceived by others and herself, eventually leads to a breakdown. This clinical example of how taxing it can be for a trans-identified person to maintain control over their own and others' perceptions helps us to understand the sensitivity and the traumatic experience of being misgendered or mispronounced by others.

Conclusion

Detransitioners and desisters often report being aware of doubts in their minds but ignoring them and pushing on. This involves a form of mental double bookkeeping as, on the one hand they push for transition, while on the other hand they question the direction of travel.

We have observed that the desire to transition is often connected to an attempt to distance the person from the psychic pain related to internal and/or external traumatic experiences. These traumas and their effects can be reawakened by more recent developmental conflicts or events in the young person's life. The child tries to control their underlying vulnerability by projecting unwanted aspects of the self into their natal body which is then regarded as the problem that needs to be changed or eradicated. At this point in their gender identity history, most young people will strongly resist any attempts to explore the psychological aspects of their presentation because they will feel any adult who questions their resolution is undermining their solution to their psychological well-being.

The initial excitement and determination in the young person's wish to transition is possibly related to the belief that their difficulties will be removed. In our clinical experience, we often find that the vulnerable part of the self, which is hated, has been captured by a part of the self that believes psychic pain can be eradicated through a transition. Ordinary doubts and anxieties about the belief system are dismissed and attacked as they undermine the concrete solution. However, once the excitement of transition wears off, the individual can find themselves disillusioned, facing the social, physical, and psychological damage done; this can lead to a re-emergence of underlying feelings of despair, sadness, and anger, now often compounded by a sense of guilt or shame for their own part in the process.

Patients who self-harm or take overdoses after medical and/or surgical gender transition treatments often report to Accident and Emergency in crisis. A common theme in their presentations is a belief that physical treatments would remove or resolve aspects of themselves that caused them psychic pain. When the medical intervention fails to remove these psychological problems, the disappointment and often anger lead to an escalation of self-harm and suicidal ideation, as resentment and hatred towards themselves is acted out on their bodies. Detransitioners and desisters can also feel angry at psychiatric and medical services who they understandably believe have not adequately assessed their motivations for requesting medical intervention. Grievances towards parental figures in the past can be reactivated and directed towards authority figures who are perceived to have failed in their duty of care in the present. Freud noticed the way early relationships between infant and parents are re-enacted and described this as the transference relationship (see pp. 207–209 for more information on the transference). In the cases of Emily and Bianca, early experiences of neglect are re-enacted with the medical authorities, who in their view have failed to carry out their duty to care and protect them. This leaves them feeling that the traumas of the past are being re-enacted in the present as clinicians unwittingly colluded with the patient's own internal attacks on vulnerable aspects of the self.

Part II

Development and gender dysphoria

Every child has their own individual characteristics, but they are also part of a family structure which is integral to their developmental journey towards adulthood. Children presenting with gender dysphoria are part of a family, whether intact or not. It is therefore important that children are treated if possible within a multidisciplinary structure that can address both family and individual dynamics. Children or their parents might be expressing something on behalf of the family and their place within it. The gender dysphoria might then be viewed as the symptom of underlying individual and/or family conflicts, which we discuss in the following four chapters.

FOUR

Early development in the context of the family

In a child's life, each developmental stage makes new demands and it is mainly the family that must support the young person through these challenges. Children respond to these challenges in different ways. For example, weaning can be a difficult time for both baby and parent, leading to an increase in crying and unsettled behaviour. Getting the infant to go off to sleep without the comfort of the breast or bottle can be tricky, as can persuading him to sleep in his room and not in the parents' bed. Other developmental challenges can include the birth of a baby brother or sister, potty training, starting at nursery where he must share toys with other children, or attending primary school when his parent must leave him at the school gate. Some young people respond by becoming unhappy and fighting any shift or separation. Others seem to be ready for change and see it as an opportunity to develop. The child's internal sense of security will largely dictate their ability to navigate developmental stages.

All these transitions can be a challenge to both the child and the parents, who require a combination of empathy and resilience in order to help the child along.

It is crucial that while the parents can tune in to the young person's anxieties, they also demonstrate a belief that the young person can manage realistic challenges. "Helicopter" parenting, continually hovering and intervening when kids face any difficulties, or "snowplough" parenting, removing all obstacles in the young person's path, tend to produce young people who do not feel confident in their own resources. They might become over-reliant on the parents' capacity to sort out their problems. However, at the other extreme, unempathetic parents can make the young person feel that their anxieties are unacceptable and must be disposed of in some way.

As well as having anxieties about how the young person will cope without parental support, the young person also has anxieties about how the parents will cope without them. Some parents give off messages that they will not survive without the young people. This can inhibit the young person's ability to separate from the family and move towards developing a mind and life of their own. These messages may be communicated in conscious and unconscious ways.

Joan, a patient in once-weekly psychotherapy, told the therapist that her mother continually emphasised the suffering she had gone through to bring up the family. When Joan was applying for university, she had an opportunity to take up a place overseas but turned it down on the basis that her mother would make her feel so guilty for leaving the country to pursue her studies.

Sexual development is another point of separation between parents and children. It is one of the areas where the teenager determines that they, and not their parents, are now in charge of their bodies. This battle for independence and the right to determine what the young person does with their body is often fought over with parents: what clothes are suitable, whether the teenager can have piercings or tattoos, their choice of friends and activities, and so on. The young person is saying to the parent, "It is my body, and I can do what I want with it!" Of course, in this state of mind, the young person can appear both supremely confident in their choices and actions, whilst also harbouring the belief that their parents will help them if something goes wrong, which it often does.

The development of a sense of self

Some older children are terrified of any development that involves a separation from the infantile state and the protection of the parents, as they move towards the demands of the adult world. They cling to a stage in their lives in which they could maintain themselves as the infant of the family, never really accepting the birth of a younger sibling. For example, one patient had a history of throwing temper tantrums whenever their therapist mentioned the patient's brother. Such young people often fear that they will not survive unless they remain the centre of attention and occupy the infantile position. Of course, in normal circumstances, it is usual to regress in protest at losses in life, and development is never a linear process, full of progressions and regressions. For example, the toddler who is potty-trained may suddenly stop using the potty or wet the bed when a new sibling is born.

Children who feel unloved may believe that things would have been much better if only they had been born someone else. They believe that their envy of their siblings or resentment towards their parents is so great that they cannot be accepted back into the family. These children might develop a phantasy that their parents are not their birth parents and they have been adopted into another family. This can lead to the development of a fantasy that they would be loved if only they were another person, or perhaps if they were of the other sex. Alternatively, the child might fantasise a new self in place of the self that is believed to be flawed. It may also lead to the development of a phantasy of the death of the self and the rebirth of a new self.

Case presentation—Sarah

Sarah was a sixteen-year-old girl with a long-standing history of anorexia, referred for psychotherapy by her mother. The mother (Mrs B) told the therapist that she had struggled to bond with her as a baby and said Sarah had been an anxious child who could not relax. Sarah had a younger sister who seemed to be getting on well at school. The father (Mr B) had a high-powered job, which took up a lot of his time and energy leaving Sarah's mother to cope with the two children on her own.

Mrs B described Sarah as a child who formed intense friendships with other girls at school but that these relationships often broke down when Sarah became too intensively dependent upon her friend. When Sarah moved from primary to secondary school aged eleven, her behaviour became more challenging and she frequently had temper tantrums which were not managed particularly well by the school according to Mrs B. The mother also described incidents in which Sarah would attack her younger sister over disputes about the television. Sarah spent increasing amounts of time on the computer, and her mother later discovered she had joined a pro-anorexia forum that encouraged her to restrict her diet and over the next few months she developed anorexia nervosa. At first, the parents tried to manage her eating disorder at home by encouraging her to eat. This led to huge rows over mealtimes, as she refused to eat or would say that her parents had no right to make her do so. The mother described an incident at her sister's birthday party, where she refused to eat anything and left the party, saying that she hated everyone and nobody understood her. Sarah was then referred to the eating disorders service, which put her on a programme of controlled eating and the family engaged with family therapy. The treatment appeared to work, and she and the family were discharged.

Two months after discharge, the mother was contacted by the school to say that Sarah had seen the school counsellor and requested a change in her pronouns. The mother was told that Sarah was now called Steve at school and that she wished to transition socially. The parents were alarmed at the pace that this had taken place and that the school had acted with no discussion with them. The mother asked to see the form teacher who told her the school had adopted an affirmative approach to gender, meaning the pupils should be free to express their gender in any way that they wished. Sarah's mother felt she had been told off and went home, where she discussed it all with her husband, who immediately phoned the school and asked for an appointment with the head teacher. The head teacher was more sympathetic in her approach. However, she said that they had been advised by the education authority to take an affirmative approach to young people who wanted to transition, irrespective of the parents' wishes. The head teacher also explained that they would be making an urgent referral to the child and adolescent service, because Sarah was often in tears and threatening to walk out of school when she felt she could not manage the schoolwork. The mother said that she hoped the child and adolescent service, which had been so helpful with the treatment of her anorexia, might help with her daughter's identity issues.

Sarah was seen on her own by a worker who was described as "the person who dealt with young people with gender dysphoria". He then met with the parents and told them in quite an abrupt manner that their daughter had gender dysphoria and he would be referring her on to the specialist gender service for an assessment. The parents mentioned her previous history of anorexia and her long-standing difficulties in coping with the demands of development. The worker explained that these would be looked at by other workers, but that it might be contributing to the gender dysphoria, and if Sarah was helped to feel that her dysphoric state was understood, this might reduce her tendency to lose her temper and present with behavioural difficulties. After the meeting, feeling completely at odds with their child and the family worker, the couple decided to ask for their daughter to be referred to another service.

New service assessment

At the first consultation the family therapist met the family together and then met individually with Sarah and Mr and Mrs B. The parents talked at some length about their concern that their daughter was being rushed into social gender transition. In contrast, her other difficulties and the influence of social media were being ignored. They mentioned the traumatic period of her eating disorder and the way Sarah had so readily adopted the advice of the internet support group. They described her as being suggestible and easily persuaded by any group that offered a one-size-fits-all solution to problems. Sarah's parents seemed extremely concerned that their daughter was being pulled into a cultish gang that would lead her inexorably towards medical and physical interventions.

The therapist asked the couple about Sarah's early life. Mrs B started crying and saying that she had suffered from a severe post-natal depression when Sarah was born, and her husband and his mother had cared for Sarah. She went on to say that she thought she was to blame for Sarah's early difficulties, and she worried that Sarah had never quite recovered from this early adversity. It was apparent to the therapist that the mother felt guilty about her daughter and perhaps had trouble standing up to her daughter's tyrannical behaviour, due to this feeling of guilt. It was also apparent that Mrs B missed her husband's support when he worked away from home for long periods.

The therapist then asked about Sarah's response to the birth of their second child. Again, Mrs B looked upset, saying that she suffered a less severe bout of post-natal depression but her second daughter was also often looked after by the grandmother. She went on to say that Sarah had an extreme response to the birth of her baby sister, going into sulks and throwing tantrums. Having been potty-trained and out of nappies, she started to wet the bed and demanded to come back into the parental bed. Mrs B said it was as if she was competing to be the baby all over again.

When Mr B was asked about his relationship with Sarah, he said they got on well, although when she was upset about something she tended to fight for his wife's attention. He said that he sometimes stepped in to stop her from violently screaming at her mother. Mr B felt guilty that he had been away for extended periods while the children were small, and he knew this had left his wife with a lot to deal with.

Meetings with the parents

Early in the therapy when the family therapist explored the relationship between Mr and Mrs B, they both lowered their eyes and said that they did not have much time for each other, as Sarah dominated the house. The therapist pointed out that there seemed no time in their house for anything but Sarah and her problems and how this placed a lot of power in the hands of one person. Although her behaviour was clearly an attempt to remain centre stage, this might make her feel that she was entirely bad for having this impact.

Over time the family therapist was able to help the parents talk about their feelings of guilt regarding Sarah's early years of life and to examine how this influenced their behaviour towards her. They were able to develop a more firm but thoughtful approach to the containment of her threats and hostile outbursts, while helping Sarah to find alternative ways to manage her anxiety and anger. Bion described the mother's containing function of the infant as she takes in and digests experiences that the developing infant cannot manage (see pp. 195–197 for more information on the mother's containing function). The parents began to feel more confident in the face of their daughter's behaviour and to stand up to her intimidation. The therapy also allowed for discussion of the family dynamics and the need for Mr B to support his wife when he was away for work. The father agreed to have regular face-to-face conversations with his wife and children who didn't normally get much of a look-in. The parents also agreed that the younger daughter did not complain about being neglected; in fact, she seemed to keep her head down as if to say, "Well, Mum and Dad have enough on their plates." This theme was explored, so that the sister could be encouraged to have her individual thoughts and feelings taken into consideration. Thus, the family was supported in finding a way to struggle with the balance between Sarah and her difficulties, and the necessity to make room for other members of the family.

Towards the end of the family therapy sessions Mr and Mrs B returned to see the therapist and said that they had left the grandparents in charge and taken their first weekend away in nearly twenty years, which had gone well. Mrs B then described a situation in which the family had been driving to a pub for Sunday lunch to celebrate the younger daughter's birthday. Sarah started to scream and shout at her mother about the fact that mum would not use her male name. Mr B said to Sarah that she was deliberately picking a fight. Mr B stopped the car, took his daughter out and quietly but firmly told her that Sarah was not to shout at her mother and that she was spoiling her sister's birthday. He went on to say that they would not continue the journey until she calmed down. After some time, Sarah calmed down and got into the car and they continued their journey.

Therapy with Sarah

Sarah agreed to meet on the basis that the therapist was trying to understand her and her difficulties without prejudice.

The therapist invited Sarah into the room. She came in with a sullen look as if she assumed that the therapist had heard about her and knew she was demanding. She sat on the edge of the chair in an uncomfortable position. It looked as if she was not sure if she was welcome or was going to stay. The therapist said perhaps she was sitting on the edge of the seat because Sarah might worry that the therapist had heard a lot of bad things about her. She nodded and looked up a little. The therapist then commented that perhaps she also felt worried about being made to feel small or ashamed.

The first few months of the therapy were characterised by long periods when Sarah was stuck in some sort of frozen state. She would occasionally show some interest in something the therapist said before sinking back into a sullen, uncommunicative state.

After several months, Sarah began to engage more and opened up, talking more about her history, including her feeling that her mother always made her think that she was too sensitive and too childish. She talked as if she felt she was being pushed too quickly to develop and grow up. The therapist said Sarah did not seem to feel her mother had provided her with the equipment she needed to grow up.

Later on in the therapy the therapist was able to address Sarah's resentment over her sister's birth, which she felt had deprived her of the exclusive relationship with mother. They explored how Sarah's need to be "the baby" at the centre of things meant that she was stuck in a position where any movement or development felt like a threat.

Clinical discussion at team meeting

In the team meetings, Sarah's therapist described the situation early in the therapy, whereby she felt unable to operate in her usual manner. The therapist said she felt that Sarah was withholding information and material in a way that prevented the development of their work. The therapist felt wary of making any interpretations that might upset Sarah, but this left them in a frustrating and disconnected state.

The family therapist thought this situation somewhat mirrored the situation at home, as Sarah's mother was endlessly trying to coax her daughter into a position where she would engage with life, while the patient hung on doggedly to her symptoms and her position as being the young person with the most needs. A colleague wondered if Sarah was preventing the parents from moving on with their lives and eternally punishing them for having another child. The team were then reminded of the patient's history of anorexia. The anorexic state of mind draws the individual into a state of manic self-sufficiency where development, and particularly any evidence of sexual development, is arrested, in part by starving the body of the food it needs to develop, grow, and function as a sexual body. It also prevents any ingestion or digestion of their emotional experience in the external world. It is also common for young anorexics to dominate the family dynamics as everyone is terrified of a deadly relapse in the patient if they upset the routines and structures that are traditionally used to control family behaviour.

After a summer break

After the summer holidays, Sarah's mother phoned to say that the patient was refusing to come back to the therapy and just wanted to transition. Sarah believed the therapy was all part of a plot to prevent her from being who she wanted to be.

However, she did return the following week, and after five minutes of what felt like punishing silence she said that the therapy was a waste of time and that the therapist was just trying to stop her from being her real self. The therapist responded by saying that perhaps she felt she had been "dropped" during the break as the therapist got on with other aspects of life, like for example when Sarah's mother had gone on to have another baby.

Sarah snarled at the therapist and said something dismissive. However, she then softened, saying that she knew her parents were disappointed in her. The therapist said perhaps Sarah thought the therapist had gone away because she was disappointed in her progress too. Sarah slumped in her chair in a way that suggested the therapist had said something that affected her.

The therapist asked her if there was an area where she thought she could give her parents some pleasure. After a short pause, when she seemed to be holding back a smile, she said she was very good at hockey. She was so good that she had played with the boys until she was thirteen, but then she was told she would have to play in the girls' team. She looked disconsolate, saying she hated playing with the girls because they bitched and complained when they got hurt.

Over the next few weeks, the therapy explored several themes focusing on Sarah's anxiety about her ability to manage her emotions without losing control. She felt threatened in any situation where she felt excluded or humiliated and would become very angry. After the second break in the therapy, Sarah became sullen and angry. She stopped talking to the therapist and started to restrict the content of the session. The therapist said she thought Sarah had experienced the break as a rejection, as if she had been pushed out into the cold. Sarah said that the therapist was just like her parents, who demanded that she cheer up just to make them happy. The therapist then said she thought Sarah wanted to convey that she was very angry and did not feel like forgiving her.

Case discussion

The working hypothesis was that Mrs B's post-natal depression did interfere with her capacity to bond with Sarah as a baby. This problem may have been compounded by the fact that after Mrs B emerged from the severe post-natal depression, she continued to suffer depression and anxiety about the impact this separation and her illness had had upon her daughter, and her guilt continued, for many years, to interfere with the need for her to develop a more robust and confident relationship with Sarah. Mr B's regular absences for work had compounded this problem as it left her without his support and help in managing the children. We believe this anxious attachment between mother and infant may have interfered with Sarah's need to internalise a mother who could help her make sense of her rage, anxiety, and jealousy. This led to Sarah trying to control her mother and her actions in an attempt to prevent any separation, as she needed an external figure constantly available to alleviate and remove anxiety. The birth of another daughter ruptured this fragile relationship, causing Sarah to regress, flying into rages as she competed for her mother's attention. It was as if she were saying, "You have no right to have another baby. I am the only baby you can have, and I will always need you to be available." Her father's absence meant there was no alternative parental presence to help Sarah triangulate in her thinking.

Triangulation is connected to the ability to separate from the ideal object (i.e. Sarah's mother) and see things from her perspective (see p. 198 for more information on triangulation). Faced with overwhelming anxiety and rage at separation, Sarah dominated the household, driven by a grievance towards the (other) baby. The combination of Mrs B's guilt about her post-natal depression and the lack of paternal support inhibited Mrs B from standing up to her eldest daughter's demands. In many ways, Sarah's dominance kept the younger sister out of the picture. These behaviours appeared to be one way Sarah tried to control the family, so she could remain at the centre of their preoccupations and thereby evade her own anxieties about separation and loss.

The fragile nature of Sarah's ego when overwhelmed with feelings of anger, jealousy, or humiliation causes her to evacuate these feelings through actions and violent verbal outbursts. Her communications are driven by anxiety and a grievance that everything would have been all right if only her parents had provided perfect conditions for her. In other words, they should have acted as "snowplough" parents paving the way for her and removing any obstacles to her well-being. It was as if she needed to believe that she should live in a perfect world with her at the centre of everything.

The therapist working with Sarah had the challenging task of empathising with how the patient felt about humiliation, grievance, and jealousy whenever there was a problem, while also exploring with Sarah how she tended to get stuck in these states. In this angry frame of mind, she believed she had no internal resources or abilities to help her come to terms with the pain of disappointment, or to enable adapting to new circumstances. The therapist had to help her work through the loss of her position in the family, while also pointing out how she viewed herself as stuck, ignoring the internal resources she possessed.

In the early stages of the therapy, the therapist often felt like she was walking on eggshells in each session. On the one hand, there was a risk of traumatising the patient by attempting to address important issues, such as loss and rivalry prematurely, which led Sarah to feel pushed to grow up, which she felt unable to manage. On the other hand, the therapist had to guard against being controlled by Sarah and colluding with her hatred of development. This is a constant dilemma in the treatment of young people with a fragile ego who can rapidly feel overwhelmed by too many psychological demands. Consequently, they rely on more primitive defence mechanisms such as denial, splitting, and projection, which rigidly protect the individual from psychic pain, but inhibit the individual's capacity to develop the mental flexibility required for the reality testing central to healthy psychic development.

Ten months into the therapy, Sarah told the therapist about the incident in which her father had stopped the car and got out to reprimand her. Sarah emphasised how unreasonable she had been. The therapist said it seemed Sarah was aware that she sometimes provoked an irritated response in the therapist and others. The conflict between the part of her that wanted to transition, and the part that had doubts, got acted out between herself and the therapist.

Gradually Sarah's desire to transition desisted and after three years of once-weekly therapy, she said that she would like to stop. Towards the end of the therapy, she proudly told the therapist that she had been made captain of the girls' hockey team and said she was also getting on much better with her friends at school.

Soon after the end of the therapy, the parents contacted the family team to say that their daughter seemed much happier. Although she still had her moments, they felt like they had been able to restore themselves as parents rather than carers of a fragile young person. The parents also had more time for each other and the rest of the family.

Links between eating disorders and gender dysphoria

It is common to find that young people with gender dysphoria also have a history of an eating disorder. We think this is related to early experiences between the infant and the mother. Problems can arise if there is a difficulty or a disruption in this relationship, which is mainly established through the mother's care and love of the baby and in particular through early feeding and weaning. In the case of Sarah, we can surmise that her mother's post-natal depression interfered with the bonding process which disrupted her capacity to internalise a good object. The link between eating disorders and gender dysphoria is also not unexpected because, in our experience, they are both developmental disorders that look to control ordinary developmental processes by employing primitive psychological mechanisms. The control of the patient's relationship with food represents their wish to control the process of bodily development and functions such as puberty. This control over the body makes the patient feel that they can also exert powerful control over their desires and appetites, which are constantly threatening to overwhelm them.

Rosenfeld (1971) described the way individuals may develop pathological organisations that offer to protect the individual from psychic pain. Pathological organisations operating within the patient may offer omnipotent solutions to the individual. These organisations promise to offer pain-free solutions to life by employing violent psychic defences. The cost is that the individual is often dependent upon the internal organisation, and any rebellion against the organisation may cause considerable anxiety about a backlash. The cost of the individual's dependence upon these organisations is that they inhibit development as they interfere with vulnerable aspects of the personality's capacity to get help.

This leads to atrophy within the personality as the individual becomes stuck. Inevitably the sadomasochist internal dynamics get re-enacted in the therapy as the therapist may be pulled and pushed into enacting different roles. Relinquishing the dependence on these roles is difficult as they require the individual to relinquish their dependence on powerful defensive systems. Sarah was controlled by an internal system that demanded devotion in return for control of her psychological state. The overvalued idea that transition would remove psychic pain and confusion is based on an idea that Sarah can control her body and her body's development. This is very similar to the fantasy of control exerted by the anorexic over their body and their body's functioning.

It is also striking that, as with the anorexic patient, the young person who wishes to transition has transferred the psychic conflict into the body, which then becomes the thing they wish to control. This is symptomatic of the fact that the individual does not feel they can manage the conflicts and psychic pain associated with development in the mind. This anxiety increases with the onset of changes that take place during puberty in relation to sexual development.

The wish to control the sexual development and functioning of the body is extremely important in both gender dysphoria and anorexia. Many anorexics have deep-seated anxieties about the transition from being a sexually immature young person to becoming a sexually mature adult. Anorexics who have amenorrhoea (meaning their periods have stopped due to weight loss) can find it reassuring because it means they cannot have children and are not reminded of the fact they can during every menstrual cycle. One can think of this as a psychic retreat, as a mental state that avoids the anxieties associated with depressive guilt on the one hand and persecutory fears of fragmentation on the other (Steiner, 1993a) (see pp. 203–204 for more information on psychic retreats).

Some young people do not feel that they have the mental equipment to deal with the transition from childhood to adulthood and unconsciously look for psychic retreats that offer respite from the demands of development. Psychic retreats attempt to stop the physical changes and associated anxieties brought about by physical and emotional development. However, by moving into a psychic retreat, the person also stops the development that occurs as a result of the changing demands of life, which lead to maturity. The psychic retreat offers powerful solutions to disturbing psychic pain. This psychic structure and the dynamic between different parts of the self need to be identified by clinicians who could help the child and the family by supporting the patient in tolerating psychic pain anxieties and conflicts rather than colluding with a phantasy that part of the self can be permanently removed through a transition.

The need for a multidisciplinary team

Any individual therapy with children and young adults often needs to be supported by other sorts of intervention, like family therapy or couple therapy with the parents. Parents might take various stances on their child's wish to transition. Sometimes, families can fit in with their child's wish to transition unquestioningly. Alternatively, one parent may be at loggerheads with their child and their plans to transition. The child often holds a central position in the family, and as we have noted elsewhere, before a young person proceeds to any medical intervention the family dynamics need to be investigated and understood. It is sometimes observed that young people who develop gender dysphoria have siblings with serious conditions that affect the family's functioning. Early separation and loss are also common in the patient's history, such as problems with a mother who is struggling to manage the break-up of a relationship or come to terms with a perinatal death. Children who have parents who abuse alcohol or drugs, or who have mental health conditions, are also more likely to develop gender dysphoria.

Meeting with the parents and wider family can help to explore the impact of these traumatic events, as well as exploring the role that the young person fulfils in relation to the rest of the family. For example, it is crucial to understand the family's wish to support transition. There are many varied reasons: it could be due to homophobia, the parents' wish for a child of the other sex, Munchausen by proxy, or it could be due to separation anxiety or the parents' anguish at seeing their child in a distressed, dysphoric state which they wish to be resolved as quickly as possible. Pressure either from parents or families should not interfere with the clinician's need to make their own independent assessment.

Child and adolescent psychiatry and psychology are other disciplines that can play an essential role in the treatment of young people with gender dysphoria. Many of the young people presenting have comorbid problems such as eating disorders; they may be on the autistic spectrum or have ADHD. It's been reported by parents and desistors that gender services often seem to look at the comorbid presentations as if they were separate from the gender dysphoria. This idea of the mind and personality as existing in silos is often supported by the young people who are attracted to "paranoid–schizoid" ways of thinking which involve splitting things apart (see pp. 189–194 for more information on the paranoid–schizoid position). The reality is that the human mind and personality are dynamic and therefore different parts of the personality link and interact. A multidisciplinary team can help to bring aspects of the dynamics of the family relationship into relief and to explain how they might have been projected into the gender dysphoric young person. The gender identity clinics need to try to develop a dynamic formulation that attempts to build a picture of the way different aspects of the personality link together (D'Angelo, 2019).

Conclusion

Each stage of life faces us with developmental challenges and difficulties. For adolescents, the appearance of secondary sex characteristics, such as the enlarging of breasts, widening of hips in women and the deepening of the voice and increase in facial and body hair in men, produce all sorts of anxieties related to sexual maturation and there may be huge anxieties about the changing body.

It is essential to allow psychological space for the exploration of the underlying issues of any presentation of gender dysphoria, not with the aim of preventing transition, but to ensure that the unconscious motives and thinking have been explored and understood. Young people can develop fixed beliefs that they are born into the wrong body and that all their problems will be solved when they are helped to transition to another gender. Services need to be empathetic with the young person's desire, while resisting the temptation to collapse into a position of colluding. This difficult clinical task is made more difficult when one or both parents are pushing for the transition. Parents do often argue that their child is distressed, and that transitioning will take the distress away. This creates great difficulties for the service as they are under enormous pressure to facilitate transition, which does not give them enough time to explore the long-term implications. It is also evident that some parents form a folie à deux with the young person underwritten by serious pathology in the parent. For example, it is commonly argued that some families would find it easier to accept their child is trans rather than homosexual. Services need to assess these influences and, therefore, ongoing assessment and therapeutic work with the family should be an essential part of any treatment service in this area.

FIVE

Separation–individuation and fixed states of mind

"When I was a child, from the age of about three years old until I was roughly ten years old, I had what would now be described as gender dysphoria. I was persistent, consistent, and insistent in my belief that I was really a boy. I knew I was very good at being a boy and that there was nothing girlish about me. I was proud of my ability to be a boy and dismissive of other girls who were tomboys—I knew I was much more than a tomboy. It just seemed fundamentally wrong that I was a girl because I was so boyish, and I was so good at being a boy. These feelings were so deep and profound, from as far back as I remember. I was an unhappy kid, and particularly unhappy as an adolescent; looking back it seems clear to me that I was manifesting the many difficulties in my family life in the only way that made sense to me.

"From the age of about ten, my dysphoria became heightened around puberty and my distress increased but became more secretive, more internalised. I realised by that age that other people thought it was silly that I said I was a boy and so I went inward. Puberty was a train wreck. And yet ultimately, it fundamentally released me from what is now termed gender dysphoria. By the time I had moved out of puberty, I had left it completely behind."

—Stella O'Malley, psychotherapist

Jane—a fifteen-year-old girl

Jane was a fifteen-year-old girl who was referred for assessment of her gender dysphoria; she had gone to her local family doctor asking to be referred to the gender identity clinic because she wished to be prescribed hormone blockers. She lived with her mother and older sister. Her parents had divorced when Jane was very young.

When she presented at the gender clinic for the first time, Jane had a closely shaven head and was wearing a checked shirt with rolled-up sleeves, a denim jacket, and Dr Martens boots. Her body language and mannerisms were exaggeratedly masculine. She sat in her chair with thighs wide apart and a defiant look on her face. It felt like a challenge to the therapist as if she were saying, "Right—do not question me—I know what I know—I am a man." She had multiple piercings on her eyebrow and nose, which gave the impression of someone with a hard attitude towards the world. It was as if she was saying to everyone, "Look how tough I am. I have pushed all this metal into my face." She was flat-chested and told the therapist that she bound her breasts because they offended her. The therapist had the feeling that her hard, macho external appearance was in order for Jane to disguise anything soft and vulnerable in herself, and that perhaps any need to be cared for had to be denied because it posed such a threat.

In the first consultation, the therapist asked Jane to talk about why she had wanted a referral to the clinic. She said that she knew she was a man and that she wanted to transition by taking hormones and eventually going on to change her name legally and have a double mastectomy. (The therapist thought this conveyed a desperate wish to get rid of any evidence of her female self as well as her female body.) They agreed to meet in order to explore Jane's feelings about herself.

The therapist saw Jane regularly for several months. Initially, Jane was defended against the idea that there was anything in her thinking that needed attention or exploration, and she was irritated whenever the therapist tried to make links between her underlying feeling of insecurity and her wish to transition. The therapist neither confirmed nor denied Jane's ideas about being "in the wrong body" but continued to think more widely with her about who she was and her life experiences. The therapist took up the fact that Jane seemed angry and suspicious of the therapist's motives.

Therapist: I think you believe that I am trying to control your thinking. But it's important to explore your thoughts and feelings about yourself, why you think you need to transition, what you want to change about yourself.

Jane slumped back in her chair, as if the therapist had stopped her and her almost physical momentum. For the first time she looked more anxious and then sad. The physical slump seemed to convey that she felt both cared about and that the therapist had been able to puncture her hard exterior, which indicated to Jane that she was serious about their exploratory work together. Her defensive physical state was like a suit of armour she wore, but for a moment the therapist felt, after months of working with Jane and her fixed ideas about herself, that something had got through. Jane began to feel safe enough with the therapist to allow her more vulnerable feelings to be acknowledged.

Over the next few months, Jane started to talk more about her life as a young child. She had experienced hearing difficulties that had gone unnoticed until she was seven, halfway through primary school. The therapist talked with her about how difficult this must have been and explored with Jane how it had affected her. Jane talked about how she had found it difficult to fit in with the girls at school, as when they laughed at things and shared jokes she didn't catch what they were saying and so felt excluded from the group. It emerged that she had also struggled academically, and her speech had been affected by the hearing difficulty. She had corrective surgery to improve her hearing, but by then she had become socially isolated. Jane also said she was chubby because she ate too many snacks and thought herself to be "too fat, not as pretty as the other girls, and very out of place".

When she went to secondary school at the age of eleven, although her academic work improved, she still had social difficulties and experienced bullying about her weight. She talked about this period of her life as a tough time: she hated herself; she hated being at school; she found social situations extremely difficult and always felt the outsider in any group. As a result of her social anxiety, she became more isolated and spent time browsing the internet. It was here that she came across ideas about transgender identity, which she felt helped explain why she had experienced all these difficulties.

Therapist: It must have been very disappointing that the hearing problem was not recognised earlier. You describe feeling like you don't fit in with the other girls in a way that makes me think it has been very painful for you.

Jane: So my mum was preoccupied with her work and earning money after dad left home. My older sister did a lot of after school activities and is a really good swimmer. At the weekend my mum and sister went to swimming galas, so I was often left with the neighbour.

Therapist: I think you feel you are only acceptable if you are physically capable like your sister and there is no room for imperfection or physical limitations like your hearing difficulty.

Jane: [*Shrugging her shoulders*] Well, what's the point in making a fuss?

Therapist: And perhaps you feel that way here too. That you think that no one could really care about your difficulties or vulnerabilities when you suspect these are unwelcome and unattractive. [*Long pause and it looked as if Jane was going to cry but then she sat up more in her chair with her chin slightly jutting out*]

Jane: What we are doing is a complete waste of time, I know what I need. I just need to be given hormones.

Therapist: It is as if you have decided that who you are now is intolerable, and there is no point in talking to me or exploring things. But I think it's important that we keep trying to understand what's going on for you.

Jane again looked momentarily sad, but then coughed and rested her head on her hand as if she was tired of talking. She then repeated that she was born into the wrong body and that's all there was to it.

This pattern of some emotional contact followed by withdrawal and irritation continued throughout the first year of therapy.

During the second year, there was a subtle change in Jane's outward appearance. The exaggerated masculine posture started to recede, and Jane became less habitually defensive and more receptive in the sessions. Her outfits also became more varied and she sometimes came without her Doc Martens or wore a colourful T-shirt rather than her previous "uniform".

Over time it began to emerge that Jane was doing better at school and on one occasion she told the therapist that she came second in a test, although she also had felt angry that she could have come first if the form tutor had not favoured the "teacher's pet". She went on to say that the teacher had also talked with her about whether she was interested in going to university, but quickly followed this by telling the therapist, in a somewhat provocative way, it was of no interest to her. She also mocked the other kids: "The swots who just wanted to get to university and do student things." She tried to give the impression to the therapist that she didn't care and couldn't be bothered. Jane went on to talk about an argument with her mother who had objected to her going to stay with friends who, she knew, took drugs, and drank, and had dropped out of school.

Therapist: I think you take yourself seriously and work hard, but then it feels unbearable when you come second and feel that somebody else has been favoured over you. Then you want to give up.

Jane: That's my life.

Therapist: I think when you say, "That's my life", you want to get rid of any worry about the way you may be damaging your opportunities and put them into me. Then you don't have to worry.

Jane: I stopped trying to be a "good little girl" years ago.

Therapist: You might have an idea that I would prefer to see "good little girls" than you and your angry, mixed-up feelings.

Jane: I just can't seem to do anything right because I always feel there's something wrong with me.

This allowed for an exploration of how Jane hated feeling unfavourable compared to others and that she always imagined herself being in competition with someone who had no flaws. The "teacher's pet" was someone like her sister, who she imagined would always come out on top. In the transference, Jane doubts that her therapist would be really interested in her as she knows she is defensive and angry a lot of the time.

Although Jane was often provocative in her nihilistic approach to life, she was able to convey to her therapist that she did not entirely believe her stance. It was as if she was searching for an adult who would try to reach her and not give up on her: someone who could make her feel that she might not be perfect but who thought that didn't mean she was completely unacceptable. At times, the therapist had to contend with being a helpless bystander as she witnessed Jane's dismissal of her actual capacities in preference for an ideal version of herself. At other times the therapist would catch glimpses of the vulnerability underlying Jane's aggrieved state.

Two years into the therapy, Jane came into the session wearing a colourful jumper and she appeared not to be wearing her binder around her chest. She said that she had started dating a girl from school and felt she was probably lesbian and not trans. The therapist explored in the transference the implications of this communication about the date. Jane had begun to look forward to her sessions with her therapist and her softer feelings about herself and others had begun to emerge. Jane now felt she had something to offer the therapist and the therapist had something to offer her.

During the remaining months of therapy, the atmosphere changed considerably. The therapist felt she was able to explore Jane's thoughts and feelings without treading on eggshells. Jane was noticeably more open in talking about her confusions and anxieties, as well as reflecting on how her mind had developed in regard to her life and identity. Jane was able to talk about her father leaving the family and how much this affected her mother. She felt constantly worried that her mother might become overwhelmed or unable to cope with two daughters alone. The therapist talked with Jane about her fantasy that she was in some way the man of the house protecting her mother, while denying her own feelings about his desertion.

Case discussion

Jane presents herself as a defensive, physically tough-looking masculine figure who is certain she is a man trapped in a female body. She is not curious about herself or interested to understand or explore her feelings around her wish to transition. The rather stereotypical presentation of a hard, male figure who is not curious or receptive is in stark contrast to the soft, disguised tissue of the breasts which have been bound. This physical presentation is quite common in adolescent females looking to transition. It is reflected in the black-and-white thinking that characterises many gender dysphoric presentations. If you like the colour pink and play with dolls, you must be a girl. If you like black and playing football, you must be a boy. Jane does not want to be a soft, little girl who can be easily bullied and hurt when left out. It is also common for young people with a presentation of gender dysphoria to be locked into a frozen state in which they have fixated on an "overvalued idea". The person can be completely obsessed by everything relating to gender, almost to the exclusion of any other dimension of their lives. It is as if they believe all their problems would be solved if only they were the "right" gender.

The idea of gender as a fixed solution can function just like a psychic retreat—a defensive state in which the confusion and anxieties caused by the inexorable path of sexual development can be put on hold for a prolonged period. These states protect the young person from anxieties about depressive breakdown on the one hand, and fragmentation on the other. This is important to understand because when the fixed state is challenged or feels threatened, it can produce a fierce defence from the individual. When faced with the challenges of development, the young person retreats into a psychic suit of armour. Then, when the therapist starts inviting the young person to take the armour off, they hate the idea for fear of being made vulnerable. The response can be fierce and off-putting for professionals as they are made to feel their attempts to work with the patient are unwanted or even unkind or harmful.

At the start of the consultation, Jane is suspicious and hostile towards the therapist. We think this is related to her assumption that if the therapist fails to adopt a stance of automatic affirmation it is because she is against the idea of transition. Therefore, Jane believes she has to defend herself and her views of herself from a therapist who already believes transition is a bad idea and will want to impose her view upon Jane. Adolescents have the task of trying to take ownership of themselves and their bodies and this often leads to conflicts with parents and adults who are in positions of authority. This is often represented by the argument: "It's my body and I can do what I like with it." Intense feelings may be provoked when the adolescent plans to take action that may damage the body or interfere with its functioning, as is the case with transition. A detached attitude on behalf of the therapist towards the patient's actions would be inappropriate, and, as with some detransitioners, eventually lead to accusations of neglect. However, a wish to control the patient's thinking or actions, rather than an open, exploratory attitude, can be equally inappropriate and may lead to a breakdown in the therapeutic relationship. This will be an ongoing clinical dilemma for professionals working in this area.

For this reason, the therapist needs time to understand what the young person is defending against and what function the psychic retreat serves. What are the anxieties that threaten to overwhelm them? The aim of exploring these ideas is not to persuade the young person that they are wrong about wanting to transition, but that by learning about their defences and vulnerabilities, they are in a better position to make decisions about what is motivating them. If this can be facilitated then, like Jane, they find their anxieties are easier to bear and they can risk leaving the psychic retreat.

All young people have to face the reality that they are not ideal and that their internal objects are not ideal (see p. 240 for more information on the internal object). This is a crucial step in the development of the individual's capacity to separate from their parental objects and make a truer assessment of themselves in relation to their peers. However, it also leads to feelings of rage, envy, and jealousy often directed towards the parental figures whom they also depend upon and love. This, in turn, can lead to feelings of persecution and guilt which are often acted out between children and parents. When young people feel that their "objects" cannot bear their hatred, or their guilt threatens to overwhelm them, they retreat to the "paranoid–schizoid position". This leads to "black-and-white" thinking, where self and other are split into "good" and "bad" (see pp. 189–194).

Grievances towards parental figures who are perceived as failing to provide optimal care can unconsciously become the locus of a developmental problem. Jane struggled academically and socially with her peers as a result of an unrecognised problem with her hearing. She held a grievance towards her parents, who may have been genetically responsible for the hearing problem. They also failed to pay attention to the problems she was having. Jane believed that she could not overcome her difficult start, perhaps compounded by her father's desertion of the family. It is painful for anyone to come to terms with a disability, and parental figures can help with this. Avoidance or denial of the disability leaves the child on their own with feelings of inadequacy, frustration, or failure. In many ways, Jane felt she could not come to terms with her hearing difficulty and subsequent losses. It was as if she wanted to reinvent herself, so she could leave behind the girl with the problems and cut off any painful emotions she had. Black-and-white thinking is a characteristic of gender dysphoria (Hakeem, 2018), and Jane was quite rigid in her thinking about male and female stereotypes.

This was demonstrated when she worked hard and came second in a test but then couldn't bear coming second and started talking about an argument with her mother over Jane spending time with friends who'd dropped out of school. It is as if she were saying, "Either I will be the best, the 'ideal' and come first—or I'm not trying at all." The rivalry for her mother's attention with her high-achieving older sister is an all-or-nothing fight; she either has to triumph completely or to refuse to compete at all. It is striking that Jane does not feel able to have the argument with her mother as she fears her rage would destroy her mother, who is on her own and unsupported by her father. Consequently, she swallows her anger, turning it inward. The underlying grievance produces a hard exterior which binds a soft, neglected interior in need of protection.

One viewpoint is that Jane needed a receptive mother who could nurture and help her develop. However, Jane believed that her mother and sister were a couple with no room for her. Instead, she is left feeling isolated and like the un-ideal one. When the hearing disability is rectified and her abilities improve, she has already become entrenched in the position of the unloved outsider of the family. This isolated, detached state gets worse as Jane realises that she does not fit in with her peers at school. She adopts this role as the hard, uncaring, unreceptive young person who is detached from feelings. She disowns feelings because they threaten to overwhelm her, and she may fear that they would overwhelm her mother.

Jane was unsure whether she would be lovable if she were difficult and her tendency to swallow her aggression meant that this issue was never tested. However, Jane was able to test this out with the therapist. At times she could be provocative when she talked dismissively about her wish to give up her schoolwork or just get rid of her breasts as if they were valueless aspects of her body. When she said these things, she often watched the therapist closely to see if there was any response in the therapist. In this way, she could project her concern and anxiety into the therapist and see the disturbance as the therapist registered the pain of realising that she was planning on having her breasts removed. The feelings this generated took quite a bit of managing in the countertransference. If the therapist were to reply that Jane should not remove her breasts, it would confirm to Jane that the therapist wants to control the outcome of the therapy. In contrast, if the therapist were not to respond at all, it would indicate that, like Jane's parents, she did not care. The challenge for the therapist is to find ways to demonstrate empathy for Jane's need to protect herself by disguising her vulnerability but to stand firm on the need for a therapeutic space where these painful aspects of Jane can be explored.

Dissociation from the body

Where there are difficulties in the relationship between the mother and infant or failures in the relationship with the father, it can create schisms in the mind because the infant fails to integrate internal experiences. If young people feel threatened by emotional experiences which they worry will be unmanageable, they develop an intellectual defence moving up into the mind and out of the body. They then look at their body from the outside in a detached way, as if they view themselves as alien. (This tendency fits in very well with the domain of social media where adolescents continually assess how many "likes" their picture gets or how many people have followed them on Instagram.) The body may be treated as if it were something they just happen to be landed with, rather than an intrinsic part of themselves; as some sort of mannequin that needs to be controlled, rather than the body through which they experience the world. We are all preoccupied with how we are seen from the outside, but this needs to integrate with how we feel on the inside.

If the individual is detached from their internal bodily experience, which they try to control by focusing on external judgement alone, it may lead to problems integrating subjective and objective experience.

The gender dysphoria is symptomatic of Jane's cut-off emotional state where all feelings are projected into the body, while she moves up into her intellect and away from the emotions that threaten to overwhelm her. Jane is looking for safe psychological ground, somewhere she can evade feeling angry and neglected. Dysphoria is a state of distress and unhappiness. We can see how Jane is unhappy with who she is, as she does not feel very loving towards her mother, whom she resents for preferring her sister. The projection of these unwanted feelings into her body augment the split between mind and body. (Projection involves pushing elements of the mind out into an external object in phantasy.) The fixed idea that she is in the wrong body reinforces the defensive structure and seems like a haven in a storm to Jane, buffeted as she is by the storms of puberty. A rationale that narrowly focuses on the preoccupation with gender also excludes looking at what she really feels and thinks. Indeed, curiosity and thought are experienced as a threat to the overvalued belief that all her problems would be solved if only Jane could have medication to stop her breasts growing and become a man. The belief she is really a man in the wrong body functions as a plausible defence against the depressive feelings that she feels lonely, isolated, unwanted, and unloved.

There is also the matter of distancing herself from her identification with her sister and mother as she feels hurt that she does not measure up or fit in. If you cannot be a girlie girl, you are not a girl at all. Again, this is based on a very rigid idea of what a girl is. It suggests that all girls are soft and preoccupied with feelings, while all boys are tough and never talk about feelings. This is a very rigid characterisation of masculinity and femininity; however, it appealed to the sort of black-and-white thinking employed by Jane.

As Jane's thinking became less rigid, her preoccupation with gender to the exclusion of everything else lessened. This enabled her to think about herself in a broader way which included other aspects of her personality and her life, such as the prospect of university and potential relationships.

When the family or clinical service too readily accept or comply with a patient's view, they are supporting the belief that psychic problems can be dealt with by medical intervention. Psychoanalyst Rosine Perelberg (2019) makes the point that there is a "confusion of registers" where the professional and the patient "are prone to getting caught up in mistaking symbolic communication and concrete action". The cost is that the individual is dissociated from their own body. Worryingly, some of the internet chat forums provide coaching for young people on how to get past the assessment in order to obtain hormone medication as quickly as possible. If achieved, this bypasses the psychological conflicts that need to be addressed (and matters are unlikely to be resolved through medication).

Beatrice—a thirteen-year-old girl

Beatrice was a thirteen-year-old girl who had been diagnosed with autistic spectrum disorder. She was referred to a gender identity service to assist her with gender transition. The school had written a report which said that Beatrice was an intelligent pupil, who was very good at maths and computer studies, but that she had difficulty with the social aspects of school and appeared to withdraw into a world of her own.

At the first family meeting, the parents described Beatrice as a quiet girl who enjoyed being at home and was not particularly involved in a social life. They also described her as very bright, who had done particularly well at primary school where she was always top of the class. However, they also mentioned that she had tended to form intense, almost obsessive, one-to one relationship with girls. Each friendship would start well but would then fall apart when her expectations of exclusivity became too demanding. For example, she travelled to school every morning with her best friend and when her friend decided to meet up with some other friends on a different route, Beatrice felt completely betrayed. She refused to go to school for several days and stayed up in her bedroom, playing for hours on computer games. She became extremely abusive towards both her parents when they tried to talk with her or attempted to stop her playing on her computer. Her school attendance was eventually solved by her mother offering to travel with her daughter into school every day, which she did for the remainder of the term.

Beatrice responded well in her private tuition classes for music and advanced mathematics but struggled to manage as part of any large classroom group, sometimes leaving the classroom if she felt she had been ignored by the teacher or if another young person had received praise. When Beatrice became upset and moody, her mother commented that she had to spend considerable time with her daughter, trying to talk and reason with her, in order to get Beatrice to join back in with life. Her mother also said that Beatrice had had a severe speech impediment when she was young and that she had been the only one who could understand Beatrice until she was three years old. Beatrice also had problems separating from her mother when she commenced primary school aged four. Her mother had given up her work when Beatrice was three, when it became clear her difficulties in communication and her fear of separation were going to need more time and attention.

During the family meeting, the therapist noticed Beatrice would look down when her mother was talking. Mother described Beatrice as liking things to happen in the house in a certain way and that she would go quiet when they did not correspond to her wishes. She also mentioned her dietary requirements which were very particular and different from everyone else's in the family. This meant that her mother had to cook her special meals. The therapist also noticed that the father remained silent and distant throughout the first consultation.

Beatrice's mother said that she had not responded well to the birth of her younger sister, Grace, and would throw tantrums and become quite physically disturbed. Grace, who was a year and a half younger than Beatrice, looked timid and spent the whole meeting hiding behind her mother.

The therapist commented on how Beatrice seemed to take up a lot of her mother's attention and that perhaps it was difficult to be able to make room for Grace, her husband, or herself. The father continued to look at the floor while her mother responded in a concrete way, saying that both the girls had their own rooms. However, she went on to say that Beatrice still sometimes came into their bed either when she could not get off to sleep or if she awoke during the night.

Beatrice told the therapist that she wanted to change her name and her school. Her father said that was fine if this was what she wanted, and her mother said she was happy to support anything that made Beatrice happy. She also said that Beatrice had started to voice a wish to transition when she was twelve years old after her friend had told her she no longer wished to be friends with her. Beatrice had retreated to her bedroom and a short time later announced her decision about her wish to transition.

The family therapist pointed out that Beatrice had reacted very strongly to the rejection by her friend, as if she felt she was no longer acceptable and had to change something completely. At this point in the meeting, Beatrice said that she had always felt she was a boy. Her mother reminded her that she did not always want to be a boy. She went on to say that she had been OK in her earlier years and had liked her primary school but had found the move to secondary school unsettling. It was noticeable that there was very little communication, either verbal or nonverbal between the parents. Instead, her mother spoke to Beatrice in most of her communications, as if she was constantly monitoring her reaction. When Beatrice became more insistent and agitated in her claim, the therapist observed that the mother seemed to relinquish her view and agree with Beatrice in a placatory manner.

Reflecting on the family therapy meeting, the team was struck by the way the family seemed to be dominated by Beatrice's moods and insecurities. The mother seemed to orchestrate herself around the wish to prevent the emergence of conflict and tension. She did this by talking in any silence. Grace was not able to contribute anything verbally to the meeting and seemed younger than her years. The father seemed to be somewhat depressed and absent. It felt as if Beatrice was still the infant who could not let go of her mother and was resentful about the birth of her sister. Perhaps in response to her sister's resentment, Grace seemed only to feel safe when she was hiding behind her mother. The team commented on how the family dynamic seemed to revolve around Beatrice and her mother. It was as if Grace did not dare develop a voice as this would create a conflict within the family. The mother also appeared to be extraordinarily concrete and dealt with most comments or questions from the therapist in this state of mind.

Individual assessment

The therapist described Beatrice as being extremely reluctant to talk with him about her feelings or thoughts, seeming locked away inside her mind. The therapist said that Beatrice spent much of the session looking at the floor and the only change in her appearance was when she looked a mixture of bored and irritated when he commented on anything. The therapist took up this irritation with him and asked her to say something about it. Beatrice said that she did not feel angry as that would not be very nice. The therapist pointed out that Beatrice did not allow herself to express any "not nice" thoughts, but wondered then what she did with her frustrations and irritations. Beatrice replied that she tried not to think anything bad.

Later in the session Beatrice brought up the steps she had in mind for her transition and wanted to talk about the active steps such as name change and school move. The therapist commented on her wish for action but that it seemed more difficult for them to spend some time thinking together about what was going on in Beatrice's mind and why she disliked being Beatrice.

Beatrice said that she hated her body because it was wrong. At this point in the interview, Beatrice became more animated, talking at some length about the fact that she did not like her breasts or her periods as she thought it was all disgusting.

This seemed to be associated with ideas of her body being out of control and changing in a way she couldn't prevent. The therapist noted that these thoughts seemed to be associated with sex and the development of secondary sex characteristics.

The second appointment had to be cancelled due to therapist illness. However, the message did not get through to the family and Beatrice was told the therapist could not make it only when she arrived at the clinic. At the next appointment, after a long period of silence at the beginning of the session, the therapist took up Beatrice's feelings about the cancelled appointment. Beatrice shrugged her shoulders, implying she did not care. The therapist pointed out the way Beatrice shrugged off any uncomfortable feelings as if she did not want to be affected by them. Beatrice responded by saying, "Well, there's no reason to get upset by things." The therapist followed up by saying that she might have been a bit annoyed about the fact that she had come all the way to the session, only to find it was cancelled. Beatrice again shrugged her shoulders, saying that it was not nice to get annoyed and there was "no point". The therapist said that it appeared that any feelings of disappointment or annoyance seemed to be either denied or located in her body that she hated.

Discussion of the assessment

The therapist was struck by Beatrice's lack of eye contact and the obvious irritation if he spoke. It could be that she felt eye contact was dangerous and that the therapist might see right inside her. His words could be experienced as unwanted intrusions into her mind. Every time the therapist tried to open up a line of enquiry, it was stopped by a remark from Beatrice that curtailed thinking or enquiry, such as "that would not be very nice" or "no point".

Beatrice seemed very disturbed by any change in her environment, be it the birth of her sister, starting school, the transition to secondary school, or reaching puberty. Should any development or change threaten to overwhelm her, she responded by exerting more control over her environment. Any examination of her feelings and thoughts seemed to pose a similar threat, as if feelings and thoughts were inseparable from actions. For example, she says she cannot afford to think that she is angry with the therapist for missing the session because that would not be nice. Beatrice seemed to live in a rigidly defined world where the complexity and strength of any emotions are flattened. It is as if she tries to maintain a safe, superficial area of emotional comfort, which nullifies the significance of issues which touch on her at a deep emotional level. It is only when her "safe area" is disrupted by the external world that her emotional safety is threatened, and she becomes psychologically destabilised. Passionate feelings are split off and projected towards her body which was held responsible for the development of secondary sexual characteristics. At other times the projected aggressive feelings and grievance towards the parents for having a second child came back in the form of violent temper tantrums that dominated the family.

Her mother seemed to have difficulty helping Beatrice to discover her own resources to help her with the loss involved in separation and development. She came across as a rather anxious woman who also dealt with anxieties and conflicts concretely. The therapeutic team wondered if this, in turn, affected Beatrice's anxieties about development as they could only be dealt with by the ongoing presence of a figure who would remove all psychic pain, rather than a mother who could help Beatrice tolerate psychic pain and develop a capacity to work things through. Her father seemed unable to help his wife separate from her over-involved relationship with her children. He presented as a figure who had absented himself from the family's difficulties as if he felt his wife was managing it all without need of his help.

It was decided to continue with the family therapy and the individual assessment in order to see if the team could help Beatrice's mother separate from her and to try to understand why her husband was so disengaged. At the same time, it seemed important to try to pay some attention to Grace and her umbilical attachment to her mother. In the individual therapy, they hoped they could understand more about Beatrice's fear of her internal world and anxieties about development in the external world.

Family dynamics as part of the assessment process

Exploring the family dynamics is an essential part of any assessment as it is important to understand what part they may play in the young person's presentation. Parents' own difficulties are bound to affect the young person and the way the young person thinks and is seen. In the case described above we can see how Beatrice's mother's separation anxiety and her difficulties dealing with both her daughters' emotions could in turn undermine their ability to develop resources of their own. Her concrete thinking also prevented her from dealing with Beatrice's emotional states in terms of psychological support rather than concrete action (see pp. 204–205 for more information on concrete thinking).

At other times, "ideals" pre-existing in the parents can often be projected into the children as a parent may worry that problems in their own relationships with their parents can be re-enacted in relation to their children. For example, Munchausen by proxy involves the parents pushing fears of their own illness into the child, then presenting them to medical services for treatment. There is evidence that parents who have a history of being abused may project their fears related to their own history into their children. Women who have been sexually abused may harbour a fantasy that their lives would have been different if they had been born male. They might then identify their daughter as being vulnerable to the same sort of abuse and actively encourage a masculine identification as the mother may believe this will protect the daughter from the cycle of abuse.

Assessing comorbid factors

Young people on the autistic spectrum are particularly prone to rigid (black-and-white) thinking and often search for concrete solutions to psychological problems. They are easily overwhelmed by changes in their environment and consequently look to reduce emotional turbulence by attempting to rigidly control their environment. In other words, the obsessional attempt to control the external environment is symptomatic of an attempt to control their internal psychological environment. Sexual development poses a threat to young people as they shift from being a child to an adult. They can feel overwhelmed by anxieties about the demands of adult life, which they don't feel equipped to manage. They tend to evacuate unwanted experiences to establish psychic equilibrium in their minds. It is widely recognised that teenagers with ASD are emotionally less mature than their peer group, tending to catch up in their twenties. These youngsters are especially prone to the promotion of ideas of transition, as it promises to remove conflicts and difficulties in order to achieve an ideal, pain-free state. Young people with autistic traits are disproportionately represented in the number of young people currently presenting to medical services with gender incongruence and it is vital that their gender identity issue is not disaggregated from their overall assessment.

The parents of children with autism face a particular challenge when their child reaches puberty. During early childhood and latency, the family has often developed their own rhythm and methods to help their child manage the usual developmental and environmental changes of a young person's life. When puberty commences, there follows a dramatic period of change, both physical and emotional. These changes cannot be controlled by either the young person or their parents, which can lead to a situation of crisis.

Conclusion

As the infant begins to separate from the mother, he or she must become aware of the mother's relationship with others. This is a developmental step as it offers opportunities for the child to develop new relationships with the wider family. Accompanying this separation is the infant's growing awareness of their primary object's (usually mother) limitations and the frustrations introduced by psychological separation. This can lead to attacks on the "bad mother/object", but through the process of integration inherent in depressive position functioning the infant can now recognise the object they "hate" is also the same object they "love" and have come to rely upon for support (see pp. 189–194 for more information on the depressive position). The aggression towards the object they love in turn leads to guilty feelings about their attack on the object. If the infant healthily manages to process their feelings of guilt for, and fears of retaliation by, the object, they can internalise a "good enough" object (see p. 201 for more information on the internal good object). However, the infant might not manage this and instead must resort to further fragmentation of the ego. Infants that have failed to internalise a good enough internal object that can help them bear the pain of guilt or the fears of fragmentation may look to powerful primitive defences designed to eradicate psychological pain.

Such individuals may grow up to develop a psychic retreat (see pp. 203–204 psychic retreats) in order to control the extent of their exposure to psychic pain and the threat it poses to the ego. These psychic retreats are often based on a grievance towards the parents who have failed to provide them with an ideal body or self. Another way of saying this is when the young person begins to discover that they are not the most attractive, or the cleverest, or the best at sport, or become aware perhaps that others are more popular, it can become the locus of a conscious or unconscious grievance. This can re-emerge in various manifestations, one of which is gender dysphoria, where the young person believes their ideal state would be something or somebody else. In phantasy, they reject the body of the sex their parents have given them, in preference for a gender and a name they create themselves. This powerful phantasy can reverse any feelings the individual might have of being small, humiliated, jealous, or rivalrous as they have become a perfect/ideal figure of their own creation, leaving the damage behind.

Psychic states which are unusually fixed require any would-be therapist to try to understand the role they play in defending the young person against anxiety. These states of mind employ primitive defences based on splitting, denial, and projection of parts of the ego used for perception and thought. So, for example, doubt and confusion about the belief that they are in the wrong body may be forcefully projected into the object, the therapist, or the parent, while the individual retreats into certainty and anxiety-free conviction. The young person then pressurises the object into agreeing with their conviction. If the young person receives unquestioning affirmation of their thinking, they do experience temporary relief. However, the cost of this solution is denied and projected into others and/or the future. Any thinking from a different perspective that raises questions and fails to endorse the plan to transition can be viewed as a hostile attack, rather than an appropriate wish to examine the underlying rationale.

Clinicians need to understand that the vulnerable part of the self may exist in a dynamic relationship with a defensive aspect of the self that promises to protect the individual from re-experiencing psychic pain associated with trauma. In effect, the defensive structure, which might have the intimidating qualities of a suit of armour, has captured the vulnerable aspects of the self and often wants to prevent it from finding a voice or being observed by others. This dynamic gets enacted in the relationship with the therapist. The therapist may spot a chink in the defensive structure, which allows the vulnerable aspect of the self to speak, only to find that the moment this is identified, the defensive system closes emotional contact down. Clinicians need to identify the part of the patient that may be silenced or being kept out of the picture while also understanding that any emotional contact is likely to lead to further resistance.

SIX

Adolescence

In Chapters 4 and 5 we considered how parental relationships early in life shape the infant's capacity to withstand uncertainty as they pass early developmental milestones. Here we are concerned with the transition from childhood to adulthood, which involves huge physiological, psychological, and sociological changes. Although we typically associate adolescence with the teenage years, neuroscientists understand adolescence to be a process that is not usually completed until an individual reaches their mid-twenties, well into legal adulthood. Meanwhile, in the body, sex hormones kick-start the development of secondary sexual characteristics (see p. 241). This change in the body is usually accompanied by profound changes in relationships with parents and the outside world. The trajectory towards adulthood presents all sorts of demands and questions to the emerging adolescent: What sort of adult are they going to be? How will they separate from the influence of their parents? How will they manage sexual relations in the adult world? These questions may not be in the foreground of the young person's mind, but they exist in the background of everyone's mind. All these shifting demands create not only excitement but also anxiety about what the future holds.

Separation and rebellion

For some adolescents, the process of separation produces fights over independent status as they challenge the adults in positions of authority who oversee their lives. The battles between young person and parent are often fought over the rights of the adolescent to control their decisions and their right to treat their body as their own.

Arguments therefore rage over skin piercings, tattoos, hair dyes, fashion choices, how late they stay out, the company they keep, their attitude to schoolwork, sexual behaviour, appropriate dress, experimenting with drink and drugs, or changing their appearance in more dramatic ways. Adolescents often live in a world where the difference between fantasy and reality has not been fully established. Although the rebellious adolescent may fight for independence, they can be distraught and break down in tears when the implications of their reckless behaviour become evident. "Leave me alone! It's my life!" can rapidly turn into, "My life is over! I've ruined everything." Parents are often aware of the dangers this period holds, as rebellious activity may result in unwanted pregnancy, drug overdoses, or fights in which an adolescent is injured, or worse, dies. The adolescent brain has a skewed notion of risk assessment in comparison to the adult brain, especially in the company of peers. Thus, they might cross a road recklessly as if they were immortal or drive under the influence of alcohol without realising the dangers. It is a period characterised by the teenager acting like a grown-up who can make his own decisions, but who needs the parents to pick up the pieces if or when things go wrong.

The importance of peer groups

Peer groups in adolescence usually become much more prominent and important as the group represents a place where the adolescent can share the journey with other kids. In the group, there is often a range of attitudes with different presentations: for example, the kids that are experimenting with sex talk within the group, while others listen in to the details. The sheepish one hides in the group, ashamed of their lack of physical maturity but gets on by being funny or cheeky. The peer group provides a place where the adolescent can experiment with different ways of being. There are leaders of the group who dominate and followers who may appear to tag along for the ride. While they may wear clothes or behave in ways that exist outside their parents' social norms, the groups often have a definite "on trend" uniform. These uniforms are the outward expression of the group's underlying values and ideologies. These adolescent groups can be underpinned by bonds of loyalty and belonging, offering an alternative to their family of origin. This is part of a normal process of separating from the parents and the family and finding an individual identity.

Fear of adulthood

Some adolescents, perhaps terrified of the adult world, cling to an infantile attachment to their parents as if they are still little children who could not possibly make any decisions of their own. They might not join a peer group fearing that they are not ready for the separation from their parents. Parents may be faced with the opposite problem to the reckless tearaways, as the teenager needs cajoling into adulthood. They may be anxious about their sexuality and the demands of adulthood, hiding behind their parents' views and sticking closely to the family or locking themselves away in their bedrooms. More formal groups, like school trips, or clubs, can provide a halfway house where the young person can separate from the parents, while the group is organised by teachers or adults who act *in loco parentis*.

Adolescent development

For most adolescents, they are both fighting to establish their own identity by rebelling against their parents, and also in some way struggling to incorporate their parents' ideals. The projections and projective processes underlying this process are unconscious—the young person is usually unaware they are doing this—but these projections can have a disturbing effect on others. The boy who argues with his parents, stating that he does not care about his upcoming exams, projects his anxiety about his future into his parents, who are left carrying the worries.

The adolescent is also usually extremely self-conscious and is compelled to compare himself against others. The world of social media has increased this tendency as Facebook, Instagram, TikTok and similar exploit teenagers' strong urges to find out how popular they are, how handsome, or how funny. Facebook began, after all, as a method to compare the desirability of girls on the campus at Harvard University. "Likes" on certain accounts have been scientifically shown to alter brain chemistry by stimulating the brain's reward circuits and promoting the release of endorphins.

The focus on the external environment is often driven by the wish to manage internal anxieties. The adolescent may fall back on primitive, defensive states of mind to manage their internal states, which is why teenagers are notoriously moody and changeable. They project a lot into the external world in order to master their unruly feelings. These projections can sometimes be accompanied by actions designed to provoke a response in others. In this way, an internal conflict is now acted out in the external world. So, for example, the girl who goes out with older men is dismissive of her mother's concerns about whether she will be hurt or led astray.

The adolescents' sense of themselves is extremely volatile as they can quickly be overwhelmed by anxieties, so their functioning fluctuates between being grown-up and integrated on the one hand and feeling very infantile where the world is too much and wholly against them. Parents sometimes struggle in managing the provocation, while trying to understand the underlying conflicts, as their child may present them with reminders of their own conflicts and struggles in their childhoods. The professional working with adolescents has to be prepared for the dramatic changes in mood a patient can present with. The work requires patience and resilience in the face of sometimes overwhelming or frightening provocation.

The transition from childhood to adulthood is a crucial threshold moment in the development of the individual, throwing up all sorts of psychic conflicts, confusions, and challenges.

Disdain towards authority

Rebelliousness against parents can be represented in the adolescent choice of political affiliation, and disdain for the older generation and authority. It is an important stage in de-idealising the parents and a way of saying, "You lot do not know what you are doing. When the new generation are in charge, then we will create a better world."

Meanwhile, drugs and alcohol are often used to deal with anxiety by changing the brain state to escape from underlying feelings of persecution or confusion.

Powerful defences

The immature ego deals with anxiety by projecting any persecutory thoughts, threatening internal desires, and psychic conflicts into the external world. It also often splits the world into all-good and all-bad states.

A fifteen-year-old boy who has recently had to resit his exams goes into a rage at his father's incompetence at texting. Thus, feelings of humiliation are projected into the father. The son is left feeling completely in control and in charge, while his father has been identified as the stupid one.

Conversely, a fourteen-year-old girl, who lacks confidence and fears responsibility and separation, continually asks her mother to do things that she is fully capable of doing herself. In this way, she plays the role of an anxious infant that depends on her mother totally, by projecting her capabilities into her mother. There is an avoidance of the reality that she is becoming an adult who should be expected to take responsibility for her actions.

In both these examples, an internal conflict has been projected and acted out in relation to another. Parents can struggle to see clearly that these interactions are driven by unconscious projective processes designed to provoke strong emotional responses in the recipient.

Exploration of gender: a normal part of development

Childhood and adolescence are developmental processes, and all individuals experiment with different identifications, both male and female. This can stir up all sorts of confusions, doubts, and conflicts which drive the individuals to employ powerful psychic defences such as denial, splitting, and projection. When these forces become overwhelming, they may push the individual to focus on a fixed solution in an attempt to reduce feelings of confusion—one of which might be, "I'm not the sex I was born, I am the other gender." In adolescence, the experience of being dislocated from one's body, which is changing rapidly, is common. It is these experiences that will secure the link between mind and body in the mental life of the adult to come. In many ways, adolescence involves making your body your home and "moving in".

When considering the more recent trend of ROGD teenagers (i.e. rapid-onset gender dysphoria, rather than the more traditionally reported group of younger children), there are several factors worth investigation. The general thinking behind the ROGD cohort is that they are children who expressed no earlier ideas about their gender confusion, hence "rapid-onset". A sudden presentation might have multiple and connected origins. Young children fantasise about many identities (e.g. dinosaur, princess, pop star, footballer, etc.), which may involve being another gender in their imagination. Children also often play in mixed sports teams and boys and girls can easily pass or be mistaken for a child of the opposite sex. Some children may harbour a conviction that they are of the other gender and this particular belief is easier to maintain for the young child, due to the more minimal differences in physical appearance and abilities, with the absence of secondary sexual characteristics (see p. 241). There is also a societal acceptance of children displaying more gender non-conformity, for example tomboy girls or "girly-boys".

In younger children these fantasies are more commonly transitory and fluid, whereas some children develop a more fixed belief system in connection with how they view themselves. However, as the child moves into puberty, under the influence of a surge of sex hormones, the body develops secondary sexual characteristics. At this point the contradictory ideas and beliefs the child had are more difficult to maintain and the young person is faced with the consequences of these changes to their body and its implications for their biological sexual role. The little girl who enjoyed life and was accepted as a tomboy may find her female identity more apparent as her body develops in adolescence. We could therefore regard ROGD as a response to the trauma of the reality of puberty, together with the loss of the freedoms of childhood identity.

In the medical treatment of gender dysphoria, puberty blockers are used to stop normal physical development, thus putting a blanket over the young person's sexual development. This may reduce their anxiety in the short term—hence the alleged improvement in mental state. The difficulty of administering early treatment of blocker hormones to children is that the influence of the natal sex hormones on the body and mind during adolescence is interrupted. The influence of natural sex hormones on the body are clear to see, but they also have key roles in brain development and maturation and are likely to be the crucial components which influence the behaviours and emotions of young people.

Fantasies of adolescence

The adolescent may have all sorts of fantasies about the ideal self they would like to be in order to deal with the difficulties and demands associated with the adult world. They may feel persecuted by their failings and fall into morose states when faced with limitations or deficiencies. They may develop grievances towards their parents who have failed to give them the ideal body or mind or temperament they feel they need to succeed in the adult world. This can lead to arguments and conflicts where the adolescent blames the adult for their shortcomings.

Hatred of the sexed body

The adolescent's anxiety can lead to feelings of dissociation as they locate irritation at imperfections or desires into the body, while distancing themselves mentally from these experiences. This can lead to an increase in the fantasy of, "If only I'd been given the ideal body/mind then everything would be OK," or, "If only I could return to being a young person, then I could escape from all these adult responsibilities." This state can lead to a feeling that the body is no longer loved or wanted but is treated as if it was responsible for the failing of the self. Hatred of the body may become so great that the adolescent feels that their body is a separate entity and no longer anything to do with them.

The developing sexual characteristics increase anxiety and are treated like an unwanted visitor. Eventually, the adolescent can feel that their body is an alien thing or that they are a prisoner in a body they no longer identify with. At this point, the young person's body now contains all the emotional persecutions and insecurities. The young person's questions about their future sexual roles in adult life are then postponed, as they have become utterly preoccupied by the idea that they have been "born in the wrong body". The trans-affirmative script goes something like this: "You feel at odds with yourself. You lack confidence and suffer from social anxiety. This is because you have felt you have been born into the wrong body—you might be trans."

Our minds naturally like to protect us against psychic pain and unconsciously we try to find less painful, arduous routes to psychic resolutions. The "trans-identifying" adolescent starts to become more fixed in their belief that this is the answer to many of their problems. If only they could transition, the distress would resolve and everything would be all right. When a fragile ego is under pressure, it tends to focus on the idea of one problem with one solution, as the individual fixes on a very narrow field of mental life. A very similar process is evident in the anorexic's fixed preoccupation with their weight, or in the obsessional compulsive's preoccupation with cleanliness.

Control of the identity by enactment

The fixed belief about being trans can give the adolescent a powerful feeling of control as they believe that they can design their own perfect body. For many, transitioning also involves changing their given name. Thus, they have revenge upon their parents by rejecting the name they have been given as infant. The developing adolescent feels exposed to painful and humiliating aspects of life and may feel deep grievance towards the parents for being made to feel this way. In many ways, this is an omnipotent mental state as the young person develops a phantasy that he/she can recreate themselves and dispose of their unwanted identity.

Dagny (2019), a detransitioner, has recently published an article about her experience of transitioning. She highlighted the influence of the online site Tumblr and described the ways she internalised the ideals of the website.

> One of these unhealthy beliefs I held was the belief that if you have gender dysphoria, you must transition. And anyone that appeared to stand in my way was a transphobe—an alt-right

bigot. If I, myself, questioned my actions, I was suffering from internalised transphobia. No matter how much genuine concern others may have had for me—by now, a miserable 16 year old—they were committing an unforgivable act if they just asked me, "Why?" Why do I want to be a boy? Why do I want to change my body?

The development of gender dysphoria or a "trans-identification" appears to be based on a split between the individual's natal sex, which is disowned and rejected, and the attractive belief in a newly created identity which can usher in the creation of an ideal self. The fantasy that the individual can sculpt the body according to his/her wishes adds to the feeling of power and control over the body and everything contained within it. The now self-diagnosed "trans person" can put enormous pressure on family, school, and clinical services to join unquestioningly with them in the belief that transition is the only solution to their problems.

Splitting in the family

Eva was a fifteen-year-old girl referred by her family doctor to a child and adolescent mental health service after saying that she wanted to transition. Initially, the team saw the family together, and it was evident that the parents were split over their daughter's wish to transition. At the first meeting Eva's mother asked the family therapist whether she thought they should go along with Eva's wishes to use a boy's name in place of her given name. The father added that he did not think that there was a problem with it and said that he wanted his daughter to be happy; the mother replied that she wanted to understand why Eva was not happy with who she was. The therapist asked Eva what she thought about her birth name and what she thought would change with the new name. Eva talked in a matter of fact way, about a feeling that she had never really liked her name and couldn't think of herself as an Eva. The therapist said that it would be helpful to try to understand more about Eva and her family as well as the ideas behind her wish to change her identity. The family therapist agreed to meet the family once a term.

Eva started in once-weekly psychotherapy which ran alongside termly meetings with the family. Eva was one of non-identical twin girls, with an older brother and a younger sister. When she arrived in the consulting room, she smiled in a shy, pensive way that gave very little away about her underlying feelings. The therapist felt as if Eva was polite on the outside as a way of keeping the therapist from what was going on inside. The therapist asked Eva about her family. She said that her older brother, now twenty, had been very depressed and suicidal as a teenager. The brother's condition had dominated family life for a number of years as the parents always had to deal with his rages and tantrums.

While she said all this, there was very little expression in her voice or face. The therapist commented that it sounded like the brother's illness took up quite a bit of the family's time. Eva shrugged her shoulders in uncommitted agreement. The therapist asked her about her twin and younger sister. She said that her twin was very bright, and her younger sister was very pretty and popular. The therapist tried to explore with Eva how she felt about herself in the family with her cleverer twin and prettier younger sister. Eva smiled and shrugged her shoulders but said that she didn't really think anything about it. This tended to be the pattern of exchanges between them for several months, as if Eva had no intention of exploring her emotions and thoughts.

The therapist became aware she was doing most of the work in the session, in taking various imaginative leaps in response to how the patient seemed to be keeping them both in the dark.

After several weeks of therapy, the therapist said that perhaps Eva's reliance on the therapist to do all the thinking and talking in the session was like her somewhat hidden position in the family. In other words, Eva mirrored the way she felt hidden within her family as the "odd one out" who didn't quite fit in by hiding her thoughts and feelings on all matters relating to her family. The therapist's comment produced a small smile and another comment about having no thoughts on what the therapist had just said. After a brief silence, the therapist went on to say that perhaps Eva was hoping the therapy could help her to express her hidden thoughts and feelings. Eva shrugged her shoulders at this comment but this did seem to allow a subtle change in the session as Eva started to be more talkative about her outside life at school and her sports team.

Then in one session shortly afterwards Eva told the therapist that her mother did not want her to change her name or her school and that was why she wanted Eva to attend the therapy. This was said with a tiny hint of irritation. The therapist said that maybe Eva felt annoyed that her brother had received so much attention from the parents, while she gets sent to a therapist. However, Eva responded to this by denying any feelings of annoyance.

At the beginning of the next session, Eva looked at the therapist and asked what she should talk about. The therapist said she was free to say anything and that the therapist was interested in whatever was on her mind. Again, she smiled politely while falling silent. She then talked about an incident in which she remembered her older brother had screamed and shouted at her mother until the mother cried and Eva hated seeing any of this. Eva went on to say that the atmosphere was terrible as everyone was walking around on eggshells. The therapist commented that it must be difficult for Eva to express any irritation or anger herself, when the atmosphere felt so tense, and asked what she did when she got frustrated. She replied that she went to her room and contacted people on the internet in order to play online games or she would put her headphones on and listen to loud music so she couldn't hear if anything more was happening downstairs.

The therapist said it sounded as if Eva was afraid to talk to her parents about any of the thoughts and feelings she was having, and it seemed as though her question to the therapist at the beginning conveyed that she also felt that way about her sessions. The therapist wondered with Eva if she was keeping others happy, rather than having any real expectation that she could get anything out of it for herself. She smiled more warmly at this, as if the therapist had rumbled this polite way of keeping herself at a distance, and therefore hidden. Eva then remembered that the therapist had said when they first met that she talked about an early memory she had and she mentioned that once she had been left in the car by the family. She said she was too tired to go on the walk, but they had got lost and were gone for hours. The therapist asked how she had been in their absence. Eva said that she knew she had to distract herself and she kept telling herself the same nursery rhyme repeatedly. When they returned, she said nothing to them about feeling afraid or angry at being left alone for so long and the incident was soon forgotten.

The therapist commented on her need to soothe herself as if she had to manage all her distressed feelings on her own. She can never feel frightened or anxious or neglected. Eva looked challengingly at the therapist and said, "What's the point of feeling that way?" The therapist said that perhaps Eva did not expect anybody to be interested in her feelings or that it was worth the risk for her to shed light on what was going on deep inside her. She replied, "Feelings just cause pain; I cannot see the point in them." Eva then retreated into a sullen state, repeating that she had no expectations of the therapy. The therapist also talked with Eva about how she imagined that Eva had probably felt scared and upset in the car but had managed her emotions by distracting herself with the repetitive rhymes. Even when the parents returned, she did not feel able to cry or complain.

During the following months of therapy Eva continued in this somewhat detached state of mind, causing the therapist to feel a mixture of either being shut out or frustrated, but there were occasions when Eva became more engaged. The therapist learned that Eva was sensitive about how she was viewed by others and how she tried to fit in with the girls at school. She did not feel like she was one of the prettiest or the most intelligent. She was able to allow the therapist to explore and notice her sensitive and vulnerable feelings. However, there was a pattern which developed whereby progress in the therapy would be followed by Eva becoming suspicious of the therapy and pulling back from emotional contact.

Eva would shut down and then go back to saying that she just wanted to change her name and move to a different school. It was as if this issue was used to disconnect from any other emotions/feelings and to flatten any discussion about her as a person. Indeed, the therapist developed a view that part of the fantasy of transition for Eva was that she would get rid of this sensitive girl who left her exposed to feelings of vulnerability and a sense she couldn't measure up. During these periods of the therapy, Eva sometimes talked about her mother's attempts to engage her in discussions about life or how she was getting on. She described going along with her mother, placating her, while inside she said she did not feel moved at all.

A few months into the treatment, Eva told the therapist that the class had been shown a film about child slave labour where they were exploited and treated badly by merciless bosses. Most of the class had been very upset and cried during the film. Eva said she was unaffected and did not get upset. However, she did comment on how different she was. The therapist said perhaps she identified more with the cruel bosses who neglected these young people and mistreated them in a sweatshop factory. This seemed to hit home with Eva because she looked uncomfortable and the therapist observed this.

Eva said, "Mmmm … but I do not like to think of myself as being so cruel." Then, with a flash of anger, she said, "I just can't see the point or what you want from me—you just want me to cry or be sad." The therapist wondered whether Eva thought the therapy was a form of exploitation, as now the therapist was like the factory boss who was just trying to make Eva feel dependent and needy. "Yes," said Eva. "You just want me to feel unhappy or guilty, and I don't see the point of all those feelings. Where does that get you?" The therapist replied that by ignoring her own needs, she was also cold and cruel to the part of her that wanted warmth.

Over the next few months Eva would sometimes be more open about her underlying hostility, occasionally pointing out the therapist's deficits or mistakes. This was interspersed with moments of more humour or warmth.

Six months into the therapy, Eva came into the session complaining that the man who had come before her had left a terrible smell in the waiting room and that the therapist should do something about it. The therapist said it might feel to Eva just like her mother at home who lets her brother dominate the household with his outbursts. She said with real anger that her father did not do anything to help when her brother went into one: "He just stands by and watches." The therapist went on to say that perhaps Eva also felt her therapist was useless to her when she was silent about her difficulties, leaving her on her own without any support, just as she had been left in the car on her own. Eva did not reply but she sighed, her shoulders slumped, and she looked away at the bookcase as if trying to control her emotions.

A few weeks later, Eva was telling the therapist about how her week had gone. She mentioned that her father was a keen sportsman and used to take Eva to tag rugby when she was very small. Her twin sister did not want to go, and her other siblings were not that interested. The team had been mixed sexes until nine years of age when physical contact started. Eva's father enjoyed the fact that she was so sporty and that she was a match for the boys. When she was about eight years old, she remembered him saying what a relief it was that he had somebody interested in sport, because the brother had not been. She said he was disappointed that her brother took no interest in sport. The therapist said Eva's father's comment about wanting a sporty boy seemed to have made quite an impression. Eva seemed pleased that her father and she had something in common and it made him happy.

A year into the therapy, Eva arrived in the session in obvious pain. Eva mentioned nothing and after a short time, the therapist enquired about her injuries. She said she had been hurt in a rugby match but had not wanted to go to the casualty department as she didn't want to have to wait to be seen. The therapist commented on the way Eva wished to ignore the pain her body was in, as if it was nothing to do with her. Eva replied by saying that the pain was only in her body and that she was almost sure she had not broken anything. Her only concern was that she could be fit in time for the cup match in two weeks' time otherwise her coach would be angry.

The therapist thought Eva located all pain and desire in her body, which she then disowned. Eva then seemed to live with her mind cut off from her body. Instead of feeling the pain of a little girl who wanted her Mummy to take notice of the fact that she was hurting, she felt she could get rid of this part of her mind by transitioning into being a man. Eva said that girls are always crying and overemotional, always hurt, but she wasn't like that.

During the next months of therapy, Eva and the therapist were able to explore the way Eva had developed a belief that she would be acceptable if only she could get rid of her grievances, desires, and pain located in this little girl that she believed was unacceptable. The man she thought she would be was someone who would get on with life, and had no need of love or passionate relationships. This was repeated in the therapy, as Eva tried to control the distance and contact between her and the therapist, in an attempt to manage any intense feelings that threatened to emerge during the sessions.

In the second year of therapy Eva became more able to express her emotions and talk about different aspects of her life. She also reported that her relationship with her twin sister and mother had improved. She became a bit more critical of her father and his tendency to stay out of family arguments.

Two years into the therapy, with a small grin, Eva told the therapist that she had been asked out, by a guy at the local rugby club. She had turned him down, "Because I'm not sure I'm into men, but it felt nice to be asked."

In the third year of treatment, Eva started to talk about how she no longer thought she fitted into the categories described on the trans affirmative websites and rarely talked about her ideas of transition. Eva said that she had realised that the websites were not real life and no longer held any interest for her. The therapist said she thought Eva had realised that she was allowed to feel different things and express herself in different ways. She no longer had to be silent herself when she felt angry or had loving feelings. There was also talk about Eva's application to university. Eva said she felt worried about how it would go, that university was a big step, but she wanted to believe she would manage. She was reluctant to leave her current small friendship group and start again. The therapist began to talk more about the end of the therapy and next steps for Eva. They agreed the therapy would end that summer.

At the next session, Eva suddenly announced that she wanted to change her name; her father was happy about it and it was only her mother who was being difficult. The therapist was taken aback by this announcement as this subject had not been an issue in recent months, but started to try to look with Eva at what had brought about this idea. Eva seemed much more wary and unwilling to explore her thinking in this session.

The therapist drew attention to the fact that they had agreed an ending date at the last session. She said she wondered if the "little girl her" felt upset about the loss of the therapy and now perhaps Eva wanted to distance herself from these feelings. Eva said in a dismissive way that it had nothing to do with the ending of the therapy and that she was fine with stopping.

After a long pause Eva said that her brother had had one his outbursts during the week and her mother had been trying to calm him down. The therapist said that Eva might be feeling she would be replaced by the patient who used to leave smells in the waiting room, as her brother had taken her mother's attention. Eva replied, "It is what it is—I'm used to that." The therapist said that although in life it is not possible to avoid losses and the resentments they cause, they could pay attention to Eva's feelings about it.

In a team meeting the following week the family therapist said that the termly meetings with the family had been going well but then at the last meeting a row erupted between Eva's parents over her wish to change names. She thought there was obviously a lot of animosity between the parents over the issue and they didn't seem able to discuss it in a reasonable manner. The therapist pointed out the way Eva and her father seemed to back each other up, while Eva's mother's point of view was not sought out. They all agreed that this often happened, as Eva's mother was very involved with the brother and her twin sister while the father was closest to Eva. The therapist made the point that Eva might feel she missed out on a close relationship with her mother. In response to this comment, Eva sat in silence. The therapist felt this comment hit home.

During the last phase of the treatment Eva described her excitement at going to university; she was sad to leave the therapy but felt much more settled in herself. Arguments in the family between Eva and the parents seemed to have settled down and Eva described herself as having a slightly better relationship with her mother who now took more care to spend some time with Eva.

Case discussion

Eva had not been able to manage her feelings of neglect, especially by her mother, who was preoccupied with her older brother's illness. She inhibited herself from expressing her anger and hostility as she worried it would damage her mother. Her father's tendency to hover in the background when the brother was difficult meant that she did not believe her father was sufficiently robust to support her mother. Instead, Eva cut herself off from her claim to a place in her mother's heart, believing that she had no time for her. This turned into a grievance against her mother for failing to make room for her and against her father for failing to support her mother. She tried to eradicate the hurt, sad, angry little girl by identifying with a tough, masculine character who was all action, with no soft feelings. This structure developed further when she spent time with her father, who also admired her toughness and athleticism.

The underlying grievance towards Eva's mother was represented by her wish to remain hidden in the family. This dynamic was repeated in the therapy as Eva tried to stay hidden by remaining almost monosyllabic and keeping her thoughts to herself. We have often found that a patient's wariness is driven by a belief that the therapist is against transition; a repetition of the conflict with one or both of the parents about whose version of the child will survive. Trans-identified children often believe that their parents do not accept their trans identity because their parents want them to submit to the parents' view of who they are or should be. Many of these children already believe they have failed to measure up and fight against the imposition of the parental ideal: "You can't force me to be a version of you! I am my own person." This dynamic is often repeated in the transference, as the patient believes that the therapist is against transition and is aiming, by coercion, to persuade them to give up their wish to transition. In Eva's case, the therapist represents the mother who refuses her daughter's chosen name.

The idea of her transitioning gathered momentum when this somewhat neglected little girl, so desperate to be loved and accepted, cottoned on to the idea that her father would have liked a sporty son. In this way, the fantasy would be that she would become a tough little boy who had no feelings at all. This deep-seated yearning was the cause of so much anger and pain, feelings that had gone unacknowledged by Eva or anyone else until she started therapy. In its place, she developed a cold, hard, defensive structure which protected her from any feelings of vulnerability.

This was conveyed in the session when Eva talked about the film shown at school. It became apparent to the therapist that Eva was more identified with the cruel boss than the vulnerable young people in the factory. The therapist felt herself carefully watched by Eva as she told the story and noticed that Eva smiled at the cruelty she was describing. In this way, the cruelty was re-enacted in the session. It was as if Eva was saying unconsciously, "You thought we were working together in my therapy, but really I just exploit your softness and enthusiasm for the work. I am more like the boss who exploits vulnerability than the poor young people who are being exploited."

In his description of perverse organisations, John Steiner (1982) reveals the way that vulnerable aspects of the patient who needs therapeutic help may be controlled by sadistic and cruel parts of their personality. He describes the way this perverse structure can be acted out in the transference/countertransference (see pp. 207–209) as the patient cruelly attacks the vulnerability and softness located in the therapist. The therapy's task is to expose the way sadistic aspects of the personality hold vulnerable aspects of the personality to ransom and that this needs help and attention to resolve.

The therapy provided a space where the professional team could examine what was going on for Eva, exploring the fantasies behind her wish to transition, including the origins of her hatred of her gender. The deep-seated nature of Eva's difficulties meant that it took a long time for her to emerge from her psychic retreat. She also needed to experience the support of the therapist in exploring her feelings concerning the therapy in the first instance, then in relation to her family of origin. The cycles of engagement and resistance had to be endured, explored, and challenged. It was important to take up the role Eva's cold hostility played both in relation to the therapist and towards her own development.

Eva started therapy wanting to be transitioned into a new identity. She felt this would eradicate the unmanageable feelings she felt towards her parents for failing to provide her with a proper place within the family. She wanted to change her gender and her given name to enable this. However, the therapy offered a space where she could explore her internal world and find another solution to her conflictual feelings towards herself and other members of her family. Over time, Eva was able to see she could express irritation and aggression when she was disappointed with her therapist and that this did not amount to a disaster. Being more in touch with her negative feelings allowed her some room for development. She was also less fanatical about her plans to eradicate the little girl in her.

The announcement of the end of the therapy revived the argument about changing her name again. This caused a rift between the mother and the father. Initially Eva, perhaps unconsciously, provoked an argument between the mother and the father as a way of externalising her ambivalence about her wish to transition. This would protect her from arguing in her own mind as to whether she wanted to distance herself from the rather unhappy little girl who felt she had lost her mother to her brother. The argument between the parents represents the two parts of herself. Her father's position says, "Escape painful feelings of loss," while her mother's position can be in touch with the experience of loss as part of the mourning process. The conflict emerged again temporarily due to Eva's fear of losing the therapist who had supported her to a better understanding of herself. Eva had increased her capacity to think about things rather than act them out, and her social relationships and sense of herself had improved as a result so that she was less isolated both in her own mind and also in her external life.

Discussion

As Money-Kyrle wrote in his 1971 paper on the facts of life, some children find anxieties about the difference between the sexes and the difference between the generations difficult to manage and they find themselves being pulled into psychic retreats that offer illusory control over the developmental process. Part of the developmental struggle in adolescence is to come to terms with the reality of who we are, including our natal sexuality and the different roles demanded of us in reproduction.

"A normative developmental task is to integrate pubertal change into a revised and satisfactory body image" (Laufer & Laufer, 1984). This transitional stage often stirs up conflicts over control and who is responsible for the child's body and mind. Is it the child, with grievances towards the parents for their failings as parents, or the parents, who may be struggling to conceal a sense of disappointment or concern about the child? To avoid this conflict, the therapist may take the affirmative approach in saying, "Whatever you think and makes you happy." However, as detransitioners point out, they often believe this amounts to a collapse of professional responsibility. Meanwhile, therapeutic work relies on the therapist's ability to find a way to explore the child's underlying defences, motivations, and feelings, with the knowledge that the child will ultimately decide on how best to lead their life.

Conclusion

We also have found that the desire to transition often is related to a wish to control sexual development, and perhaps to defer it entirely, including, in a literal sense, through the use of puberty blockers. It's interesting to note that many detransitioners report that there is little talk about sex on pro-transition websites, or in the medical care they received. Under the current "affirmative" model of treatment (which might more aptly be called a "belief-confirmation" model), some services may be tacitly providing reassurance to young people that their anxieties about sexual development will be removed through gender transition. We would argue, however, that adolescent confusion and distress is a normal and even necessary part of development. And over time, the adolescent can be helped and supported to become an adult who might enjoy what their natal sexual body has to offer. However, a defensive structure that wants to put a lid on sexual development can be very appealing to children who feel threatened by the demands of a changing body. The transition may be seen as a way of stopping and controlling the doubts and anxieties raised by puberty. The child may also hope they can be supported with their feelings through periods of anxiety, confusion, and uncertainty, as they come to terms with the implications of sexual development.

Those in positions of authority in relation to the adolescent may often feel they are being provoked into retaliating, on the one hand, or collapsing into agreement on the other. The concrete nature of the communication can provoke concrete reactions and a projective system is set up as unconscious communications get pushed backwards and forwards between patient and therapist. It is especially difficult to maintain a calm, reflective state of mind when the patient is threatening to take drastic actions that the adult/professional may (rightly) perceive could be damaging. It is challenging when pushed to offer black-and-white responses or asked to give concrete direction in a "for or against" manner. Supervision is essential when working with these disturbed and disturbing states of mind as even the most experienced therapist can be provoked into enactments. Supervision can change a dyadic projective system into a triadic one as the supervisor can retain the potential for restoring the capacity for symbolic thought. The adolescent needs parental figures and therapists to help them think about the underlying issues that might be driving them towards action.

SEVEN

Excitement as a psychic defence against loss

In the preceding three chapters, we have discussed the developmental challenges and the ways in which anxieties associated with sexual development and separation might present with symptoms of gender confusion and dysphoria. In this chapter, we discuss a particular use of manic, erotic excitement which defends against the physical development of puberty and the inevitable loss of the primary relationship, which in phantasy threatens to be catastrophic for the individual.

As the baby develops, the physical process of being more separate from the mother enables the baby to see her more clearly as an "other" person. The developing visual capacity is accompanied by a curiosity about the world the baby is living in, as he/she becomes aware of the mother's relationships with partners, siblings, and the outside world. This can lead to feelings of smallness, jealousy, rivalry, and envy which the child needs to integrate with more loving feelings. This is the first dyadic relationship and it needs to be a robust attachment to allow the infant to internalise a good enough relationship and develop ego strength (see p. 239 for more information on the ego).

As the child's mind develops, he/she becomes aware of the anatomical differences between boys and girls. This leads to questions about sexual differences and how babies are made. A boy has to come to terms with the fact that he will have to penetrate a woman if he wants to make a baby. Penetration may bring up all sorts of phantasies about damaging or being damaged by the woman. Conversely, a girl has to come to terms with the fact that she will have to allow penetration if, as an adult, she wants to conceive a baby. The girl may also have phantasies of being damaged by the boy's penis and fears about pregnancy. The knowledge of these different sexual roles becomes apparent over time and the requirements may cause anxiety, which can result in an adolescent wishing to withdraw from their increasingly adult sexual body. One upset seven-year-old returned home after attending a sex education class saying that he was "too young to hear about all that stuff and someone might get hurt".

In many ways, the developmental process from childhood through adolescence to adulthood faces the individual with challenges, opportunities, and anxieties. Children need help and support as they go through these stages. Problems arise when a parent is unable to support them into the next stage or when the child feels unprepared or unable to let go of the primary and often idealised dyadic relationship.

We are now going to describe the assessment of Chris, a young man who found that he felt "more real and alive" when dressed in "girls" clothes. As a result of his feelings, he had diagnosed himself as transgender. However, he did not complain of severe discomfort with himself and his male body and although there was some idea that he might wish to physically transition in the future, this was not a pressing feature of his presentation.

Chris

The service received a request from Mr and Mrs Y to see their sixteen-year-old son, Chris. They said he had recently disclosed to them that he had been experiencing gender dysphoria since he was five, although they had seen no signs of it. Two members of the team offered to see the family in the first instance. The team explained to the family that the aim of the assessment consultations was both to gather factual information about the family history from them all, and then for a therapist to explore with Chris individually whether he could benefit from a psychotherapeutic approach.

First family consultation

The therapist leading the family interview was struck by the way the mother sat next to her son encouraging Chris to talk and anxiously checking on his well-being. However, there appeared to be very little warm engagement between the mother and the father. Indeed, Mr Y seemed irritated whenever Chris' mother mentioned her concerns about Chris.

The couple explained that they had married late and Mrs Y had experienced difficulty conceiving and had undergone several miscarriages before Chris was born. It was clear that this had been a traumatic period and Chris was described as a miracle baby. The mother added that she was a rather anxious person and used to worry all the time that Chris would stop breathing in his cot.

Therapist: Can you tell me what Chris was like to feed?
   Mrs Y: Chris wouldn't settle. He had eczema, which made him uncomfortable, and I just couldn't get him to settle well when feeding on the breast.
Therapist: That sounds distressing.
   Mrs Y: Yes, it was upsetting, and Chris wasn't gaining weight. In the end, the health visitor suggested we swap to the bottle.
Therapist: What about sleeping? How was he going to sleep and throughout the night?
   Mrs Y: He used to only go to sleep when he was snuggled up next to me.
   Mr Y: We struggled to move him into his bedroom. Our nights were very broken and, consequently, I moved into the spare room and Chris would sleep in the bed with my wife.
Therapist: And how do you sleep now, Chris?
   Mrs Y: [*Before Chris can answer*] We try to make sure he goes to bed at a reasonable time but he is often on his mobile after he should have his lights out.

Therapist: How did Chris get on at school?

Mrs. Y: [*Looking at Chris*] He was reluctant to go to primary school initially, but he soon settled in and was very happy there. But he struggled with the move to secondary school. He felt a bit lost at the much larger school. Also, the school is big on football and Chris hates doing any sport.

Therapist: How do you find your secondary school, Chris?

Chris: [*Looking down at his feet as if he doesn't want to be part of the meeting*] Dunno. Alright.

Mr Y: Well, Chris used to be top of his class at primary school but his grades have slipped over the past few years.

Chris: [*Sighs*]

Therapist: Did you find it hard to adjust to your secondary school, Chris?

Chris: [*In a slightly dismissive tone*] No, not really.

The assessment continued in this vein, with Mrs Y. answering most of the therapist's questions and responding much of the time on Chris' behalf.

Before the end of the first family meeting, the therapist suggested a plan for further work. He would meet weekly with Chris, while other members of the team would conduct family meetings every six to eight weeks. In response to the therapist asking what Chris thought about this plan, he shrugged his shoulders and simply said, "OK."

Discussion of the family consultation

The clinical team discussed the case history, noting the difficulties the parents had with the miscarriages. Mrs Y came across as a rather anxious woman who found any separations from the miracle baby, Chris, difficult. This seemed to be a point of contention between Mr and Mrs Y as he looked irritated whenever she talked reassuringly to Chris. There was also the issue of him not being able to latch onto the breast and the difficulty he had sleeping without physical contact with his mother. It was as if she had difficulty taking him in and psychologically containing his communications when she was so anxious about him and his survival. One wonders if this anxious atmosphere conveyed itself to Chris, thereby inhibiting his capacity to settle and relax. One also wonders if he was able to internalise a good primary object that could help him metabolise his experience. With this foundation of anxiety between them, it seemed that he had difficulty letting go of his mother, with every new stage of development seemingly reigniting his separation anxieties. In contrast, Mr Y seemed rather intolerant of his wife's anxieties about her son and tended to distance himself from them both. Rather than helping Mrs Y with her difficulties in letting go of Chris, while supporting Chris in finding his resources, Mr Y seemed to back away into the "spare room" of family life, leaving his wife and son to manage their anxieties between them.

First individual consultation

Mrs Y and Chris arrived at the consultation on time and she remained in the waiting room until the end of the session. The therapist asked Chris when his feelings of uneasiness about his body started. Chris said that he had fantasised about being a girl since he was a very small boy. He said that he didn't hate being a boy, but he couldn't imagine being a man. He thought that being a man was quite boring and uninteresting in contrast to the idea of being a girl, which gave him a great deal of excitement and pleasure. Chris told the therapist that he felt happiest when he was able to dress up in girls' clothes. The therapist was struck by how Chris was both animated and amenable to sharing his thoughts and feelings, as if he were demonstrating how much better he was when free to discuss his wish to transition.

Therapist: Can you say more about why you think the idea of being a man is so dull and boring, compared to the fun of being a girl?

Chris: I don't know really. I've just always thought their clothes are better, with more variety and colour and stuff, and their shoes are just so much nicer … like, ever since I was young … My mum loves ballet and we've been to quite a few shows together. I always liked the women's costumes, I didn't even notice the men on stage much; they always seemed in the background. I used to sometimes imagine being a dancer on stage, but only as a girl.

Therapist: I notice the way you seem to come to life when you are talking about the ballet shows.

Chris: Well, there is something about being in a show. I'm in all the school productions and I love it. I've also attended a kind of performing arts club in the school holidays a few times. I love it and think I'd like to do something like that when I'm older.

Therapist: You love it—could you say more?

Chris: I just love being on stage with an audience, pretending to be someone else.

Therapist: Perhaps pretending to be someone else helps you to get away from something difficult in yourself?

Chris: [*shrugs*] Maybe.

Therapist: How do you feel about being an only child?

Chris: I've never thought about brothers and sisters. I like being the only child. I can't imagine having a brother or sister so I don't miss it, I don't think.

Therapist: What's your relationship with your parents like?

Chris: It's OK …

Therapist: How do you feel they have they responded to your wish to transition?

Chris: Well, Mum fusses a bit and worries a lot, but she is very supportive of what I'm doing. She hasn't said anything negative. My dad runs his own business, so he is busy a lot of the time. Most of the time we get on OK, but I don't think he reacted very well when I came out. He was a bit more critical and asked loads of questions, so I was disappointed about that.

Therapist: Disappointed?

Chris: I think he disapproves of me and that's annoying.

Therapist: Do your parents know that you dress up in women's clothes?

Chris: I think Mum knows because she caught me once, but I don't think she's said anything to Dad.

Therapist: So, you think maybe it's a secret between your mum and you?

Chris: [*Smiles at the therapist and studying him closely*] Yes.

Therapist: I noticed you smiled when I asked you about that. I wonder if you like to have things with Mum that Dad doesn't know about?

Chris: No, it was just a bit embarrassing when she caught me.

Therapist: You perhaps felt she had found out your secret?
Chris: Suppose so …
Therapist: Tell me something about the issues that arose in your secondary school.
Chris: [*Looking more troubled, less animated*] It was just difficult …
Therapist: Your Dad said you were the brightest in primary school but found it hard to adapt when you weren't always top of the class in secondary school. Sounds like that was quite hard for you.
Chris: [*His face brightens*] Better now, though—I've made friends outside school and we meet up at weekends and have a laugh.
Therapist: I noticed how you looked troubled just now when you said that secondary school is difficult for you, but your mood changed when you started to talk about your new friends.
Chris: They accept me—it's more comfortable and fun with them—unlike the others at school. They help me be myself and accept me as transgender, so life is just better.
Therapist: It seems like you have an idea that living as a man would be a disappointment.
Chris: I can't imagine myself as a man, whereas I can imagine myself as a woman. I just feel more comfortable, there's something right about it.
Therapist: I think that maybe you try to get rid of uncomfortable feelings by thinking of yourself as a girl, rather than the boy, Chris, who is having difficulty liking himself.
Chris: It's much more comfortable being a girl.

At the end of the session, the therapist and Chris agreed to meet again in a week.

Second individual session

Therapist: Do you want to start Chris? What's on your mind?
Chris: [*Looking down and worried*] I don't have anything on my mind.
[*Short silence*]

Chris: [*Shrugging his shoulders*] I've got a lot of homework to catch up on, but that is all boring.
[*Another short silence*]
Chris: Can I put my jewellery on?
Therapist: I wonder why you ask—do you think it will help?
Chris: Dunno—I'd just like to put it on … Is that OK?
Therapist: It's as if the excitement of putting on jewellery helps you get rid of some difficult feelings.
Chris: [*Looked intently at the therapist, waiting for an answer to his jewellery question*]
Therapist: It seems as if you feel you need my permission, but perhaps we need to understand this more. We need to think about why dressing up as a girl makes you feel so good and why just being you, sitting here with me, without jewellery, feels so uncomfortable.
Chris: [*Looking angry and bored at the talk, as if he just wanted a simple answer to a simple question*] It's just a matter of yes or no.
Therapist: I understand what I have just said feels difficult, but we need to try to think together about the meaning of why you want to do certain things.
Chris: [*Silence for a few moments*] So, it's OK to put the stuff on? [*He takes some jewellery out of his jacket pocket and puts it on, together with a floral Alice band. He smiles, while looking at the therapist intensely. He then adds, rather defensively*] I just feel better and free when I put stuff on. [*His demeanour becomes more lively*]
Therapist: I wonder if we can think about what gives you that feeling of freedom and feeling better?
Chris: [*Again, looking intently at the therapist, watching his every response*] I don't know, I just love the feeling and it changes me.
Therapist: It seems to transform your mood, as if you leave behind your worries. Perhaps I am left to worry about why you have difficulty feeling comfortable with yourself as you are?
[*Chris remains silent for a few minutes staring at the therapist*]
Therapist: I'm struck by how you watch me, as if you are trying to read my reaction?

EXCITEMENT AS A PSYCHIC DEFENCE AGAINST LOSS

Chris: You are probably like my dad. He doesn't know I do this, but I reckon he would not be happy if he could see me now.

Therapist: And your mum? How would she react?

Chris: OK, I think—she just wants me to be happy.

Therapist: I think you watch to see how I react because you aren't sure whether I would be like your mother and say, "Whatever makes you happy," or your father who would be unhappy with you. I'm struck by how any conflict or concern about what might be going on in your mind seems to reside in me.

Chris: Not really. It doesn't matter what you think.

Therapist: There is something about you feeling that you are uncomfortable not just in your own body, where you tend to locate the problem, but also in your mind. It doesn't seem that you ever feel very at home in either your body or your mind.

Chris: [*The rather excited and detached state of mind seemed to crack, and he physically shudders at this comment. He remains silent for a while with eyes downcast*]

Therapist: I wonder where your mind is now?

Chris: I sometimes can't see a good way out of this.

Therapist: Although you get very excited putting on the jewellery and your girl's clothes, you also seem to be self-conscious and perhaps ashamed of your actions?

Chris: I dread my father catching me dressed up.

Therapist: So, you have an idea you can keep this as a secret between you and your mother?

Chris: [*Nods, looking down at the floor*]

Therapist: How do you imagine your future? What are you wanting to happen?

Chris: [*Looking more positive again*] Well, I am going to start taking hormones as soon as I can and maybe other stuff later on.

Therapist: You seem to be focused on the physical plans for your body, through getting into the fantasy of being a woman, while trying to leave behind some feelings of disappointment you have about yourself.

Chris: [*Looking quite sullen*] I do sometimes worry I won't pass as a woman.

Therapist: You mean that people might see through the fact that you aren't everything you appear to be? Like people will see the rather unhappy boy you are trying to get away from.

Chris: [*Looks briefly upset, but then his expression appears to harden as he looks away from the therapist*]
[*A few minutes of silence*]

Therapist: What do you think about what I just said?

Chris: [*Looks quite contemptuous, as if this is all a waste of his time*] I've no thoughts at all.

Despite this difficult ending to the second session, Chris agreed to meet weekly with the therapist.

Thoughts about the second individual consultation

Chris starts the session by briefly stating he was behind with school-work and this leaves him feeling bored and frustrated. The therapist was reminded about how easy Chris had found primary school work but that his grades had slipped since moving to secondary school and enquires about this. Chris then seems to want to transform himself away from his difficulties with the jewellery and Alice band. He is no longer a man who will be measured against his father's expectations but can escape into being a woman.

The request from the therapist to think with him about what the jewellery represents seems to produce a distant contempt. Chris is interested in the actions that will help him evacuate his worried, self-critical state of mind, replacing it with a more excited state. Any thoughts about what this action might represent are located in the therapist, who is left thinking about the meaning of the dressing up. The therapist is also left with the concern that he is watching Chris enact a phantasy solution to his problems. It is as if Chris could get rid of this "male Chris", and whatever is believed to reside in him, and inhabit the female persona, who is believed to triumph over all anxieties. Chris seems aware that this proposed action fills the therapist with all sorts of feelings about it, as he stares at the therapist intently in an attempt to make him give an answer. The therapist feels that if he agrees to the dressing up, he is giving up on the opportunity to think with Chris about the meaning of this action, but if he tries to stop the action in the name of thought, he will be seen as rejecting or disapproving.

The clinical team was struck by the contrasting presentations in Chris. Before he put on the jewellery, he looked flat, unconfident, and avoided eye contact. After he put the jewellery on, he appeared more animated, confident, and looked straight at the therapist. It was as if the change in appearance produced this dramatic change in his presentation and mood.

Clinical discussion

It seems that Chris might have developed an excited "if only I could play the part of a girl" daydream as a way of distancing himself from anxieties about separation and loss. In this daydream, he transcends his identity as a rather anxious little boy by playing the part of a mesmerising female figure that could hold an audience transfixed. In many ways, Chris appeared to be happiest in the session when he could put on his jewellery and perform.

The therapist was also aware of the way in which Chris watched his reaction intently. The clinical team thought that Chris unconsciously projected his internal conflicts into the therapist, then watched to see how the therapist managed them. One part of him hopes to resolve his separation anxieties, by literally getting into his mother's clothes and shoes and leaving behind the sad little boy; while another part had doubts and concerns about the cost of this solution, represented by his thoughts that he would not pass as a woman. This split was also represented in the split existing in his relationship with his parents. Chris felt that his mother seemed to secretly support his wish to transition, while he believed his father would be critical and disapproving if he knew the full extent of it.

Chris' wish to get into his mother's identity is perhaps based on an early, insecure relationship with the mother. This insecurity and failure to internalise his mother as a good internal object mean that he has difficulty separating from his actual, physical mother. It might be that he feels he does not have the internal emotional equipment necessary to manage the loss of the dyadic relationship with his mother to the triadic oedipal relationship with the external world (see p. 198 more information on the oedipal situation). This seems to be a repetition of the infantile situation, as the baby Chris found it difficult to latch onto the breast and take in its life-giving properties. It might be that from early on, he could not bear to be dependent on his mother's care. Instead, he takes over his mother's identity in order to avoid his problems of difficulty in separation. Thus, in phantasy, he doesn't need the breast because he creates his own. The addition of female clothes, shoes, make-up, and hairstyles help him to sustain this idealised state. He exerts a considerable amount of control over his parents, with his mother attending to his anxieties while his father angrily looks on.

In many ways, his "transexual ideal" seems to represent a way of taking over his mother's identity so that he triumphs over feelings of dependency on and need of her. This manic solution makes him feel excited and triumphant, as he projects anxieties, doubts, and conflict about his solution into his therapist and his parents. This powerful defence also seemed to be represented by the idea of a magic potion (hormones) that would enable him to triumph over separation anxieties and the worry that he wouldn't be able to measure up against his father. Chris might feel his father to be successful and out of reach in some way, that he can never measure up to his father, or gain his support as a man. But Chris is also aware at times that his father carries and voices his own doubts about his solution to his problems—to transition.

It can seem easier, and perhaps even kinder in circumstances like this, for professionals to simply accept the apparent improved state of mind when Chris inhabits his female persona. However, in supervision, the therapist is helped to see his countertransference, and hold in mind the doubts and anxieties in Chris' communications, both verbal and nonverbal. The therapy aimed to see if the therapist could find a way of getting beneath the manic defence in order to attend to the rather anxious little boy who was worried that he did not feel able to be himself.

Britton (1999) describes the way the hysteric tries to actualise the Oedipus complex as a cure for their difficulties, rather than give it up. The hysteric intrudes into the parental couple's creativity. This inability to separate from the parents' sexuality interferes with the development of the child's own sexual identity. Britton describes imagination as a place in the child's mind where the parents' intercourse takes place when the child is not present. Room for the development of imagination in the child's mind comes into existence when the child can tolerate the idea of the parents' sexual relationship going on elsewhere—behind the bedroom door. It is the place where the object spends its time when the child is not present.

In our experience, many children with gender dysphoria have a problem employing their imagination or thinking symbolically. Indeed, many describe difficulties establishing a mind that can think about their own emotional life and their relationship to other members of the family. It is as if they fear the development of a mind that might begin to think about the meaning of their wishes, desires, and phantasies.

In therapeutic relationships, the hysteric patient might demand the therapist's exclusive love, while attacking and undermining the therapist's relationship with others, including their internal relationship with psychoanalytic theory and practice. Patients in this state of mind can fill the consulting room with action designed to saturate the therapist's mind and induce them into reacting, rather than thinking. Thus, the therapeutic setting and the therapist's capacity to think are threatened by the patient's erotised enactments. A particular problem can arise with this patient group because any curiosity expressed by the therapist or mental health professional can be misinterpreted by the patient as erotic interest in them.

Chris' therapist feels he is under pressure to go along with Chris' wish to dress up, as a solution to underlying feelings of anxiety. If he goes along with this pressure to collude, he re-enacts the seductive relationship Chris has with his mother in the transference, which fails to examine the underlying meaning of Chris' symptoms. However, if he questions Chris' motives and wishes, he is felt to re-enact the paternal relationship with a father who judges and criticises Chris from a distance without understanding his underlying anxieties. When the therapist takes up either position, he unwittingly re-enacts these relationships in the transference. Therapeutic work in the future would depend on the therapist's capacity to avoid this split and bring these aspects together. The therapist needs to help Chris explore the meaning of his behaviours, while understanding the nature of his underlying anxieties and urgent compulsion to enact his phantasy solution.

Although Chris is addicted to "dressing up", he is also aware that this is an illusory solution, because he worries he will not pass as a woman.

Although he does find the exciting, seductive nature of his sexualised defence difficult to resist, in another part of his mind, he hopes he can find someone who will help him understand the addictive effect of this manic solution that has captured him. There is a hope that someone can help free him from the enveloping psychological solution with all its unseen and unacknowledged costs. However, the therapist is also aware that Chris' defences are necessary to protect him from anxieties that threaten to overwhelm his ego. Chris will need his therapist to act as a robust but humane figure who understands that he needs his omnipotent defences to protect him from overwhelming anxiety.

Summary

In this chapter we have tried to explore a particular psychic defence arising from difficulties experienced in the relationship with the primary caregiver (usually the mother but not always). In these cases, the child can be left feeling insecure and unprepared for the challenges of becoming a separate entity. In ordinary development any form of separation from the primary caregiver provokes feelings of envy, rivalry, jealousy, love and hate in the infant towards them, but an infant who has experienced some form of trauma in relation to the primary object may struggle more to manage these overwhelming, conflictual feelings towards the person they rely upon most. They may fear that the primary caregiver is too fragile to accept them and survive. At this stage a phantasy may develop that the child can inhabit the mother's space, assume her identity, thus providing a refuge from the unbearable feelings aroused by separation. The defensive function is often enhanced through concrete actions that accompany the phantasy, such as getting dressed up in clothes and other items associated with mother. In this way they believe they have overcome the difficulties of dependence. As this goes on the child might also come to believe that their phantasy solution is supported by one parent, who is then involved in a collusive relationship, while the other is excluded, thus recapturing the idealised exclusive relationship. We suspect that this collusion might also come about due to the primary caregiver having pre-existing difficulties in this area. This collusive dynamic is then re-enacted in the therapeutic relationship.

There is a group of patients who develop erotised defences against the pain, confusion, and anxiety provoked by development. The concrete acting out of fantasies designed to triumph over anxiety might have an addictive quality, as it gives the individual a feeling of power and control over their own minds and sometimes provokes predictable responses in others, who are left feeling inadequate, threatened, helpless, or unwanted. The compulsive nature of this type of defence, which also involves evacuation of parts of the ego associated with awareness and thought, creates technical difficulties for the therapist. Misunderstandings, frustration, and hostility may arise in the therapeutic relationship if the therapist tries prematurely to push insights back into the patient. Instead, the therapist has to recognise that the therapist is having aspects of the patient's mind pushed into him/her while the patient watches for the impact of these projections. It is this dynamic between them that needs to be addressed by the therapist. Once progress has been made in this way, the therapist can move on to interpretations designed to return the projections back to the patient. In other words, the patient needs the thinking and understanding to take place in the therapist's mind before they can begin to take it in themselves. In cases such as these, supervision is key to enable the therapist to process these projections.

Part III

Gender dysphoria and comorbidity

We wish to re-emphasise the importance of not separating gender dysphoria from any other aspects of a person's mental functioning. Many of the young people presenting with gender incongruence have comorbid problems; as we have already discussed, they may also be on the autistic spectrum or have ADHD, have eating disorders, depression and anxiety, or obsessional thoughts, etc. The recent ideological drive to separate all gender incongruence from mental illness leaves some individuals vulnerable to mistreatment. The denial of the psychological factors influencing the desire to transition can unwittingly lead the patient and the service to look towards concrete, affirmative solutions, whilst omitting important consideration of the individual's mental health and any potential link between their underlying condition and gender dysphoria. In the following three chapters we will discuss patients who have presented both with intentions or actions of trans-identification and with serious mental health conditions, some of whom were being cared for within the mental health system.

EIGHT

The link between suicidal ideation and gender dysphoria

Stekel (1910), a colleague of Freud's, proposed that anyone who kills themselves has wanted to kill another or wished the death of another. The fundamental truth of this statement has persisted throughout the development of psychodynamic and psychoanalytical perspectives on suicide. Freud theorised that murderous impulses against others are turned on the self to precipitate suicidal thoughts. We believe that the wish to transition can be connected to a wish to kill off the natal body and biological sex inherited as a result of the parent's sexual intercourse. This is related to a sometimes unconscious, often deeply concealed grievance towards the parents who have failed them in some way. This grievance might be as a result of more obvious parental failings but often the trauma of such failures and the subsequent grievance are subtle and not consciously acknowledged by the child or the parents.

First, some definitions

1) Suicide occurs when the person knowingly brings about his or her death.
2) Parasuicide is a non-fatal act of self-injury (for example, taking an overdose that does not kill you).

3) Suicidal ideation means experiencing suicidal thoughts and impulses in response to a crisis; or engaging in suicidal thoughts for a long, sustained period. This third group may develop a suicidal attitude towards their life while denying active thoughts of suicide, for example, in anorexia nervosa, extreme obesity, or alcoholism.

In this chapter, we are going to focus on the meaning and use of suicidal ideation in relation to gender dysphoria.

David—a twenty-three-year-old man

David's mother phoned a therapist wanting a psychotherapy consultation for her son. He was a twenty-three-year-old young man who wanted to transition. She said she had been unaware that he had any idea of wanting to change gender, but he was now saying that he had been having these thoughts for many years. She said David had had a history of anxiety and depression including suicidal ideation over the past five years, but that these thoughts had stopped after he decided to transition. The mother told the therapist that her son had overdosed on paracetamol after failing to get into medical school. The therapist agreed to see the patient, but emphasised it should be David who made contact, which he did the next day.

The first meeting

David was a short, slim, attractive man with long, straight hair. He started the session by saying that he had long-standing difficulties with anxiety and depression but had been feeling much better since he had decided to transition. He went on to say he was not sure what the point of the meeting was but that he was attending because his mother had suggested and encouraged it.

The therapist said that although his mother had talked about David, she would like to hear from him.

> David: [*Angrily*] Didn't my mother tell you everything you need to know?

Therapist: Your mother did tell me something about what's been going on and your decision to transition, but I would like to hear more from you about your life.

David: [*Shrugs his shoulders as if he didn't care—silence*]

Therapist: You seem to indicate that there is nothing to say or think about.

David: [*Again, shrugs his shoulders*] No, not really, I've already made my mind up.

Therapist: Perhaps you could tell me a bit about your history.

David: I have an older brother and a younger half-sister. My father left home when I was seven years old and my mother remarried and had my half-sister with my stepfather. [He then rushed on to talk about something else, but the therapist went back to his father.]

Therapist: I suspect it might have been difficult for your mother, your brother, and you being left by your father?

David: My mother found it very difficult at first and my older brother was very upset. He used to cry and scream at her that it was her fault. There was a lot of drama between the two of them.

Therapist: It sounds like there was no room for you to be upset?

David: My mother and I were very close until my stepfather moved in.

Therapist: Leaving you feeling you lost your close relationship with your mother?

David: Well, my younger sister was the golden girl. [He went on to say that after his half-sister was born, he gave up on his family and asked to be allowed to move away and live with his aunt and her family on their farm. Initially, his mother said no, but eventually she agreed, and he went to live in another part of the country when he was eleven years old.]

Therapist: It sounds like you couldn't stand the situation at home?

David: I didn't feel like I belonged.

The therapist then asked how he managed at school. David said he was reasonably successful and that he had had a long-standing plan to train as a doctor, but this was thwarted when he failed to get into the medical school of his choice. At this point in the interview, David looked uncomfortable and explained that after this failure, he became depressed and withdrew from all social contact for a prolonged period. He eventually applied to a different medical school and around this time he moved back in with his mother, who had by now separated from his stepfather. On the morning he received the rejection letter from the second medical school, he described taking an overdose because he felt so ashamed and infuriated.

Therapist: It sounds like you were devastated not to get into medical school and unable to bear those feelings.

David: [*Looking at the therapist in a slightly challenging way, as if he thought the therapist was saying he was weak*] I put the period of withdrawal down to an unrecognised virus. The letter was the last straw.

Therapist: [*Asks him to say a bit more about the overdose.*]

David: I took paracetamol from my mother's bathroom cupboard and intended to kill myself, but my mother came home and found me unconscious in my room.

Therapist: It sounds as if you wanted your mother to find you—dead or alive.

David: No—I just wanted to die—I didn't think about any of that.

Therapist: There seemed to be a lot riding on you getting into medical school and the failure to get in seems to have stirred up some terrible feeling of anger and shame?

David: [*Remains silent*]

Therapist: I am thinking about your comment "the last straw" and I think that there were other "straws" in your life which have made you feel so disappointed or angry. Firstly, your father leaves the family, and then after all your hard work taking care of your mother, she marries your stepfather—leaves you feeling hurt, left out, and unappreciated.

David: [*Angrily*] Oh, here we go … typical shrink. "It's all your mother's fault."

Therapist: Perhaps you did feel angry with her though and your overdose was a way of getting her to care for you or to regret her actions over you.

David: You are just like my dad always telling me what I'm thinking or why I'm doing things.
Therapist: You feel like I'm saying I know what you are thinking and doing.

David went on to explain that his father would often lecture him about his life and his choices, but as far as David was concerned, his father had lost all rights to an opinion about David's life when he left the family home. Although after a long list of complaints about his father's behaviour, he did concede that he enjoyed days out with his father because they had two season tickets for a cricket club and they would often go together to watch matches. However, he made it clear that this was done on the basis of being "mates on a day out" not a father–son relationship.

At the end of the session, the therapist suggested meeting again before discussing treatment options. David seemed much more open to this suggestion than the therapist had anticipated, and agreed to return.

Discussion of the first session

At the beginning of the session, David seemed quite detached, as if he was only attending the appointment to keep his mother happy. Indeed, he seemed to want to show off his nonchalance as if he was determined to convey the fact that he had no anxiety at all about himself or his decisions.

In response to his parents' separation, it seemed David withdrew from contact with painful feelings of anger and loss. His mother was left in a fragile state as she struggled to deal with the loss of her husband, combined with the demands of a young family. David again felt a great sense of loss when his mother remarried, and his half-sister was born. The loss of his mother leads to a deep-seated grievance towards her for marrying and having his half-sister. At this point, he seems to cut off emotionally from his family.

When assessing a suicidal patient, the assessor needs to understand the pre-suicidal psychic structure, including their phantasies and the relationships that support their psychic equilibrium. Campbell and Hale (2017) highlight the importance of the core complex in suicidal states.

The nub of the core complex is that the individual has phantasies of merging with an ideal object—in the unconscious this is the mother who, once upon a time, could solve all the infant's problems. This phantasy acts as a psychic retreat from painful reality. But the suicidal phantasies are provoked because the individual feels betrayed by their ideal object.

David developed a view of himself as being his mother's partner when his father left home because he stayed close to her, looked after her, and didn't express any anger, unlike his older brother. However, he felt utterly betrayed when his mother remarried and had his younger sister. This was the nub of his deep-seated grievance against both his parents. He seemed to cut off from his feelings and from any wish to be cared for by them. He went into a deep freeze emotionally by detaching himself from any need of warmth or familial love. The request to leave home and move in with his aunt seemed to be part of the rejection of his mother and half-sister. As he said, he developed a fantasy that he did not belong in the family. In this way, he experienced a cut-off, self-sufficient state where he is removed from feelings of anxiety, doubt, or conflict.

The hope of becoming a doctor may have been driven by a wish to project need or vulnerability into others and then cure the problem in the patient. It may also have been related to a wish to cure his mother of her pain after the divorce, when he was a boy and was left feeling out of his depth and emotionally responsible for her fragility. When he failed to get into medical school twice, his idealised solution broke down; he felt he was useless and collapsed into a depression. Then he turned to more drastic psychological solutions. If only he could become somebody else and get rid of this collapsed useless man, he would feel much better. His wish to have his masculinity removed seemed connected to a wish to distance himself from his father, whom he blamed for his family's collapse.

Second session

David looked a little more annoyed and irritated. He sat looking at the therapist in a somewhat defiant way as if he felt he should do something.

Therapist: You are waiting for me to start.
David: Well, you are the expert. [After a short pause David went on to say that he had visited his older brother during the week. His brother was doing very well after leaving university and had a girlfriend. He said that he was sure they would get married soon and start a family. With a quite dismissive tone, he said that finally somebody would make his mother happy.]
Therapist: It doesn't sound like you anticipate making your mother happy.
David: Although my mother doesn't say it to me, deep down inside she is looking forward to grandchildren. [He went on to say that his family had been such a mess and he had no intention of following in his parents' footsteps. This was all said in a dismissive and angry tone.]
Therapist: You're not sure whether our meetings are going to produce anything creative.
David: Well, my mother made me attend—she's the one who is against my transition.
Therapist: You seem to locate any concern about your planned transition into those around you as if the potential losses don't concern you, as if you want to distance yourself from anything to do with them.

David replied that his friend had often commented on the fact that he did not get excited or passionate about anything. Again, he said this with a considerable amount of pride. He went on to say that people made a lot of fuss about things that do not matter. Nothing mattered to him apart from his cricket team. He said that he loved watching the matches because he felt alive. The therapist asked him what he liked about the matches. He said that you never knew which way a match was going. It was the "parry and thrust".

The therapist pointed out the way he seemed to have withdrawn from the "parry and thrust" of life since his failure to get into medical school, as if he could not bear to be passionate about something as this might lead to disappointment and loss. This was true in most areas apart from his cricket team where he did allow himself to feel passionate and risk being disappointed.

David nodded sombrely saying that he had his heart set on training at a medical school and that he was devastated when he did not get in. It was humiliating. The therapist said that he seemed to have shut down since that time and David agreed, saying that he thought he could not see the point of anything.

Therapist: The overdose seemed to be a way of killing the pain.
David: [After a few moments when he looked upset, he seemed to pull himself together and in a breezy way, announced that he did not care anymore, and this seemed to be a better way of coping with life—to "take it easy".]
Therapist: It seems as if you really struggle to recover from these disappointments.
David: After failing to get into medical school, I just decided that I had given up.
Therapist: It sounds like you feel you are surrounded by fragile, broken figures like your mother and your brother when you were both children. Becoming a doctor might be connected with a wish to cure these fragile figures.

David scoffed at this, saying, "Oh, you have all your fancy theories," but then went on to say that he used to have fantasies about making everybody better when he played doctor and nurse with the girl next door. He then said that he was not sure what relevance any of this had to him now. He said it was clear that he was born by mistake into the wrong body. Moreover, this could easily be rectified. The therapist asked him what he did not like about his male body and his male identity. He said that he had always thought penises were ridiculous. David went on to say that he used to hear his mother crying to herself at night, and he remembers praying at night that his mum would be alright and then feeling disappointed with God the next time he heard her crying. The therapist said it sounded as if he was praying that a powerful figure could sort everything out, but when the therapy failed to sort out the problems immediately, he slumped into a feeling of disappointment.

At this point, David looked straight at the therapist as if he was suddenly engaged, saying that his brother really struggled and was hit very hard when his father left, and his mother was in pieces.

Just before he went off to live with his aunt, he remembered thinking, "I am never going to expect anything from my parents. I felt free after that decision."

Therapist: So, you are on your own, you don't need any help, and yet you must be worried that your detached state, apparently free of anxiety, leaves you vulnerable to making decisions without really thinking through the implications.
David: No, not really, I don't care that much.
Therapist: I think you have dispensed with the need for parents, and therapists that you worry are working for parents, but I also think you have dispensed with the need to worry or think about anything going on in your life. It's like nothing matters.
David: So now you think you know everything; think you know me better than I know myself, just like my dad.
Therapist: You are very angry with your father for leaving the family. I also think you are unsure whether I am more interested in my fancy theories than really trying to help you through difficult times.

This seemed to hit home to the patient. He said that his mother was overanxious, but at least she did not desert the family.

Discussion of the second session

Rosenfeld (1971) described the way destructive narcissistic structures in the mind function like a pathological gang who offer a retreat from the pain of reality, using an omnipotent, psychic mechanism which enables the patient to deny reality rather than to face it. This destructive internal structure seduces the individual into believing that loyalty to the internal gang will protect them from all pain caused by loss, dependency, conflict, or vulnerability. Rosenfeld outlined the way parts of the internal gang promise to deal with the individual's problems in a pain-free way by employing manic defences of triumph, control, and contempt. In his paper, "Who Is Killing What or Whom", Bell (2001) highlights the way some individuals project unwanted aspects of themselves into their body, which they then attack.

David seemed wedded to a powerful internal structure that dealt with the anxiety and pain of life by projecting it into his body, which he then treated with contempt. The option of suicide, which he kept in reserve, provided the ultimate defence against psychic pain. Thus, the patient harboured a relationship with suicide and self-harm as a way of managing painful situations. He said in a challenging way, "Well, we are all going to die in the end anyway." He felt to do otherwise would overwhelm his ego and lead to fragmentation or collapse.

Campbell (1995) believes the unconscious suicide phantasy is a "psychotic" one because the individual believes that the attack on their own body will not result in their death, as an observing part of the self will survive. The suicidal act itself reveals a significant confusion between the body and the mind, for it reveals the patient's reduced capacity to know reality, meaning that if they kill their body their mind dies too. Instead, the body is used to get rid of extreme states of mind. Psychoanalytic theory argues that the body represents the hated primary caregiver (mother) who is an ideal object that needs to be punished for her failings.

In the case of David, we can see how his cruel indifference to his body and his life is used as a reproach to his mother. In fantasy, he gambles with the idea that his mother will find him unconscious and feel appropriately guilty for getting on with her life. His sense of triumph accompanying the conscious fantasy of his mother finding his overdosed body was palpable in the session.

Third session

At the start of the third session, David began by saying that he remembered crying in his room when his mother confirmed that he could go and live with his aunt. He said that this was the last time he remembered crying.

Therapist: I think you felt there was nowhere to take your feelings of disappointment and anger with your parents. Perhaps that is why you became detached from yourself, locking the feelings inside your body which you no longer acknowledged as your own. [*At this point, he seemed to slump*]

David: [Said that he had become extremely self-conscious and had developed suicidal thoughts around the time he started puberty and moved to his aunt's. He hated the fact that he started becoming hairy, and his voice got deeper.]

Therapist: [Pointed out that he appeared to be distancing himself from his masculinity as if that was something he wanted nothing to do with. The therapist also returned to the link with his grievance towards his father, who had left the family.]

David: Well, the bloke is just a selfish prick.

Therapist: A prick that can make two babies but a man that cannot stay around to look after his family.

David: Well, some men are just selfish like that.

Therapist: You still like watching the cricket team with your father and admire his knowledge of the team.

David: [Said that they had a very talented bunch of players but that that can mean they get lazy, taking their talent for granted. But currently, they had a great coach who seemed to inspire them, did not let them drift, and kept them working hard.]

Therapist: Perhaps you hope I will be like this honest coach who could help you think hard about yourself and your situation—not let you drift into lazy thinking.

David: [Smiled and after a period of silence, said that he was dreading telling his brother and half-sister about his plans to transition because he thought they would question him and express their doubts.]

Therapist: Your dread about your siblings' doubts represents a part of you that knows there is something in your plans that needs to be thought about.

David: [Shook his head at this comment indicating that he did not agree, then went on to smile in a mocking way. He went on to explain with some pride that his friends would often comment on how he was not affected by things in the way that other people were.]

Therapist: [Pointed out that David seemed to be distancing himself from his own doubts and his capacity to critically examine his own thinking.]

David: [Looked as if something the therapist said caused him to reflect. After a long pause, he said that the decision that he had made to transition had in fact resolved all the suicidal feelings. He said that his mother was delighted as she felt that he was better since making the decision.]

Therapist: So, it seems that you believe that transition is the solution to all your suicidal feelings which are connected to your anger and resentment towards your parents.

Case discussion

The "ideal self" is the self that the individual desires to be. This aspect of the self is a depository for all the desires and aspirations that the individual is aiming for. The "real" self is then weighed against the "ideal" self by a combination of reasonable judgement located in the ego and the sometimes harsher, more primitive judgement located in the superego (see pp. 239–240 for more information on the superego). The ego's judgements are based on the individual's capacity to reality-test, whereas the superego makes judgements based on how things should be in a perfect world. All of us struggle to accept the painful reality that our performance and the performance of those we are intimately involved with rarely lives up to the ideals we are hoping for. Reality-testing involves recognising our own qualities, including our limitations and deficits, in relation to others. In that struggle we have to find a way of acknowledging we would wish things "ideally" to be, while tolerating and accepting ourselves and our objects as they really are. Our assessment of ourselves varies according to our personality traits. For some with a harsh superego, failure or imperfection are particularly unbearable, irrespective of their capabilities.

For some individuals a way of managing a harsher superego is to project the critical judgement into others, who are then felt to be observing in a disapproving way. At other times people may project the ego's more realistic judgement into others, in order to avoid facing any questions or conflicts in themselves. In the clinical example of David, it is his siblings who contain the split-off doubts which would threaten his belief that transition is the only answer to his difficulties. To be clear, these are his reasonable doubts which he has projected into the siblings and he "dreads" their return if they should express them to him because this would confront him with the doubts and conflicts he is trying to rid himself of.

The individual with a fragile ego and a punitive superego struggles to manage the pain involved in rivalry, competition, envy, and disappointment—those normal bumps and bruises of dependence and development. These experiences can be overwhelming for the mind, leading to feelings of humiliation or fragmentation. The individual may retreat from the painful anxieties involved in comparison and competition into the daydream world where if-only phantasies start to become increasingly influential.

The idea of transitioning for David seemed to be connected to a wish to punish his parents for their failings. He would deprive his mother of the grandchildren she wanted and his father of his son. In fantasy, he would return to being the non-sexual young person partner of his mother before his half-sister was born. David may have seen the idea of transitioning as providing a solution to his anxieties about his future life, with its inevitable comparison with ideals and the torment of not meeting those ideals.

When assessing patients with suicidal ideation, it is important to consider the unconscious as well as the conscious meanings associated with the suicidal act. If the suicidal ph/fantasies are not understood and worked through, the individual remains in danger of resorting to suicide as a means of dealing with their conflict, pain, and anxiety. Freud (1920g) described the way internal conflicts that have not been made conscious are enacted and re-enacted by the individual. He coined the term "repetition compulsion" to describe the way these unconscious conflicts emerge as actions until they have been consciously understood. This process is often evident in acts of suicide and parasuicide, as unconscious phantasies and conflicts are repeated in the individual's current life (D'Angelo, 2019). The links between the conscious and unconscious conflicts are often revealed by the triggers for the suicidal act which link the current situation to the historical facts. This understanding can then illuminate the relationship between the individual's psychic structure and their suicidal action.

For example, David tries to "save" his mother by becoming a doctor as he had tried to do as a boy when his father left the family. When this application fails, it leaves him feeling humiliated and deprived of the ideal relationship he craves with his mother. He then wants to punish his parents and so the suicidal act is his way to express his profound sense of grievance towards both of them.

The fantasy of transitioning is often connected to a grievance towards the parents whom the individual believes have failed to provide the ideal mental and physical equipment that could protect the patient from psychic pain. It may be related to an idea that the person can create the ideal self, that will provide protection from feelings of anxiety, jealousy, and disappointment. The defence is based on an idea that they can somehow triumph over the usual vulnerabilities which can be located in the body. Medics and mental health professionals can collude with this illusory solution to the person's vulnerabilities by promising to deliver some sort of ideal self.

David threatened his mother that he would commit suicide if she did not go along with his wish to transition. When she agreed to support his wish to transition (which is understandable following the apparent improvement in his suicidal state once he declared his wish to transition), she was also joining her son in an alliance against his father, who, he subsequently told the therapist, would be unlikely to support such a move. The pressure he placed on his mother to agree with his resolution was also present in the relationship with the therapist. If the therapist failed to go along with his wishes, he would threaten suicide, or repeat the suicidal act in the therapy by cutting off contact—thus punishing the therapist for any active examination which he might associate with a parental function. The therapist is thus put under pressure to go along with the idea that transitioning would solve David's problems. Perhaps David had an unconscious belief that he would be restored to being his mother's ideal partner before his stepfather's arrival on the scene by becoming once more his mother's prepubescent child, the one he believed she loved before anyone else.

The symbolic meaning of "deadnaming"

In the transgender communities "deadnaming" may be regarded as offensive, invalidating, or hurtful. Deadnaming is when somebody either inadvertently or intentionally uses the trans-person's birth name,

d body. The mind may then develop a hostile and uncaring
ards the body, which is mistreated and abused often with-
ught or feeling for the consequences. Thus, the childhood
h its dynamic interplay of the abuser and abused, is inter-
 enacted between the patient's mind and body. This might
sly to self-harming behaviours, suicide attempts, body dys-
orexia, and also gender dysphoria and trans-identification.
mples described in this chapter are all people who seemed to
 they could deal with their internal conflicts and self-hatred
g their bodies and gender.

Case example: the collapse of an ideal

erapist assessed Michelle, a trans-identified woman in her
ies. She had a diagnosis of borderline personality disorder,
rous admissions to hospitals in crisis after overdoses and/or
berate self-harm. (We will refer to the patient as Carl (he/his)
ribing his history pre-transition and as Michelle (she/her)
ition.)
 health services had previously known Michelle as Carl in
ns. Then shortly after his twentieth birthday, he changed his
rder to socially transition in preparation for sexual reassign-
ery. It was recorded in the notes that Carl had been involved
ative sexual relationships as a young person. He hoped that
ssignment surgery would help him manage his feelings of
ity and fears of sexual exploitation.
time of the current presentation, Michelle worked as a pros-
rder to maintain a drug habit. She felt exploited by the pimps,
ers, and the clients. She would often arrive at Accident and
y following an overdose and subsequently be admitted to the
r mental health wards.
e occasion, Michelle had taken rat poison after an argument
ent. The assessing therapist asked her what had provoked the
. Michelle said there was nothing to say and there was noth-
nk about. The therapist said that he thought this comment was
s something that had been upsetting. Michelle told the thera-
ck off and that he had no right to ask questions about her life

rather than their "affirmed" name. Some trans-identified individuals may have an extreme emotional reaction to deadnaming, and it can lead to powerful accusations and hostility towards the person who deadnames. The idea of transition can be thought of as an attempt to triumph over the limitations of the reality of the body as if the person can kill off an unwanted aspect of the self. This is also connected to a wish to kill the child who their parents gave birth to, perhaps unconsciously in order to punish them for their shortcomings as parents. Parents can deny the aggression implied in the child's wish to transition by describing them as heroic or stating how proud they are of them for coming out as trans. Parents, of course, are faced with a painful realisation because if they question their child's wish to transition, services and/or the trans charities may criticise them, or they may fear becoming estranged from their son or daughter, sometimes encouraged by the groups who support the young people.

Conclusion

A wish to transition is often based on a belief that the individual has been "born into the wrong body" and consequently deprived of the ideal. The ideal is the self that would either be loved and accepted by others or be loved by themselves. In this ideal state, the individual would be free of the usual sorts of mental pain, the conflicts, and humiliations. This ideal structure is also related to an unconscious or conscious grievance against the parents who failed to provide them with the ideal love, support, and care. The whole idealised fantasy gets concretised through the idea that they can literally be rid of their natal body and their genetic inheritance. The gender transition can include an idea of killing off the old self and replacing it with a self-created new version. Sometimes this fantasy involves being able to witness their parents suffering for their failures in the past. It also potentially deprives parents of the possibility of becoming grandparents, which could be viewed as a further punishment for perceived failures.

Threats of suicide can be a way of putting pressure on services and therapists to agree to medical interventions. However, the threat also contains a psychological truth as the individual believes that they can't live with the unwanted aspects of themselves represented by their natal body and they want to have them eradicated. Although the individual might be able to alter the body, they can't eradicate either their natal identity or their genetic inheritance. Indeed, the suicidal ideation is often connected with a wish to kill off vulnerable aspects of the self that feel humiliated or unlovable. In this way, it is seen as a solution to the problem of psychic pain. However, in phantasy, the individual often believes that the suicidal act will restore the ideal relationship or position they feel they have lost. Some part of the suicidal patient believes that they will survive and be reborn in some way through the suicidal act.

Therefore, the professionals need to take any suicidal threats seriously, but such threats should not be used as a reason to close down a thorough psychological examination of the patient's underlying motives and beliefs. Suicidal ideation often develops as a defence against unbearable psychic pain and if these underlying reasons are not addressed, it is highly likely that, even after a transition has occurred, the suicidality will re-emerge when psychological pressures increase.

rather than their "affirmed" name. Some trans-identified individuals may have an extreme emotional reaction to deadnaming, and it can lead to powerful accusations and hostility towards the person who deadnames. The idea of transition can be thought of as an attempt to triumph over the limitations of the reality of the body as if the person can kill off an unwanted aspect of the self. This is also connected to a wish to kill the child who their parents gave birth to, perhaps unconsciously in order to punish them for their shortcomings as parents. Parents can deny the aggression implied in the child's wish to transition by describing them as heroic or stating how proud they are of them for coming out as trans. Parents, of course, are faced with a painful realisation because if they question their child's wish to transition, services and/or the trans charities may criticise them, or they may fear becoming estranged from their son or daughter, sometimes encouraged by the groups who support the young people.

Conclusion

A wish to transition is often based on a belief that the individual has been "born into the wrong body" and consequently deprived of the ideal. The ideal is the self that would either be loved and accepted by others or be loved by themselves. In this ideal state, the individual would be free of the usual sorts of mental pain, the conflicts, and humiliations. This ideal structure is also related to an unconscious or conscious grievance against the parents who failed to provide them with the ideal love, support, and care. The whole idealised fantasy gets concretised through the idea that they can literally be rid of their natal body and their genetic inheritance. The gender transition can include an idea of killing off the old self and replacing it with a self-created new version. Sometimes this fantasy involves being able to witness their parents suffering for their failures in the past. It also potentially deprives parents of the possibility of becoming grandparents, which could be viewed as a further punishment for perceived failures.

Threats of suicide can be a way of putting pressure on services and therapists to agree to medical interventions. However, the threat also contains a psychological truth as the individual believes that they can't live with the unwanted aspects of themselves represented by their natal body and they want to have them eradicated. Although the individual might be able to alter the body, they can't eradicate either their natal identity or their genetic inheritance. Indeed, the suicidal ideation is often connected with a wish to kill off vulnerable aspects of the self that feel humiliated or unlovable. In this way, it is seen as a solution to the problem of psychic pain. However, in phantasy, the individual often believes that the suicidal act will restore the ideal relationship or position they feel they have lost. Some part of the suicidal patient believes that they will survive and be reborn in some way through the suicidal act.

Therefore, the professionals need to take any suicidal threats seriously, but such threats should not be used as a reason to close down a thorough psychological examination of the patient's underlying motives and beliefs. Suicidal ideation often develops as a defence against unbearable psychic pain and if these underlying reasons are not addressed, it is highly likely that, even after a transition has occurred, the suicidality will re-emerge when psychological pressures increase.

NINE

Patients with emotionally unstable personality disorder and gender dysphoria in mental health settings

As previously stated, the proportion of individuals with a combination of gender dysphoria and comorbid problems, such as borderline personality disorder, is high. In borderline personality disorder the person usually demonstrates a lack of capacity to maintain symbolic thinking as their ego can quickly fragment under emotional pressure. There is a tendency to resort to black-and-white thinking (paranoid–schizoid thinking), and to use the defences of splitting, projection, and denial. In this fragmented state, there is a lack of capacity to think symbolically about emotional difficulties, and the search for concrete solutions takes over. This state of mind is also frequently observed in those with symptoms of gender dysphoria and those who are trans-identified.

Otto Kernberg (1975) argued that some patients who go on to develop a borderline personality disorder have experienced relationships with hostile, aggressive, and abusive carers in infancy and childhood. These early relationships may be taken into different parts of the patient's mind and body where they continue their hostile relationship with one another. Patients can dissociate themselves from their feelings and sense of responsibility for their body or actions, developing a split between the mind and body. The mind may then develop a hostile and uncaring attitude towards the body, which is mistreated and abused often without any thought or feeling for the consequences. Thus, the childhood trauma, with its dynamic interplay of the abuser and abused, is internalised and enacted between the patient's mind and body. This might lead variously to self-harming behaviours, suicide attempts, body dysmorphia, anorexia, and also gender dysphoria and trans-identification. The case examples described in this chapter are all people who seemed to believe that they could deal with their internal conflicts and self-hatred by changing their bodies and gender.

Case example: the collapse of an ideal

A psychotherapist assessed Michelle, a trans-identified woman in her mid-twenties. She had a diagnosis of borderline personality disorder, with numerous admissions to hospitals in crisis after overdoses and/or acts of deliberate self-harm. (We will refer to the patient as Carl (he/his) when describing his history pre-transition and as Michelle (she/her) post-transition.)

Mental health services had previously known Michelle as Carl in his late teens. Then shortly after his twentieth birthday, he changed his name in order to socially transition in preparation for sexual reassignment surgery. It was recorded in the notes that Carl had been involved in exploitative sexual relationships as a young person. He hoped that sexual reassignment surgery would help him manage his feelings of vulnerability and fears of sexual exploitation.

At the time of the current presentation, Michelle worked as a prostitute in order to maintain a drug habit. She felt exploited by the pimps, drug dealers, and the clients. She would often arrive at Accident and Emergency following an overdose and subsequently be admitted to the medical or mental health wards.

On one occasion, Michelle had taken rat poison after an argument with a client. The assessing therapist asked her what had provoked the argument. Michelle said there was nothing to say and there was nothing to think about. The therapist said that he thought this comment was to dismiss something that had been upsetting. Michelle told the therapist to fuck off and that he had no right to ask questions about her life and background. She said he was making her "feel worse and interfering with my human rights". The therapist said Michelle seemed to think it was dangerous to think about things, as if it threatened her mental state. She said that she had seen loads of therapists: "All they want to do is make you feel bad about yourself." The therapist then said he accepted that it was upsetting to talk. However, he thought it would help to understand what had provoked the overdose. By examining the circumstances more thoroughly, this could help them to decide what sort of support and help she might need.

At this point in the interview, Michelle seemed to calm down. She said that the argument had been caused by a client who refused to pay. The therapist said that perhaps Michelle had felt devalued and humiliated. She said that she did feel devalued and that the client laughed at her when she started to undress. He said that he liked her face but that he did not want to sleep with her as she had scars under her breasts. The therapist said he thought she felt hurt by these very personal comments about her body and that she must be sensitive about her surgical scars. She said that she felt like a fraud and that she was so angry with the client and she wanted to punish him.

The therapist asked Michelle to tell him about herself. She said that she was brought up by her mother after her father left. However, Michelle (at this point, still called Carl and living as a boy) rowed with his mother, especially after his mother met and married the man who became his stepfather. At one stage, during a furious row, his mother told him that Carl reminded her of his father. Michelle described this as the final nail in their relationship and he left home after being sexually molested by an uncle. He moved in with his father for a short period of time before arguing with his stepmother, after which Carl had to leave: "My father was and always has been useless." He lived homeless for several months and became addicted to amphetamines. He started working as a sex worker (as Carl), in order to make money and in order to support his drug habit.

Michelle told the therapist that the pimps used to withhold Carl's money. This was when Carl decided to transition, believing that, as a female prostitute, he would get more business and be valued more highly. Once she changed her name from Carl to Michelle and socially transitioned, she had several years where she took fewer overdoses and was less involved with the mental health services.

The therapist asked Michelle to tell him how things had been since she transitioned. She said that she initially felt pleased and relieved but then was disappointed with the results. When she looked in the mirror, she tended to focus on the scars and imperfections. After recovering from the operation, it took her a long time to pluck up the courage to go out on the streets again. She was worried that punters would spot the fact that she was not a biological female. Most of the time, she tried not to undress. The incident with the recent client was the first time Michelle had been asked to undress. When the client had laughed, she felt terrible, humiliated, and damaged. She worried that she would not be able to earn money in the future and planned to kill herself.

It was evident to the therapist that she wanted to get rid of the pain of realising that her dreams and wishes had not provided the answer she had hoped for. At this point in the interview, she burst into tears, saying that she was in despair. After talking for a while, the therapist said it was almost time to end the meeting but that he could see Michelle the following week.

Michelle: You are like a robot or something, with no compassion, one in, one out.
Therapist: You think I'm like the punter you describe, getting you to mentally undress in front of me just so that I can point out your mental scars and make you feel inferior.
Michelle: You lot are all jobsworths, just picking up your pay packet. You don't actually care; you're not really interested.
Therapist: I think you are hoping to find someone who could think with you about your difficulties. I understand you feel let down now, but we can meet again and explore what sort of help you might need.

This seemed to settle Michelle and she agreed to come back to further appointments.

Case discussion

Michelle's mind was dominated by a belief that she was either the ideal, with no imperfections, or else she was useless. Carl had felt betrayed by his mother who had sided with his stepfather and failed to protect him from abuse by the uncle. Carl developed a deep-seated grievance towards his mother and threw himself into a life of prostitution and drug use as a way of punishing his mother for the lack of care. The transition to Michelle occurs to him as potential for an increased appreciation of his value via monetary means. However, it might be viewed as a concrete solution to kill off the devalued and worthless boy, Carl.

When the pimps withheld his money, they made it clear that Carl was less valuable than the female prostitutes, and it ignited an old illusion that his life would have been different if he had not been the son that reminded his mother of his father. He developed an idea of changing sex, perhaps unconsciously as a way of getting rid of the unwanted aspects of himself. Carl may also have associated his male homosexual identity with the sexual assault from the uncle.

Many patients start to transition, expecting to be restored to an ideal state, and they put pressure on medics to act as an omnipotent figure who can remove all their problems. The medics may also play the role of "creators" who can sculpt the body according to the patient's wishes into some sort of ideal state. When this ideal state fails, the patient can sink into further self-hatred which is often enacted through self-harming behaviour or suicidal states. In any therapeutic work, the pressure is applied through the countertransference (see pp. 207–209) on the therapist to provide omnipotent solutions. The patient fears that the extent of their difficulties cannot be solved by ordinary means, and hence they seek magical solutions. However, when a patient senses the therapist accedes to or colludes with the patient's wishes he or she may become wary, feeling that the therapist has become corrupt or lost their mind or is somehow placating them in a disingenuous manner. Patients who have a personality disorder can be extremely sensitive to the level of genuine engagement with them by the clinician and can sometimes see the clinician's affirmation as a short cut to getting them out of the clinical setting.

The difference in expectations between the therapist and the patient can lead to conflict and a sense of frustration. The patient believes the therapy should restore them to an ideal state, while the therapist is trying to help the patient come to terms with their normal imperfections and difficulties.

At the start of the consultation, Michelle was suspicious of any therapist, believing they used their position in order to make themselves feel superior. The therapist's ability to see her sensitivity to feeling diminished or judged enabled Michelle to open up and talk about herself. However, towards the end of the consultation, the atmosphere in the interview dramatically changed and Michelle reverted to her previous, suspicious state of mind. It was as if she felt the therapist had managed to get her to expose and explore her difficulties by giving her support. When the therapist mentioned the end of the meeting, she immediately felt rejected as if she again reverted to being the unloved and unwanted young person that was made to feel so unwelcome. This feeling of rejection quickly passed when the therapist offered further meetings. Michelle is hoping to find a therapist who is prepared to stick around and support Michelle in coming to terms with who she is and how she feels about herself.

Case example: my way or the highway

A clinician within a mental health supervision group presented the case of Jessica, a trans-identified woman with a personality disorder who had been treated on a mental health unit for several months but showed no signs of progress. (We will refer to the patient as Robbie (he/his) when describing his history pre-transition and as Jessica (she/her) post-transition.)

The patient had a history of deliberate self-harm as she was cutting herself seriously and alarmingly, requiring medical care. When the group supervisor asked the mental health professional (MHP) to describe the patient's history, she said that she was completely in the dark. Apart from the patient saying that her father had sexually abused her, Jessica refused to talk about her history, saying it was too traumatic. The MHP knew from the referral that Jessica had been cared for by various other psychiatric services over a number of years. However, Jessica was adamant that she did not want the MHP to contact these other services.

The supervisor talked to the group about Jessica's wish to control the treatment setting by making the staff feel they would be betraying her if they contacted the previous services. They said they worried that Jessica would feel traumatised to be reminded of her own history. In the countertransference, the staff were made to feel as if they were the abusing father in the patient's mind if they went against her wishes.

Jessica said that she feared being ganged up on and judged if the current MHP talked to the previous mental health team. She was anxious that the full picture would be used against her, to dismiss her claims for care and interfere with her control of the treatment situation. It was important to understand that the patient feared she would lose out if they were able to piece together a picture of her which was not controlled by her. It was almost impossible for her to believe that the staff might want to piece together her history in order to understand her more and to help her.

Although the supervisor did not know the history, they thought the patient was like a child who felt she had to keep the parents apart. She feared that the parents coming together would lead to her being ganged up on and blamed. The supervisor talked about the need for a broader assessment of the patient, including her history, the history of contact with other services, and possibly even of her estranged family. The supervisor added that the MHP and clinical team needed to talk to Jessica about her fears of being dropped and discounted as the unlovable young person if other versions (of reality) came to light. Even if there were conflicting accounts of her history, it did not mean that the current team would dismiss her. Jessica needed to feel that knowing more about her life would help the team to support her going forward.

Several weeks later, the staff reported back to the supervisor that they had discussed the issue of talking to Jessica's previous care teams, saying that they needed to gather more of a picture. Jessica became extremely agitated, saying that she was worried that other services would lie about her and present her in a bad light. The staff said to Jessica that although they were interested in what other services had to say about her history and her treatment, they also wanted to understand her version of events. They reiterated that they were trying to get as complete a picture of the situation as possible to develop a fuller understanding of the patient and her difficulties. Jessica agreed to allow a member of the team to contact the mental health units that had previously looked after her. The team discovered that Jessica was previously known as Robbie. He was a disturbed young man with a long history of acting out. He had been brought up in care homes on account of being taken away from his mother by social services at an early age.

The supervisor discussed Jessica's wish to leave her depressing early history as Robbie behind, the little boy who had felt unloved and unwanted. With the help of further discussions within the supervision group and by gathering various pieces of information together, the clinical team was able to establish a picture of a very vulnerable, traumatised, and deprived person. The clinician could also see that although Jessica attempts to control the clinical picture, it is driven by her wish to distance herself from her depressing and traumatic early history.

Discussion

Therapists are required to respect their patients' wishes regarding their treatment and rights to confidentiality. However, problems arise when services adhere to their patients' requests and wishes in a literal or unquestioning way, ignoring the clinical needs of the patient. In the case of Jessica, the patient was controlling the therapist's method of gathering information in order to make a meaningful assessment. This meant that the different aspects of Jessica's clinical care were being split off and kept apart. Mental health professionals need to feel free to explore the patient's difficulties by gathering the fullest possible picture as part of their mental state examination and risk assessment.

The countertransference provides valuable information about the patient's state of mind. Patients with personality disorders have difficulties dealing with the psychic contents of their minds and tend to evacuate undigested elements of their minds through action. They also put considerable pressure on mental health practitioners to act, rather than think. Ideally, the function of the MHP with this group of patients is to use their verbal capacity to reverse the process and turn the action, and pressure towards action, back into words with an emotional content. However, if mental health professionals or therapists prematurely push insight back to the patient or rush the patient's development, it can cause a rapid fragmentation. Progress is often dependent upon supportive relationships, even if the patient plays down the significance of these relationships. People with personality disorder do not like being reminded of their underlying fragility and dependence upon others—yet also hate for it to be forgotten.

The discussion in the supervision group helped the MHP and his clinical team free themselves from the effects of the countertransferential fear that they would be retraumatising an already traumatised patient if they went against her wishes. Instead, they were able to discuss the issue of her fears and beliefs as a clinical problem, thus changing a conflict between staff and patient into an opportunity for a clinical discussion with Jessica about the nature of her beliefs. In her case, this was the idea that she could eradicate her depressing early history and life as Robbie by changing gender. This meant all feeling of loss, depression, or sadness had to be evacuated rather than tolerated. By liaising with previous clinical teams, a developing clinical picture helped the clinical team to understand and be more sympathetic to their patient. It was also important for Jessica to be able to reflect on and understand the painful feelings and experiences located in Robbie, which she had attempted to leave behind.

Case example: the hysterical defence

A ward manager, from an inpatient unit, presented in a supervision group the case of Candice. She was a forty-five-year-old trans-identified woman with multiple diagnoses, including schizophrenia and borderline personality disorder. The ward manager said the patient was causing havoc and splitting the nursing team, and he was worried that they could no longer manage the patient on the ward. He told the supervision group that there had been a pattern of care in relation to Candice's previous admissions. She would be placed on a Mental Health Act section and admitted as an inpatient, following a drug overdose and other self-harm, but within days on the ward her mental state would settle down and she would appeal against her section. When her section order was subsequently removed, she would leave the ward but return several hours later in an intoxicated state. The staff suspected Candice supplied other patients with drugs, thus creating an atmosphere of excitement and mania on the ward.

When the team made a discharge plan or referral on to a rehabilitation hostel or therapeutic community, the patient would respond with self-destructive or violent acts, which undermined the discharge plans. The ward manager confessed that they usually discharged Candice in an unhelpful way, as the staff had lost patience with her disruptive behaviour. After being discharged, she would start sex-working the streets to support her drug habit, whereupon her mental state would quickly deteriorate. She would then be readmitted to the inpatient unit, via A&E, after taking a large overdose in a manic and euphoric state.

The ward manager said that Candice had formally complained about several members of the staff team and consequently they felt intimidated and angry. She was charming towards the staff she liked, but threatening, violent, and vindictive towards the ones she did not. A division developed in the staff team between those who felt sympathetic to her difficulties and others who thought she was manipulative and bullying. Her primary nurse said that Candice talked to her about a figure called John, who instructed Candice to do self-destructive things. The supervisor asked her if she had noticed any pattern in Candice's "acting out" behaviour. She said that things seemed to get worse whenever she mentioned a discharge plan, as she would take an overdose or smash up her room. The primary nurse then said she thought that Candice was quite attached to the ward.

History

Candice was born Sam but had transitioned in his mid-twenties. (We will refer to the patient as Sam (he/his) when describing the patient's history pre-transition and as Candice (she/her) post-transition.)

Sam's parents had both suffered from severe and enduring mental illness and he was taken into care when he was very young, where his carers and foster parents abused him. When he left home at the age of fifteen, he started taking drugs and supported his habit by working as a male prostitute. Around this time, he also developed an abusive relationship with a man called John, who supplied him with drugs in return for sex. In his case notes, it said Sam had a delusional belief that he was Jesus and a long-standing history of hypochondriacal anxieties and self-harm. He was sent to prison on one occasion, for grievous bodily harm.

Thoughts on history and presentation

In his paper, "On Arrogance", Bion (1958) described patients in borderline psychotic states who showed evidence of a catastrophic breakdown in their relationship with the primary object. He argued the maternal object has been unable to take in and digest the infant's preverbal communications. Instead of the infant internalising a good object that helps make sense of raw experience and becomes the basis of a healthy ego, the infant internalises an "ego destructive superego": one that hates all emotional links and experiences. This sort of internal object persecutes the patient (see p. 240). This internal structure can then become part of a destructive narcissistic structure, which employs omnipotent manic defences designed to avoid, rather than face, internal and external reality.

"John" may have represented a psychotic part of Candice's mind that was always on hand to offer manic, sexualised solutions in order to deny her underlying difficulties. An example of this included the tendency to hand herself over to strangers with no thought for her safety or protection. Over time, this orgy of dissociated sadomasochistic sex led to a fragmentation of Candice's ego. Her way of abandoning herself to others in such an excited and reckless way pushed psychiatric services into a position where they had to step in and take responsibility.

Once on the ward, a split would develop between those members of staff who felt sympathetic to her behaviour and those who thought that she was trying to extort some secondary gain (an advantage that occurs secondary to illness). Candice encouraged the split by provoking conflict between the two groups. She complained to the "sympathetic" staff that other clinicians were uncaring and unprofessional, while treating the "unsympathetic" group with contempt. Staff opinion was widely varied, from a view that Candice was manipulative and "knew what she was doing" to the belief that she was "being victimised by the psychotic voice called John". This split shifted the focus of attention away from conflicts within Candice's mind and the nature of her difficulties, into an argument between the polarised "sympathetic" and "unsympathetic" staff. The strength of the split engendered such strong feelings that the staff did not come together to discuss the patient, but rather remained split and blaming one another.

Anxiety about a patient's self-destructive behaviour can sometimes push mental health services into taking over responsibility for their care, whereupon the patient can become malignantly dependent upon that care. An unhelpful spiral of self-destructive behaviour and further care can develop until the patient is eventually detained under mental health legislation and put on continuous and close observations to prevent further self-mutilating behaviour. This situation frequently leads to a malignant regression as staff are made to feel entirely responsible for protecting the patient from him- or herself. Any attempt by staff to reduce the amount of one-to-one surveillance leads to further acts of self-mutilation and escalating self-destructive behaviour, which ensures that the patient remains at the forefront of the staff team's mind.

Candice unconsciously encouraged a split in the staff in order to prevent the clinical picture from coming together. The reality was that the split in the staff was an external manifestation of the divisions within Candice. She tried to portray herself as an integrated woman, capable of managing her own life. This presentation denied underlying fears of fragmentation and collapse. Candice was closer in function to the level of a traumatised three-year-old child than a grown adult. The secondary gain may have been related to her wish to control the treatment situation, as she denied the real level of her dependence upon the mental health service via her mania, while entrenching her dependence as a patient on an inpatient ward.

Despite the bad atmosphere on the ward, the supervisor listening to the presentation was struck by the team's compassion and concern for Candice in the face of considerable provocation. The supervisor thought the ward staff had done a good job and, in many ways, they were victims of their success. Candice did not want to leave the ward because she felt she had finally found a family that thought about and cared for her, despite her provocation and destructive behaviour.

Although on one level Candice denied her anxiety and dependency, at another level she needed the staff team to understand her anxieties about mania and self-destructive behaviour. In the group, the supervisor discussed the need for the staff to be reunited, and helped to recover their professional objectivity and interest in the patient through thoughtful discussion. In this way, they were able to gather together different and more honest views and opinions held within the staff team. A discussion arose regarding the need for a multi-professional case conference to consider clinical challenges and care planning. This would enable the multidisciplinary team to share the problems together while accepting that there were no magical solutions. In any similar case where there is a likelihood that the patient will complain or become litigious, senior managers must be encouraged to understand some of the headaches faced by the front-line clinical staff. Front-line staff are unlikely to risk implementing unpopular or more boundaried care plans with patients who complain if they do not feel that management are supportive. For this reason, it was important to invite senior management to the case conference, as they needed to hear about the clinical difficulties faced by the ward team.

The supervisor said to the primary nurse that it would be helpful for her to develop a long-term view of the patient's needs by talking to Candice about the way in which she tended to act out to eject her unmanageable feelings. The nurse also needed to demonstrate she understood that the likelihood of acting out would increase whenever the word discharge was mentioned to Candice, but for Candice to get on with her future life they needed to work together towards her discharge in a planned and realistic way.

Several weeks after the case conference, the ward manager presented Candice to the supervision group again. The clinical picture had changed considerably. Even though the Mental Health Act section on Candice had been removed, the patient remained on the ward for most of the time. Candice had stopped bringing drugs onto the ward, her self-harming behaviour was less frequent, and the difficulties between her and the staff team had reduced. The primary nurse reported that she had spent some time talking to Candice about her difficulties and worries about being discharged. She said that it had become clearer in her mind that Candice was very anxious about this, but they had begun a dialogue. The primary nurse made sure they talked through these anxieties and tried to help Candice tolerate her feelings more by encouraging her to vocalise her thoughts in their one-to-one sessions.

Over the next couple of months, a discharge plan was instigated in which it was agreed that there would be a handover period between the ward and the hostel that Candice was being transferred to. The primary nurse escorted the patient to the hostel on several occasions and met with the hostel staff to discuss her care and some of the management challenges the team had learned about during Candice's care. Three months later, the patient transferred to the hostel and appeared to have settled in and continued living there.

General discussion

Patients with gender dysphoria in borderline states of mind project in ways that affect the other, and mental health professionals often complain that these patients "get under their skin" or "drive them mad". The nature of the projection also pushes the object to cohere with the projection, so staff are often nudged into a response that confirms the patient's projections. Indeed, the forceful and concrete nature of the projections often provokes a knee-jerk response in staff and an unhelpful cycle of action and reaction can develop between patients and staff. For example, if the patient is denying and splitting off their anger, the staff member who is provoked into feeling anger needs to think about the projection they are in receipt of, rather than react angrily or act precipitously.

In many ways, it is true to say that these patients draw and push the therapists into dyadic relationships dominated by projections. These projections affect the staff's capacity to think in an objective or imaginative way. The therapist may become split between a moralistic stance, based on reminding the patient of their responsibilities, and a sympathetic stance which is in danger of colluding with the patient in order to deny their difficulties.

The professional's capacity to think about and make sense of patients who present with borderline clinical features is a dynamic process, relying upon numerous factors, including the team's capacity to verbalise and integrate the different views of the patient. This is a potentially turbulent process, requiring a constant examination of the mental health professional's contact with the patient, within an atmosphere of curiosity and openness. Teams need to work hard together, even if their views are different, to contribute to a clearer, more holistic clinical picture of the patient's internal world. This requires disagreements and criticisms within the team to be understood as a possible aspect of the patient's internal world, which has been split up and projected into them.

Melanie Klein (1946) highlighted the need for the infant to internalise the primary object as a good object, which in turn forms the basis of the infant's ego (see p. 201 for more information on the internalisation of the good object). Patients with personality disorders have sometimes had an abusive or neglectful relationship with parental figures so that damaged and fragile relationships populate their internal worlds. This fragile and persecutory internal state is always threatening to fragment the ego and its objects. When this happens, the patient may quickly feel overwhelmed by persecutory anxiety, which splits the ego into ideal and unwanted aspects of the self. These unwanted aspects are then violently projected into others to evacuate the problem. One version of this is,

"If only I could be 'other', everything would be all right and I would stop experiencing feelings of humiliation." They might tend to believe they can get rid of problems in dramatic ways to reduce pain and in order to achieve their ideal. Individuals with a fragile ego structure tend to be prone to the black-and-white thinking that looks for concrete rather than symbolic solutions. All the above makes them very prone to the rigid ideas and stereotypes of gender identity which tend to be promoted by pro-trans educational materials and websites.

The violent, concrete, and wholesale nature of the projections is also designed to have an impact on the recipient of the projections. Indeed, patients in borderline states of mind require the recipient of their projections to act in ways that confirm that the projection has hit its target, as this provides reassurance that the unwanted aspect of the self now resides in someone else. The evacuative and projective process is also often accompanied by actions that force the object to respond in a concrete manner. This cycle of action and reaction can drive the therapist and patient into polarised positions, which keep the underlying conflict or problem obscured.

In his paper, "Subjectivity, Objectivity, and Triangular Space", psychoanalyst Ronald Britton (2004) describes the patient's difficulty in bringing together his/her subjective self with an objective view. Borderline patients fear the integration of subjective experience with objective thought as this heralds painful realisations about a reality that might interfere with their psychic equilibrium. Patients in borderline states of mind are sensitive to any communication that contains an objective assessment of their behaviour, as this is felt to threaten the patient's subjective experience.

The role of supervision

Regular psychodynamic or psychoanalytic supervision can help staff in mental health settings process their feelings about their patients as well as examining the transference and countertransference relationship. Supervision can help both individual therapists and staff teams to separate from the effect of the projections by turning a dyadic two-person relationship into a triadic one as the supervisor forms the third point of a triangle and can offer an objective view. The triangle provides space for an objective examination of the clinical picture, which includes the professional's subjective view. This type of objective examination helps to provide some psychic space, which frees the therapist from the narrow psychic state created by the subjective dyadic relationship that often develops in the treatment of patients with a borderline personality disorder. This triangular space also creates room for staff to think in an imaginative way about the underlying meaning of the communications and re-establish their capacity for symbolic thought. When working with a patient who has a personality disorder with a presentation of gender dysphoria or trans identity, clinicians may be caught up in concrete thinking and concrete solutions with the patient. The clinician needs to rediscover the capacity to think about the emotional conflicts which underlie the patient's wish and pressure for concrete solutions.

It is also important in the treatment of borderline patients to establish a long-term view which takes account of the patient's latent fragility. Individual episodes of acting out need to be seen within the context of the overall clinical picture and include an assessment of the borderline patient's personality structure. Psychoanalytic supervision can also help therapists integrate clinical facts about their patient's history and personality structure with the current clinical picture by developing a long-term view in this way. Although knowledge of the patient's history will not necessarily prevent these re-enactments, forewarned is forearmed, and knowledge of the transference and countertransference may help the therapist tolerate the effect of the virulent projections. It can also help to address adverse countertransferential responses.

People with borderline features need to feel that others listen to them and take their difficulties seriously. In many ways, it is true to say that these individuals are looking for a "marsupial pouch" to offer psychological support and gradually gather the disparate aspects of themselves together. However, staff who are the recipients of these projections also need help in separating from the effect of the projections. Ideals that the individual aspires to often persecute patients with borderline features and the premature interpretation of behaviour by staff can lead to the patient feeling assaulted and overwhelmed (Steiner, 1993b). Teams need to consider what it is appropriate to say to patients in borderline states of mind, in what sort of clinical setting, and when to say it. The team also needs to take into consideration the likely impact of the insights upon the patient before saying it. However, insights should be used to help with clinical management and the assessment of risk in staff discussions.

It is helpful to think of a therapeutic relationship as having two elements: a caring element and a treatment element. Steiner (1993b) describes two phases of analytic work. In the first phase, the therapist takes in the patient's view of things and tries to understand how they see things. In the second phase, therapists need to separate themselves from the patient's view and come to their own understanding of the patient and their problems. This involves a process of being affected by the patient and their perceptions and then separating to develop an objective view.

However, the second stage of the therapeutic process can easily overwhelm the patient with feelings of guilt about the damage done, which leads to fragmentation. The patient needs to feel that the therapist cares about them and their lives. Patients get anxious if they feel that they are with a therapist who is emotionally cut off or oblivious to their suffering. You could say the patient requires the therapist to combine objective thought with empathy. Patients need to feel that they are being cared for by someone who contains a parental couple that can come together to treat and care for a troubled infant. Helping the therapist maintain their internal couple will depend on many things, including an opportunity to discuss the inevitable obstacles that arise in treatment. This, in turn, helps the patient reduce their reliability on violent projection as a means of dealing with psychic pain.

In our experience of working with gender-questioning or trans-identified patients, it is very unhelpful if the clinician/therapist is also under political pressure to affirm the patient's view without having the possibility to provide thorough psychological exploration and thought. People with borderline personality disorder live on a mental knife-edge as their perception of themselves oscillates between ideas of triumphant success and catastrophic failure. The ego-destructive superego governs this state of mind. Lucas (2009) thought the process of therapy was to provide support and help build a perspective so the patient's ego can separate from the influence of the superego. Thus, the mental health professional's objective is to turn the patient's ego from balancing on a knife-edge to something a little wider—a gymnastics bar would be an improvement!

Conclusion

Patients with borderline features who have gender dysphoria have difficulties in dealing with the psychic contents of their minds and tend to evacuate undigested elements of their minds through action. They can also seek to resolve psychic conflicts through concrete/physical solutions. Different parts of the patient are projected into different parts of themselves and the social structure surrounding them. These communications often take the form of concrete communications that fill their recipients with feelings that either provoke actions in return, or make the object feel that they cannot think clearly about the patient. Individuals with gender dysphoria often feel dissociated from their biological sex which has come to represent an unwanted aspect of themselves. Patients who operate on the border between psychosis and neurosis can find it hard to manage the feelings of guilt and loss associated with the depressive position and instead resort to paranoid–schizoid thinking (see pp. 189–194 for more information on the paranoid–schizoid position). They project unwanted aspects of the self into the object and then put pressure on the object to concur with their wishes. For example, the individual's confusion regarding their gender identity can be projected into the therapist, who then contains the doubts and concerns about the individual's wish to transition. If the therapist tries to push these doubts back into the individual prematurely, it can lead to an unhelpful situation whereby the internal conflict is now externalised and enacted between the therapist and the patient. At times the therapist may attempt to completely avoid introducing any view that might traumatise the patient. By absorbing the projections, this can lead to collusion. Neither scenario is helpful in the longer term and the therapist needs to attempt to remain alert to the potential moments of receptivity available in the patient, while respecting the patient's defences. Clinical supervision that understands the black-and-white thinking in borderline states of mind is extremely important as it helps to avoid the pitfalls of collusion with concrete thinking or acting out in the countertransference.

In our view this kind of supervision is not a luxury but an essential part of a good clinical service for any mental health patients, and one which should be free of political or ideological bias.

TEN

Comorbid mental health conditions and gender dysphoria

There is a growing body of knowledge which connects the development of gender dysphoria with psychological factors. Individuals with a personality disorder or severe and enduring mental illness have fragile mental structures that can be overwhelmed by psychic pain. *DSM-IV* stated that in rare incidences, gender dysphoria may coexist with schizophrenia and that psychiatric disorders are generally not considered contraindications to sex reassignment therapy unless they are the primary cause of the patient's gender dysphoria.

Below is an account of a consultation with Paul, a man in his mid-twenties who was referred for psychotherapy. Paul had a long-standing psychotic condition and there was no mention of his desire to transition from male to female in either the referral letter or in discussions with the consultant.

His consultant psychiatrist referred Paul for treatment of his negative symptoms and withdrawal from life. The patient had a diagnosis of paranoid schizophrenia. He had had several previous compulsory admissions for his paranoid delusions. Although he remained symptom-free if he took his antipsychotic medication, he lacked motivation. He had spent several years in his bedsit watching reruns of *Pointless* (a television game show) and smoking marijuana. At the same time as the therapy referral, the consultant also referred him to the day hospital as part of a rehabilitation programme.

Case presentation—Paul

Paul was three years old when his father left home; the mother had to raise him and his younger sister alone. He occasionally visited his father, who had started a second family. He did well at school but suffered his first psychotic breakdown when he was nineteen years of age at the point of leaving home to attend university. While in a paranoid state, he threatened to shoot his mother with a replica rifle and was subsequently compulsorily admitted to hospital.

The referral letter to the therapist also stated that the patient had suffered from impotence for four years, but he had found the investigations into this very humiliating and it was unresolved.

At the time of the referral, the patient lived on his own but was dependent upon his mother to look after and care for him. She was instrumental in the request for psychotherapy as she was worried about her son's dependence upon her and his withdrawal from life.

The therapist wrote to the consultant saying he would be happy to see Paul but wished to confirm that the psychiatric team would go on providing joint care cover. The therapist also made it clear to Paul that he would discuss his care with the consultant if there was any concern about a relapse in Paul's mental state.

Initial consultation

Paul was a very tall and extremely thin young man, dressed from head to foot in a woollen army coat, even though it was a warm day. The coat, which looked too big for him, gave the impression he was hiding something.

The therapist started the consultation by asking Paul to tell him something about himself and what he hoped to get from psychotherapy. Paul said that he lacked motivation and spent long periods in his bedsit watching daytime TV and smoking marijuana. The therapist said that he seemed to have withdrawn from life into a lifeless world since his last hospital admission, as if he was afraid that engaging with the world was too much and might expose him to further breakdown. Paul looked briefly in pain but then smiled and explained that he was first admitted to a psychiatric hospital as a result of paranoid thinking. These voices came back from time to time if he stopped taking his medication. Paul went on to explain that he used to live with his mother but had to move as he became paranoid about his living circumstances. He smiled again. The therapist was reminded of the incident in which he threatened his mother with a rifle and decided to ask him about this, in part to help in the assessment of his risk. Paul tried to dismiss the incident as a misunderstanding. The therapist said he thought Paul was worried that he did not know how to manage his aggressive feelings, mainly if he felt threatened. Again, Paul looked briefly troubled, staring at a corner of the room and twitched as if he was expelling some painful thought, then looked up quickly and smiled.

The therapist asked him to tell him about an early memory. He recalled pushing a girl away at a party when he was six years old. It made him feel horrified that he pushed her away. The therapist pointed out that this also seemed to be happening between them, as he had noticed Paul smile after any painful area had been touched upon. Perhaps his smile was used to push something painful away as if he felt that the therapist were pushing something painful into him? Again, he winced, looking depressed, then smiled in the same distancing manner he had before.

Discussion of the consultation

The therapist's initial impression was that Paul had withdrawn from life into a world of his own. In his bedsit, he controlled his contact with the world using cannabis and daytime TV. Painful questions he might ask about his life must have been projected into his mother, who then had the anxiety of worrying about what the future held for her son. This concern was represented by her request for him to have psychotherapy. If she looked after him, acting as his auxiliary ego, he could remain in his "pointless" retreat. One imagines Paul must have felt threatened by any suggestion of separation from his mother. The comment about him being frightened of the feelings of violence towards his mother seemed to hit home. However, this feeling seemed to be quickly evacuated by the smile.

The replica rifle he used in the first breakdown perhaps represented his feeling that he was not a potent man who could manage his relationship with the external world. He seemed to have a feeling that he had been deprived of some essential piece of equipment that would allow him to lead a satisfying life and this seemed to be the basis of a grievance towards both of his parents.

Paul needed some psychiatric support, an exoskeleton, to support him in the struggle against the negative symptoms of his illness. It was vital for him to attend the day hospital as it seemed he needed some structure in his life and support in engaging with the external world. The therapist explained that a condition of the consultation was that he had requested ongoing psychiatric follow-up and that he would want to speak to the psychiatric team if he became concerned about Paul's mental state.

First session

Paul started the session by casually slumping into the chair. Then with a smile on his face, he mentioned that he wanted to have a sex change and wondered if the therapist could refer him to the gender identity clinic. The therapist was surprised by this revelation, as there had been no prior mention of this as an idea. The therapist asked him how long he had been harbouring this thought. Paul started to smile in a rather vacuous way, saying he had had these thoughts for many years. The therapist took up his smiling, nonchalant attitude towards the referral and the operation, as if he had no doubts or concerns about the request. At this, Paul became angry, saying that the therapist did not know him.

Paul went on to explain that he had dressed up in his mother's clothes for many years and these episodes were accompanied by the belief that he was being watched. However, he triumphantly announced that since he developed the idea of having a sex change, the paranoid voices which he regularly experienced had stopped.

Therapist: The watching eyes made you feel there is something wrong with you dressing up as a woman.

Paul: [*Smiles*] There's nothing wrong with it. It's what I'm supposed to be.
Therapist: So, you believe the feelings of persecution will be cured if you can get rid of any evidence of your masculinity.
Paul: I have never liked my body. I have always despised it, and it has made me want to laugh. [*Looks sad*] I have regrets I didn't request hormone treatments earlier as I have got such big knuckles and feet.
Therapist: The idea you have is that hormone treatment could have removed these big features that make you feel so uncomfortable and remind you of how big you are.
Paul: [*Looks upset, then smiles*] I want to get away from my mother. Because I rely on her to tell me to do everything, she must get me up in the morning and tell me to brush my teeth. Mind you, I think that I would stay in bed all day if she didn't get me up.
Therapist: You worry you don't have the right equipment to survive in the outside world.
Paul: Well, relying on her so much makes me think what the matter with me is. Why do I need her so much?
Therapist: And that is upsetting for you.
Paul: [*Looks in pain*] I went to the day hospital the other day, and I hated it and decided not to go back.
Therapist: It disturbs you when you think you have a problem that needs so much help, the day hospital reminds you of that.

Towards the end of the session, the therapist explained that he was going to speak to Paul's consultant as he was worried that Paul was breaking down.

Case discussion

The therapist was struck by the triumphant and decisive manner of Paul's announcement regarding his wish to transition. The nonchalance of Paul's approach seemed to function as a reprimand, as if the therapist was trying to force his concerns into him rather than think with him about the serious issues related to gender transition.

The therapist's confusion and shock were in stark contrast to the apparent certainty of Paul's thinking. Paul became angry after the therapist questioned his wish to transition. The therapist's response, which questioned Paul's thinking, caused a hiatus in the therapeutic contact. We think the therapist wanted to cure their own confusion caused by the shock of hearing this previously unmentioned thinking. These feelings are likely to be there because the patient has projected them into the therapist. But the therapist needs to assess the patient's ability to cope with feelings of doubt before returning them to the patient. Returning unwelcome feelings prematurely is a common problem when treating this patient population that therapists need to guard against.

The persecutory eyes Paul remembers when dressing up in his mother's clothes perhaps represent the projected, non-psychotic part of his mind, mockingly observing his psychotic mind attempting to climb into his mother's identity. The anxiety that he could not survive without his mother's support represented his fear that there was something wrong with his psychological equipment. At the same time, Paul's statement about being too reliant upon his mother seemed to represent his fear of being unable to separate from her and the fear of recognising himself as a man (with his big knuckles and feet).

Paul tries to avoid feelings of humiliation around his dependence on the mother's care by getting inside her identity and getting rid of his own. The day hospital might have reminded him of the reality that he is a patient with a chronic psychotic condition. This perhaps left him feeling depressed about the extent of his need for help and support. He is caught in a terrible situation where he feels completely reliant on his mother to look after him, but both resents, and is humiliated by, his dependence upon her. Rey (1994) described psychotic patients' oscillation between claustrophobic and agoraphobic anxieties. On the one hand, the patient wants to be inside the object, while on the other hand, they quickly feel trapped within the object. Paul finds life outside his mother impossible to bear and has an unconscious fantasy that living inside his mother would make things manageable. However, he then fears being trapped inside with no life or mind of his own. This state of mind causes resentment, which can lead to violence or threats as he feels she tries to dominate and control him.

Following this session, the therapist had phoned the consultant and asked if Paul had any history of wanting a sex change. He said it was the first he had heard of it. The consultant mentioned that the patient's negative symptoms seemed to be lifting and his mental state was improving. Is it possible that, like the suicidal patients who often become relaxed once they have decided on a plan to kill themselves, Paul becomes resolved and detached from his difficulties once he has made his decision to transition? If this change is taken at a superficial level, one might announce an improvement in mental state. However, it is important to understand why this unworried state has materialised and how it is devoid of any expected level of doubt or anxiety.

Second session

At the start of the session, Paul slouched in the chair in a relaxed manner and sat in silence. After a few minutes, smiling, he said "So?"

Therapist: So, all the thoughts and questions about your thinking are in me.

Paul: Well, you talk to me as if I am mad. [*Smiles*] Have you spoken to the consultant? He is not interested in my wish to be referred for a sex change. He says I should discuss it with you.

Therapist: You worry that I will interfere with your referral, depriving you of the surgery which you believe will remove your paranoid thoughts.

Paul: [*Getting angry*] Well, you treat me as if I am mad, but I am not psychotic. I have not been psychotic for several months. However, whenever I say that, no one believes me. I get fed up because this has nothing to do with the psychosis. There is nothing wrong with me.

Therapist: The idea that you need to have the sex change operation has pushed out the paranoid thoughts that torment you. Then you feel I am trying to push disturbing questions back into your mind, as if I'm trying to make you worse.

Paul: [*Looks in pain and then smiles and says nothing*]

Therapist: I think your mind has gone blank again and you smile because you felt suddenly overwhelmed with upsetting feelings but want to silence them.

Paul: Since I developed the idea of having the sex change, I have had this nightmare. These people are looking at me and I am terrified, but they have no eyes. [He went on to say that he used to be fascinated by the Elephant Man as a young person.]

Therapist: I think the process of us looking at you here in therapy leaves you feeling threatened, as if you feel that you are hideous or unacceptable.

Paul: I have always seen myself as a bit of a joke. [He went on to talk about a film he loved called *The Grudge* and explained that it was about a brother and sister in a haunted house. He said he used to watch it with his sister, and she hated it, as it frightened her.]

Therapist: I wonder if you hold a grudge towards your sister whose birth took your mother away from you before you were ready.

Paul: [*Looks hurt*] Yes, I don't know who I am, and I have never felt ready for the world.

Therapist: [*Thinking of the replica rifle he had threatened mother with*] I think you didn't feel you had the necessary equipment to cope with the world, whereas you seem to believe your sister did.

Paul: I remember going sailing with my father but feeling he seemed to be more interested in the boat than me.

Therapist: You felt he had no interest in you. [At this point in the meeting, Paul looked angry. This quickly turned to a smile.]

Paul: I went to the dentist to have some work done and I did not need any painkillers, whereas in the past, I had had to have injections to numb the pain.

Therapist: You believe you have developed a way to master your painful feelings of humiliation, by getting rid of your male identity and transitioning.

Paul: I will be left with nothing if I give up my wish to be a woman.

Case discussion

At the start of the session, Paul projected all thoughts into the therapist, leaving his mind blank. The sort of smile he made at these moments often seemed to convey a sense of triumph when he evacuated thinking: triumphing over his feelings and over the therapy, since the therapy stands for wanting to know about his feelings. The nightmare he tells may represent two fears: 1) that the therapist cannot see what he is like—a disfigured man with a grudge towards women. Moreover, 2), if the therapist does see him, they will see something hideous like the Elephant Man. Paul sees himself as a damaged man who is ill-equipped for the world, unsupported by his father, while his sister and mother are the ideal figures free of the troublesome masculinity that in his mind causes him so much pain.

Oppenheimer (1991) points out that non-recognition by the father is experienced as a narcissistic castration. The vacuous smile seems to represent Paul's projection of the troubling aspects of his mind, which leaves him empty-headed. When he says that he is worried about what would happen to him if he gave up wanting to be a woman, he may be expressing his fear of remaining a damaged man with severe psychological difficulties. The "illusion of another life" offers a magical cure to his emotional pain.

After this session, the consultant psychiatrist telephoned the therapist and said that the patient had asked for a second opinion some time ago. The second psychiatrist had said that he did not believe the patient was suffering from a psychotic condition and that he supported the referral to the adult gender service. In response to this second opinion, the therapist wrote a letter saying he was concerned about the change in diagnosis and thought the treatment team needed more time to think things through with the patient.

Third session

The following week Paul came into the room in a threatening and aggressive state, saying that he knew about the letter from the second psychiatrist and he accused the therapist of interfering with his life and ruining his chance of happiness. He said he was seeing this other psychiatrist who had agreed to refer him to the gender identity service, and that it was his body and his life and there was nothing anyone could do to stop him. He then got up and said he would not be returning to the therapy.

After the session, the therapist felt worried that the psychotherapy had stirred up powerful internal forces that required the employment of powerful defences. It is possible that the therapist had become the accusing eyes that watched him, pushing doubts and questions into him in a maddening way. The psychotic part of his mind felt threatened by any sane questioning of his thinking and state of mind. Quinodoz (1998) highlights the importance of "psychotic and neurotic mechanisms in the treatment of a transsexual patient".

Clinical discussion

Paul had withdrawn into a depressed state since being admitted under the Mental Health Act section. He was so humiliated and frightened by the psychosis that he withdrew into a world of his own, marooned in his flat, although he was dependent upon his mother to go on acting as his auxiliary ego. He hated acknowledging his dependence upon her because it drew attention to the extent of his difficulties. The flat seemed to function as a psychic retreat, a womb he could withdraw into while his mother looked after his needs (telling him when to brush his teeth, etc.). In this womb, he could live in an idealised dream world of his creation, protected from painful contact with the external world. Perhaps his non-psychotic mind does know this, which is why he watches endless reruns of a show called *Pointless*. In his paper on "Time and the Garden of Eden Illusion", Steiner (2018) describes phantasies of a perfect time before problems began. This seems pertinent to Paul's case.

> It is extremely common to have phantasies of a perfect time we once enjoyed, a Garden of Eden, in which every need was fulfilled and which we assumed would go on forever. In these phantasies, paradise commonly represents a period of blissful possession of the mother with undisturbed and unlimited access to the breast. If disillusion is too abrupt or too brutal, we feel prematurely expelled from paradise, sometimes robbed, and sometimes even

castrated. The idealisation may extend to time inside the womb and give rise to the idea that we were born before being ready for the world, and that getting inside the mother can restore the unique relationship. The loss of perfection may then be experienced as a forcible expulsion or a premature rejection often associated with humiliation, which then plays a critical role in defensive organisations. (p. 1274)

The birth of Paul's sister may well have been the event that expelled him from paradise. He may not have been helped by his parents to separate from his mother, to leave room for his baby sister. Steiner (2018) comments on the way the good object can be replaced by a spurious substitute to avoid the frustrations of depending on the breast. Paul developed a grudge towards the parents' sexual relationship, which produced the sister that replaced him as the baby of the family. He was left feeling he had to survive in the world outside paradise, unprepared for the abruptness of the separation and with inadequate equipment. The importance of the replica rifle seemed to be connected to a grudge towards his father for failing to support his development. It may be the replica rifle represented a potent phallic symbol to compensate for his feeling that he had been given inadequate equipment: a damaged phallic object which broke links, rather than an ordinary penis that made links (Birksted-Breen, 1996).

For example, his father's penis helped create his sister, who separated him from his mother. Paul's biologically male body may have represented a hated phallic identification with the father who gives his mother a baby, but with no care or thought for the existing baby; a penis that impregnates the mother but does not stay around to support the mother–infant couple. This is something the patient apparently rejects and hates in himself and his father. Oppenheimer (1985) remarks on the wish for transformation being related to a hatred of the penis. The patient rejected his masculinity as he felt his father had rejected him.

Dressing up in his mother's clothes represented Paul's wish to get back into the womb, a fantasised, blissful state before the trauma of his sister's birth. He then misidentifies the penis as responsible for aspects of his male sexuality which has come between himself and his mother. In this state of mind, he is persecuted by the reality-based part of his mind that mocks him for taking his mother's identity. This awareness is projected and represented by the eyes that stare at him in an accusing way. Paul develops a belief that he can get rid of the persecutory gaze of his own projected thoughts if he can surgically remove any evidence of himself being a man. This is a magical solution because although he can have his male sexual organs removed surgically, he cannot remove the knowledge he has of his biological identity.

A more reality-based awareness of his disturbed state threatens to cause another psychotic breakdown or depressive collapse. In order to defend himself from this, Paul develops the fantasy that he can completely remove any evidence of his masculinity, which he feels is a source of mockery and damage, and subsequently immerse himself in the idea of being a woman. He can achieve this, he believes, through gender reassignment surgery.

In the consultation, Paul felt the therapist was saying that his wish to have surgery was psychotic. In contrast, the patient believed that thoughts of the surgery were protecting him from the persecutory experiences. Patients in psychotic conditions experience psychic pain when they become aware that their mind fluctuates between psychotic and non-psychotic states of mind. They often attempt to resolve this issue by trying to eradicate either the sanity or the psychosis. It is common for patients to become suicidal when they fear they are relapsing, to kill off the psychosis. Alternatively, they can try to immerse themselves in an overarching rationalisation (i.e. a form of encapsulated delusion), a belief system that explains everything, which is, in fact, a retreat into psychosis. They then project doubts into an external object that is then experienced as a threat. These doubts are very often projected into the staff working with the patient.

General discussion

Fixed states of mind and belief systems are designed to provide coherence to a collapsed and fragmented ego. As Freud (1911c) pointed out, the delusional system is the ego's attempt to repair itself from fragmentation and collapse. Delusional systems are often centred upon powerful grandiose figures with great power, for example like Jesus, the Madonna, or Muhammad. These figures represent manic aspects of the personality that claim to be able to cure the collapsed or fragmented state.

It is important to understand that the patient holds to their fixed beliefs because they protect the patient from anxieties associated with fragmentation or depressive breakdown. There is no reality testing in the delusional system because this would expose the individual to the precise anxieties and conflicts they are trying to avoid.

Bion (1957) described the way a split can develop between a psychotic and a non-psychotic part of the mind. The psychotic part hates any knowledge of psychological pain, vulnerability, damage, or weakness and tries to solve complex emotional problems through concrete physical actions. The psychotic part of the mind attacks the part of the mind that can experience psychological pain and conflict. The ego's capacity to perceive and think is attacked, fragmented, and projected into the external world. Thus, the person feels that the external world contains a fragmented element of their mind that threatens to re-enter them violently.

The vacuum left by the fragmentation and projection of parts of the ego is then filled with an all-powerful and all-knowing delusional system. The delusional system is an attempt by the individual to repair a fragmented ego in order to provide coherence and continuity. Propaganda emanating from the psychotic part of the personality is used to deny the reality of what has happened to the ego. The ego integrates perceptions and is aware of the nature of the individual's relationship with the internal and external world.

The non-psychotic part of the mind has the difficulty of dealing with emotional problems while being undermined and attacked by the psychotic part of the personality. The psychotic and non-psychotic parts of the patient's mind are in a dynamic relationship and wrestle for control. Sometimes the psychotic patient will project the non-psychotic part of the ego, in order to free themselves from the pain of the conflict between the two parts of their mind. The pain of this conflict can be difficult to bear so the patient may try to resolve it in dramatic ways—such as suicide, religious conversion, or perhaps gender reassignment surgery. When these attempts fail, it can lead to a further breakdown or depressive collapse. Denial and rationalisation are powerful psychic states and may be successfully employed in persuading clinicians to support the patient in pursuing magical solutions. Indeed, clinicians can often feel they will threaten the therapeutic relationship if they fail to support the patient's concrete thinking in demanding surgery.

The problem for the patient who suffers from an ongoing psychotic state is that they cannot remove either the "sanity" or the "psychosis". Some patients in psychotic states try to remove the sanity through immersing themselves in rigid belief systems and emphatic doctrines. Although patients with long-term psychiatric conditions go through different stages of their illness, they often need to try to learn to live with both psychotic and non-psychotic aspects of their personality. To accept their psychological frailty brings them up against feelings of inadequacy. If the patient becomes aware of the damage the ill part of their mind has done to their saner part, this can cause a depressive reaction. The depressive pain may then push them back into the grip of psychotic solutions based on the evacuation of psychic pain followed by a withdrawal from contact with painful external and internal realities—producing more negative symptoms.

Paul harboured a grievance against his parents for making his mind a house built on sand. The phantasy underpinning the sex change was perhaps the following: "I am a damaged person, made so by the sexual union of my parents. I can become perfect by creating myself anew by changing gender, thus denying the biological reality we are all subject to." This chimes with Oppenheimer's (1991) view that the phantasied transformation both expresses a hatred of the parents and acts as a phantasied rebirth, dislocating and abolishing the subject's actual history of conception. Thus, Paul can become a "god" who creates himself in an ideal form by becoming a self who can define their own sex. Lemma (2013) highlights the male-to-female patient's wish to give birth to a self-sufficient, perfect body which is in fantasy a direct replica of the mother's idealised body.

Paul felt threatened by his rage and resentment towards his mother, his parents, and his sexuality. The negative symptoms and withdrawal into the daydream world of "pointless" daytime TV and marijuana may have been an attempt to kill off life and this anger. This protected him from the overwhelming feelings of violence and humiliation that threatened him with either depressive breakdown or depressive collapse. It is possible that he was also worried about his violence towards his mother, whom he needed to support him. Paul often dealt with painful experience through projection. He would find himself touched by painful experience, project it into the external world, and then smile in a vacuous fashion indicating that he had got rid of painful experience. He then moved into a state of mind in which logic, detached from emotional experience, was employed to deal with psychic problems. In this state of mind, it is logical to change your gender if you experience anxieties and doubts about your male sexuality. There is no connection to any subjective experience of being attached to yourself or your sexuality or any ownership of doubts or anxieties about your actions. These are all projected into others. The therapist is then controlled and/or treated as if they were a contaminant since they contain the projected, unwanted psychic material. If the therapist tried to talk about them with Paul, he experiences the therapist as pushing painful psychic experiences back into him in an attempt to drive him mad or prove that he is mad.

The countertransference (see pp. 207–209) can be extremely difficult to manage in the treatment of patients where the psychotic solution involves a request for gender reassignment surgery. Paul suffers from anxieties about separation from his mother, and he locates his male sexuality concretely in his genitals. Paul, by requesting castration, will do permanent damage to his capacity to have children, while also assaulting the sexuality his parents bestowed on him in conception. Steiner (2018) describes the way a child may deal with frustrations related to the oedipal situation by coupling with one parent in triumph over the other. This can also become re-enacted in the transference as Paul couples with the "second opinion" psychiatrist/surgeon, leaving the first psychiatrist and therapist in the position of the excluded child/observer.

Paul seemed to be unconsciously using the second psychiatrist and the surgeon as a "mother" who is inviting Paul into an exclusive, idealised relationship with her and denying the reality of separation and disillusionment. The second psychiatrist also supports Paul in his strong need to believe there is nothing wrong with his mind or his thinking. He dreads the awareness of his dependence upon his mother and the chronic nature of his psychotic condition. He desperately believes that the operation will provide him with a permanent cure.

Comments to the psychiatrist about the change in diagnosis and the need for more time to keep working with Paul infuriated the patient. In his mind, this threatened his mental stability as the therapist seemed to be acting just like his father, who made judgements about him from a distance without really caring or taking an interest. It is possible

Paul thought the therapist was using their position of power to stop him having the treatment he believed would cure him of his difficulties. The therapist took the place of the parents who had to watch their son express his grudge towards them through his attack on his given sexuality. Lemma (2018) makes the point that the "given body" is psychically significant. We think it is important to make the same point about the psychotic part of the self. Patients with psychotic parts of the personality may try to resolve the never-ending conflict between the psychotic and non-psychotic parts of the personality by immersing themselves in a psychotic world. Alternatively, they may try to kill off the psychosis through a radical act designed to remove the psychosis. The painful fact is that some patients with chronic conditions must find a way of living with the psychosis as they cannot eradicate aspects of their personality.

On reflection, we believe the therapist did not give enough attention to the idea that Paul believed the therapist had a mad conviction that he could cure him. All the while, Paul believed he could treat himself by getting rid of his reality-based doubts. In this way, Paul and the therapist were working at cross purposes. The therapist thought he was helping Paul by getting him to think about himself, while Paul thought the therapist was trying to make him worse. If the second psychiatrist had not assessed Paul as non-psychotic, it might have allowed more time for the therapy to explore Paul's wish to become the ideal figure in his mother's mind and his fear of being unloved as a man. Unfortunately, this was not to be and once he had approval from the second psychiatrist, Paul prematurely terminated the therapy.

Conclusion

The treatment of young people who present with gender dysphoria is a highly contested area and the pressure for quick decisions comes from the individual, peer groups, pressure groups, and sometimes the family. There is currently no adequate evidence base for the affirmative model and childhood medical transition with either medication or surgery. Given this, and the larger evidence base to support the idea that most young people will eventually resolve or learn to live with their dysphoria without medical intervention, we need to develop our clinical understanding and improve therapeutic support. At the clinical level, we need to try to understand the motivations and conflicts driving the patient's thinking and beliefs. This includes differentiating between psychotic and non-psychotic forms of thought. Patients who are prone to psychotic solutions to their difficulties may easily be seduced by ideas of radical, concrete cures that promise to remove psychic pain. Clinicians need to understand that the psychotic part and the non-psychotic part exist in a dynamic relationship to one another and although the psychotic part of the patient may appear to be dominating the patient's communication and thinking, the non-psychotic part needs to be identified and supported.

Whatever decisions are ultimately made about active medical treatment, a thorough examination should be aimed at helping the patient to explore their own phantasies and beliefs. Importantly, this includes thinking through the individual's beliefs about the surgery and its outcome in terms of what they imagine it will do for them. Patients also need psychological support to come to terms with the different elements of their personality, none of which can be eradicated by medical or surgical interventions.

This difficult mental work can feel threatening, as it challenges the individual's often rigidly held conviction that they need to change gender. However, as clinicians, we also need to understand that creating a space for thought is often complex, and although a vital part of treatment, is also often experienced as an exertion of clinical power by those in authority. It is important for parents, families, and, where relevant, mental health professionals to be helped to tolerate the uncertainties, doubts, and confusion without jumping to premature conclusions about the long-term direction of travel. This psychological work needs to be done whether or not the individual goes forward to have medical or surgical interventions.

To reiterate, individuals with a weak ego structure and serious psychological difficulties that are prone to being overwhelmed, predominantly rely on paranoid–schizoid thinking. Any comorbid problems need to be addressed and the link between this form of thinking and their interest in transitioning should be carefully examined.

Part IV

Psychoanalytic theory, assessment, and technical challenges in therapeutic engagement

ELEVEN

Psychoanalytic understanding of gender dysphoria

As children grow into adults, they are faced with many psychological hurdles to overcome and these all offer an opportunity for development. However, any developments are accompanied by anxiety, as the child must continually face new and unfamiliar challenges. Children are heavily dependent upon the adults in their life to help them manage and survive these hurdles. Relationships with these adults are intense and stir up feelings of love, anger, jealousy, envy, guilt, and shame. Initially, the baby tries to protect the relied-upon and loved adults from hateful and aggressive feelings, by splitting the object (into ideal/loved and bad/hated) and projecting the aggression. Over time as the infant develops a capacity to manage his (or her) own feelings and suffer anxiety and guilt, they gradually rely less on projection, as they can tolerate the guilt and remorse of knowing they have hateful feelings towards the person they love.

The paranoid–schizoid and depressive positions

Klein described the healthy infant's total dependence upon the mother or primary caregiver for sustenance, care, and love in order to support the development of a strong ego and sense of self. When infants feel safe, they feel in the blissful presence of an "ideal" all-loving mother. The ideal mother is gradually internalised by the infant and forms the basis of the infant's ego as a loved and loving internal object. However, when infants feel anxious, in pain, or neglected, they feel they are in the presence of a "bad" threatening mother who fails to provide protection and care. Aggressive feelings towards this uncaring bad figure then further threaten the infant's ego and sense of security. To protect the ego and any residual good feeling towards the ideal mother that they have, the infant projects these aggressive feelings towards the bad mother out into the external world. These aggressive feelings are then felt to reside outside the infant in the external world and are always threatening to return. The bad object is then attacked and treated as a threat, which needs to be kept outside, hence all the witches and wicked stepmothers in fairy tales. This state of mind is known as the paranoid–schizoid position (Klein, 1935) and the primitive psychic defences it employs include splitting, projective, denial, and idealisation.

Over time, as ego strength develops, the infant begins to lessen the split between the ideal mother who meets their needs and the bad mother who frustrates them. Indeed, the infant starts to recognise that their aggressive and loving feelings are all directed towards the same mother. The ideal object/mother is given up and replaced by the "good enough" mother who can be both loved and hated (Winnicott, 1956). At the same time, the infant begins to realise they are dependent on the good enough mother for sustenance and life rather than relying on an omnipotent fantasy that they can summon up for food, help, and love whenever they want them and kill off the frustrating mother whenever they want to. Faced with the guilt about damage to the frustrating mother and subsequent realisation of their dependency upon the good enough mother, they internalise the good enough mother object to protect her from aggressive attacks. Under these circumstances, when the infant is able to mourn the loss of the ideal mother, Klein wrote that the infant has reached what she called the "depressive position".

The depressive position is a demanding developmental threshold as the infant or child is faced with the loss of the ideal and now has to manage their guilt about resentful feelings towards others. Guilt can threaten to overwhelm the ego. If this happens, it can cause a regression in functioning back to the paranoid–schizoid position when the individual reverts to primitive defences designed to protect the ego from depressive collapse on the one hand, or fragmentation on the other.

We believe that many young people develop gender dysphoria in response to an earlier developmental crisis on the cusp of the depressive position. This is often related to an experience that their parents are fragile and an inability to manage their rage towards them for their perceived shortcomings.

This can threaten the infant's psychological well-being. As guilty feelings threaten to overwhelm the infant's mind and provoke a depressive collapse, so alternatively the baby may turn aggression and hostility inwards in an attempt to avoid attacking the object. This is particularly likely if the parents (or carer) are fragile and unable to withstand the infant's hostility or are prone themselves to depressive collapse in the face of aggression or criticism, or if there is some kind of misconnection between the child and adult. When this happens over a prolonged period of time, it can lead to the development of an internal grievance towards the object that can never (or rarely) be directly expressed. The infant may be placatory towards the object, but internally they are endlessly complaining and harbour a grievance about the failings and shortcomings of the object.

Psychological development arises at the threshold of the depressive position as integration between the good, loved object and the hated, persecutory object produces guilt, which leads to a wish to repair the relationship with the object through a loving, reparative attitude. However, while the grievance towards the object may initially be projected elsewhere, to protect the object, the continuing avoidance of the direct external attack means that for some children the necessary depressive cycle is avoided. Indeed, long-standing grievances are often related to a failure to come to terms with the loss or shortcomings of the ideal object. They are based on a phantasy that the ideal object will return if they unconsciously punish them by continually pointing out their shortcomings. However, all these complaints go on beneath the conscious surface, often through the young person's masochistic treatment of the self. Hence a young person that bears a grievance towards his parents might attack his own body, his identity, and his sexuality, rather than attack the actual parents. Additionally, the parents might be unable or reluctant to acknowledge the young person's grievance against them and will unconsciously collude with the concealment of the complaints. Alternatively, the parents might experience the young person's motivation for transition as an invitation to witness the eradication of the young person they have raised and loved. Children will often complain that their parents' concern is a narcissistic one, which doesn't take the child's autonomy into account, rather than an expression of concern for the damage the child might do to himself.

Achieving the capacity for depressive position thinking, as described, is essential if the infant is going to be able to develop a mind capable of integrating experience. It is the relationship between the primary object/parent and the self/body that helps the infant to gather together his experience of himself, through gestures, facial expressions, and talking. Physical play is crucial in helping the infant to explore and experience himself in relation to the outside world. As the infant watches his hand (which he has limited control over) hit a cuddly toy, he shows pleasure as he recognises that it is his hand making contact. The important support of parents: "Yes, go on you can do it" is all part of the process of developing a healthy body ego. Freud wrote in *The Ego and the Id* that "the ego is first and foremost a bodily ego: it is not merely a surface entity but is itself the projection of a surface" (1923b). When there is a problem between the infant and the primary caregivers, it can inhibit the young person's integration of the mind and the body and this may prove to be a fault-line in the infant's future development.

As infants begin to perceive and think about the external world, they become more aware of other figures like partners, siblings, or grandparents. These other figures may also come between the infant and the mother, causing feelings of rivalry and jealousy. These periods of separation are necessary and important for psychological development, providing they do not overwhelm the infant with too much anxiety. The infant is faced with the fact that he is not always at the centre of the mother's world. Consequently, the infant must internalise the mother's functions, and develop the capacity to manage the periods of separation. These separations can create a crisis, as now the infant has feelings of anger and resentment towards the loved and depended-upon mother. This leads to guilt and a wish to make amends for damage done (in fantasy or reality) to the mother. The infant's solution might be to replace the loss of the ideal mother that would always be with him with a symbol that comes to represent the mother, such as a teddy or blanket. This symbol allows room for impulses to be imagined, to be thought about, and be seen to represent things, rather than be experienced as the object itself. This shifts the mind from concrete thinking, where thoughts are confused with actions, to a realisation that thought is a mental activity. Another important developmental step involves the realisation that thought is not the same as action. This allows the individual to think about things, without the worry that they are actually doing the thing they are thinking about. Thinking becomes a mechanism for exploring the world and your feelings; for example, you can think about wanting to bite or kill your mother without actually doing it.

Puberty is another period of life when the young person is faced with all sorts of new challenges as the adolescent body starts to mature. This faces the individual with sexual development and the questions associated with it. How will you measure up sexually in term of performance, what sort of sexual partner will you attract? Will you either get pregnant or make someone pregnant, what sort of man or woman will you be? All of these questions can stir up feelings about parents, and grievances can re-emerge. Many young people can feel that they are ill-equipped for this next phase of life, and some will put on a pseudo-mature front, or rush ahead into sexual activity in order to obfuscate underlying anxieties about themselves. Others hide away in childish pursuits in order to put off anxieties about the adult world. There is also a normal but considerable confusion about identity as the young person moves from feeling like an adult at one moment, to an out-of-their-depth child the next.

The depressive position is a developmental threshold that makes demands upon the ego's capacity to deal with feelings of exclusion and guilt. If the infant has had problems internalising a "good" object that can help them manage the anxieties and psychic pain brought about by contact with the external world, it can lead to a fragility in their mental health, with splits between the mind and the body, splits in the mind, and splits within the family relationships. The developmental problems can also become the locus point for grievances towards parental objects. Sometimes old splits, which seem to have been resolved, can re-emerge later when a problem threatens to overwhelm the young person's mind. This can lead to a retreat into paranoid–schizoid states of mind characterised by primitive defences of splitting and projection. The idea to transition offers an apparently simplistic solution to the problems of psychic pain and can be extremely attractive to patients who seek black-and-white solutions to their conflicts.

Projective identification

Klein (1946) used the term "projective identification" to describe a mental process in which the person gets rid of unwanted psychological knowledge or perceptions through putting pressure on objects to conform to his omnipotent view of the world. This is a mental process the infant uses as a primitive defence mechanism. This is because the infant needs to feel that he is at the centre of the mother's world in the first few months of life. When the mother does feel this way, Winnicott (1956) describes her as being in a state of "primary maternal preoccupation". This state of primary maternal preoccupation provides the bedrock of the infant's ego leading to the establishment of a secure sense of self.

Sam, a fifteen-year-old boy presenting with gender dysphoria is offered a consultation in a child and adolescent mental health service (CAMHS). On meeting the therapist, he avoids eye contact. However, when the therapist invites him to say something about himself, he forcefully looks at her and says that he wants to be referred for hormones. He then gets irritated when the therapist invites him to explore his wish, stating firmly that he knows what he wants. The therapist mentions that he is irritated with the invitation to think about himself. He says that he has already been questioned by his parents and he knows what he needs and just wants to get on with it.

The therapist notices that she feels guilty for questioning Sam's conviction, as if her questions and wishes for him to think are causing unnecessary psychic pain, rather than being an essential part of her role and task. In this way, we can see how the attitude of "non-questioning certainty" is projected into the therapist. The ordinary doubts and concerns one would have about such a momentous decision are seen as threatening a defensive state of mind, rather than as helpful thoughts designed to examine beliefs.

Container and contained

Bion (1963) developed Klein's ideas further when he developed his theory of the relationship between the container and the contained. He described the infant's dependence upon the mother for emotional and psychological development as well as physical development. He outlined the way the infant's immature ego is overwhelmed and unable to process raw psychic experiences. Bion described the way the infant evacuates and communicates these raw experiences through noises, looks, and bodily movements. The mother has the task of receiving this communication and then using her intuition and empathy to figure out what the communication might mean: Is the baby hungry? In pain? Needing a nappy change? Or feeling anxious?

The mother communicates her understanding of the infant's distress through the tone of her voice and her response. She picks the baby up, rocks and talks to him, feeds him, and/or changes his nappy. The actions convey that the mother has taken in and understood the baby's distress and discomfort. Bion described this as the mother's capacity for reverie. In order for this process to work, the mother needs to be able to be affected by communication without being overwhelmed. The mother conveys her understanding of communication through her actions and loving attitude. Thus, the mother's ability to "contain" the infant's raw emotions helps convert them into "food for thought", which the infant can now internalise and digest. This gives the infant the feeling that he is being cared for by a figure who understands him. In most situations, the infant then calms down and starts to feed or gradually starts to engage with the mother through his eyes, then his movements become more regular and he starts to relax into a more settled position.

Any new parent takes time to get to know their baby's communications and it can be distressing when the baby fails to attach to the breast, is prone to gastric reflux, or has a physical discomfort such as a skin rash or pain for some other reason. Over time in early life, the repetition of this experience of communicating in a distressed state and having the mother understand and act to solve the distress is gradually internalised by the infant until this function becomes a part of their own mind. In many ways, this internalised function is the beginning of a good internal figure (ego strength) that helps the infant to think about adverse experiences and to know that he can survive. It is the beginning of being able to manage one's own experience.

Problems sometimes arise when there is a difficulty in the communication between mother and infant. This may be due to a less receptive infant's difficulty of internalising the mother's capacity to think about him, or it may be due to less receptivity in the mother. If the mother is depressed and unable to respond to the infant's demands, or suffering from post-partum psychosis, or perhaps is overanxious and prone to being too intrusive, this may inhibit the infant's capacity to communicate to the mother. The infant turns away from an overanxious mother to avoid being overwhelmed by her anxiety. Alternatively, he may give up trying to communicate with a depressed mother. Mothers who abuse drugs or alcohol often leave the infant feeling that their attention is sporadic and unreliable, as indeed it is.

There can also be unavoidable obstacles and breaks in this early dyad. A premature baby who has to be incubated or a mother who is unwell post-partum are cases in point. Infants also have innate characteristics whereby some may feel easily overwhelmed or find frustration and/or anxiety difficult to manage. These babies can become over-reliant on primitive defences used to evacuate anxiety and frustration, like projection, splitting, or denial. These primitive defences rely on changing the view of the self and the outside world rather than tolerating and adapting to the frustrations involved in coming to terms with the nature of ourselves and the nature of the world around us.

The relationship between the infant and the mother does not have to be perfect. If it is good enough, the infant can adapt to the frustrations involved in facing reality. It is during this phase that the infant develops a relationship between himself and his body through the mother's ongoing understanding of the infant's bodily experiences. This helps to cement the link between the infant's body and mind.

The mother must be able to believe that she can be good enough, not seeking perfection, which will ultimately backfire and lead, inevitably, to disillusionment. The mother must allow the infant to make small mistakes and learn from experience, and has to forgive herself her own shortcomings. The depressive position occurs when the infant is able to reduce the split between the good mother and the bad mother and begins to realise that the mother he hates is the same person as the mother he loves, that is, he no longer needs to split her into all good and all bad. This process of integration demands that the infant has internalised a good object capable of bearing painful emotions, as well as being able to reflect upon the meaning of those emotions, to feel remorse and sadness.

Mourning the loss of the ideal self

At the start of life, the mother naturally tends to adopt a state of mind in which she puts the infant at the centre of her world. Over time, the mother relinquishes this stance in relation to the infant, as she gradually introduces the reality of how her life extends beyond the infant. This goes on through a series of gradual changes: weaning, putting the young person into his own bed/bedroom, perhaps the birth of a second young person, and a return to work. The parents must support the infant through the psychologically painful process of realising that he is not the only person in the mother's world. This reality will be repeated as he is confronted by the fact that he is not the only child in the world. At some stage, the infant will also have to come to terms with the reality of his/her biological sex. If he is a boy, he will have a penis but not a vagina, whereas a girl needs to come to terms with the fact that she has a vagina but no penis. This will be transformed into a realisation that a boy can impregnate a woman, and the woman carries the baby inside her body and feeds the baby from her breast, but that a woman needs a man's sperm to produce a baby. In other words, the child will develop a growing awareness that to procreate, you are dependent upon a contribution from a member of the opposite sex.

The mourning process provoked by the confrontation with reality is re-enacted repeatedly. Indeed, you might say it is a lifelong process, going on throughout childhood, adolescence, adulthood, middle age, and eventually old age, where the individual must face the reality of their mortality. We do not spend our lives thinking about death, but an awareness and some acceptance of loss is helpful. The wish to return to an ideal state where we can deny our limits and the demands of reality is inevitable for all of us from time to time. The question is the degree to which reality must be denied in fending off psychic pain. Some individuals can get stuck, denying the facts of life or trying to change their perception of reality. Alternatively, they may get stuck in a grievance against a failed ideal object.

The oedipal triangle and thinking

Achieving the depressive position by renouncing the "ideal mother" coincides with the emergence of the oedipal situation whereby the infant becomes aware of a "third object", usually the parental partner or father. Freud (1897) coined the term "Oedipus complex" to describe the way the young person (aged between three and five years of age) develops rivalrous feelings towards the mother's adult partner. The little boy fantasises that he would like to murder his father and take his father's place as his mother's partner. In the original myth, Oedipus unknowingly murders his father and marries his mother. Knowledge of the parents' sexual relationship creates feelings of curiosity as well as jealousy and loss. The triangular relationship between the parents and the young person closes a psychic space and provides boundaries around the young person's experience of himself.

On the one hand, infants have an experience of the mother taking in their subjective experience. On the other hand, they are aware of a third object, say the father, who is looking at the young person's relationship with the mother from a different point of view. This model allows the integration of the infant's subjective experience of being understood emotionally by the mother with the objective experience of being thought about by the father from a separate point of view. This form of triangulation is necessary because it provides a space in which the object can be thought about in its absence and paves the way for symbolic thought.

Britton (1989) emphasises the importance of the third object (psychically the father/partner) in supporting the mother-and-infant couple, while also providing room for separation and thought. The triangular situation provides a structure and model for thinking and helps to prevent the collapse into concrete thinking or enactments of a two-dimensional nature.

The role of the father/partner

The father, and/or partner, has the role of supporting the mother-and-infant couple while the infant is so dependant and demanding. This is a vital role as the nursing couple need to be able to be absorbed in what Winnicott (1956) called "normal maternal preoccupation". The father also has the job of relieving the mother when she is exhausted or when she is struggling with the infant. He can also play a role in establishing some sort of separation when the mother may feel persecuted by her wish to be the "perfect mother" or if the infant has difficulty allowing the mother to separate. This is important as the infant needs to develop his capacities to manage anxiety and separate from the mother. Infants who fail to internalise any maternal capacity to manage anxiety often struggle with separation anxiety. Any separation from the mother, who has come to function as an auxiliary ego, threatens the infant with fragmentation and anxiety. If the parent does not believe the young person can survive separation or cope with a reasonable amount of distress, then it will be extremely difficult for the young person to believe he can manage either. If the father too is overanxious, this help can sometimes be provided by grandparents who have more experience in these matters.

When there is a problem in the relationship between the mother and infant, the father's arrival can be experienced as something that threatens to take away the maternal link which the infant believes he needs to survive. Indeed, every stage of development offers the infant new opportunities to grow and develop, as well as new challenges. For example, weaning can be experienced as a challenge for some mothers and infants alike. The mother is faced with the loss of her life-giving role in breastfeeding the baby, as they move on to the next stage; meanwhile the infant is faced with the realisation that he is not the only person in his mother's life. Whereas everything appeared to revolve around him in early infancy, he may no longer be at the centre of the world. The birth of a younger sibling acts as a concrete reminder of the fact that he is no longer the baby of the family; he is now the toddler. Some young people find this extremely threatening. They fear they cannot survive without being at the centre of the mother's world. They may feel furious and suffer extreme bouts of sibling rivalry.

A toddler asked his mother if she could "take the baby brother back to the shop". This child often hit the baby when the mother was not looking.

Problems arise at this stage when the father pushes himself too quickly into the picture in a way that is rivalrous of the mother's relationship with the baby. Alternatively, the mother may be possessive of the infant and look to exclude the father. The toddler can feel that he must keep one parent to himself by pushing the other out or refusing to engage with the other parent. Toddlers will sometimes push in between the parents when they come together and try to prevent the obvious coupling between mummy and daddy. It helps if the mother facilitates the separation from her and encourages the infant to get to know the other partner. The father can represent a different sort of relationship. In many ways, it is stereotypical to say that while the mother helps the infant develop their early subjective experience, the father offers a perspective from the outside and as such is seen to represent an objective view. Problems can occur, for example, when the father lacks authority and does not intervene in a situation that is going wrong between mother and baby. Occasionally when a young person is dominating the mother in a possessive way, the father needs to stand up to the child's possessiveness and facilitate some separation. Indeed, children who are placated at every turn tend to become tyrannical as they believe that their demands should always be met. This prevents the child from developing a belief that they can wait, or allow others' wishes to come before their own, share their things, as well as tolerate envy.

When fathers absent themselves altogether, they are unavailable to support the mother and infant, or to help them manage a separation. Thus the child may struggle to develop a separate identity. There is a current strand of research exploring the aspect a child's contact with the father plays in their developmental trajectory. For instance, the rough-and-tumble games that fathers are sometimes more likely to engage in may be particularly important for the child to develop physical confidence.

The facts of life

Money-Kyrle (1971) emphasised the difficulty we all have in coming to terms with three painful realities associated with the facts of life, namely: a) our dependence on (the maternal) good object in infancy, b) the difference between the sexes, and c) the difference between the generations. We all have difficulty facing these realities because they confront us with painful truths about our dependence on others, our limitations, and our mortality. It is usual to defend ourselves against the full implications of these realities by misrepresenting them or denying them. Teenagers often act as if they are immortal or will live forever. Maturity and psychological growth are based on the ability to face, rather than to avoid, or misrepresent, the reality of who we are and who we are not. The process of developmental mourning is what allows us to modify our view of ourselves in relation to others.

Dependence on the maternal (good) object

Infants rely on the loving attention of a maternal figure to bring them into the world and care for them. The earliest carer (usually the mother) is not only the source of life but also the carer who helps the infant develop in the first few months. This (hopefully) loving and caring relationship provides a bedrock for the infant's developing mind and sense of him- or herself. Separation from the mother as a result of weaning is both necessary and frightening as the infant may feel unsure about his ability to survive. The capacity to manage these anxieties is dependent upon the infant's ability to hold himself together under the strain of separation. Some infants may try to manage an excess of anxiety by pushing it into their body or into others' as a way of attempting to get rid of it. On the other hand, the infant may develop an insecure attachment by clinging on to the maternal figure and trying to possess her. One thought is that problems in separation can lead to a wish to possess the mother by literally occupying her space.

Biological sexes—the challenge of recognition

Many people have heard of "penis envy", but the truth is there are biological realities and differences between the sexes which seem to provoke intense feelings of exclusion. As part of growing up, the child begins to recognise the difference between the sexes, "identifying" with his or her sex, while acknowledging the sex of the other. This presents the infant with the reality of who they are and who they are not and the reality of the difference between the sexes. It can be very easily influenced by clothing and appearance. This can provoke rivalrous feelings towards the other sex as men may envy women their reproductive capacities while women may desire to have a penis. Recognition of the difference between the sexes may stir up all sorts of feelings of insecurity and curiosity about sexual development: "Where do babies come from?", "Where is my baby sister's willy?", or "Why don't I have a willy?"

The psychological process of coming to terms with who we are and who we are not is a developmental step. It helps to solidify the child's sense of self. However, it does produce feelings of envy and exclusion. "If I am a boy with a penis, I'm not a girl with a vagina." A later version of this would be, "If I have a penis, I can impregnate women, but I will never be pregnant with a baby." The reality of the difference between boys and girls presents the individual with realities about their limitations but helps solidify a positive sense of who they are. The young person may avoid the reality of their limitations by denying the difference between the sexes. This deprives the young person of the security that is derived from integrating their natal biological reality with the socially agreed construction of their gender. The term non-binary splits gender from biological sex and can be associated with a fantasy that the individual can triumph over not just rigid social stereotypes but also biological realities.

The attack on the differences between the generations

Another reality relates to the difference between the generations. This introduces the reality of time and ultimately each individual's mortality. Many parents whose children are transitioning often say that the "trans" state of mind seriously damages their relationship. Some say that this schism is encouraged by services which condemn parents if they fail to adopt a gender affirmative approach to their child. In her chapter on "Rapid Onset Gender Dysphoria", Littman (2018) writes: "Just as transgender-identifying young people are encouraged online to view their parents with suspicion as 'transphobic bigots' if they question self-affirmation, they can be encouraged to alienate themselves from family members by medical practitioners too."

In this way, the link between the generations—between parents and children—is attacked. The protective environment that should be provided by parents for their offspring is undermined. The medical treatment of gender dysphoria may ultimately cause sterility, thus preventing the creation of future generations. The denial of biological differences and the attempt to disconnect sexuality from gender may be related to an unconscious hatred of the difference between the sexes and the generations, and a fear of sexuality and its relationship with reproduction.

In our experience, some families immediately fit in with their child's wish to transition to avoid their anxieties about the young person growing up. In other situations, one parent affirms while the other fights. Parents have their own ideals and desires for their children, who may be highly attuned to them, whether they are consciously expressed or not. Family therapy can be extremely important to understand the family dynamics and the roles the children play in relation to their parents and the ideals they hold.

Psychic retreats

Steiner (1993a) described a "psychic retreat" hidden in the patient's mind that acts as a resting place from anxieties associated with fragmentation on the one hand, and development on the other. Although psychic retreats provide an important defensive structure that can protect the individual's ego from depressive collapse, this defensive structure comes at a price. Psychic retreats prevent the sort of reality-testing that accompanies development, and the individual can get stuck there. Indeed, some individuals spend their life in a form of psychic retreat, as they find that life outside is unmanageable, and they accept the restrictions imposed by the retreat as part of the cost of the solution. The psychic retreat often promises to offer protection to vulnerable aspects of the self.

We believe that gender dysphoria is a psychic retreat, which most young people if left to their own devices will grow out of or, with support, come to terms with. Indeed, the evidence is that 61% to 98% plus of children resolve their gender dysphoria if provided with essential psychological support and care (Steensma et al., 2011). However, those individuals who become entrenched in a psychic retreat will likely need long-term psychotherapeutic treatment. The part of the self that has been captured by the idea of transition needs to be identified and given a voice so that the conflict between the part of the self that wants to transition and the part that feels it's being bullied into submission can be fully explored. These communications might take the form of a subtle comment, smile, or gesture. On other occasions the patient may talk of a voice in their head casting doubts on their wish to transition or saying they will not pass in their chosen gender. The therapist needs to listen to these communications, which the patient might want to ignore or dismiss. In practice, this is a painful oscillating process as the patient moves towards the therapist and emotional contact and away from the therapist and back into the grip of defensive structures and thinking.

Therapists also need to be aware that emerging from a psychic retreat is a frightening and threatening experience for individuals and it cannot be rushed, requiring patience and understanding from those involved.

Concrete thinking

Some of these psychic retreats become a central organising force within the individual, narrowing the focus of the individual into a preoccupation, even an obsession about gender, as everything is seen through the lens of "being trans". The view held is that if only their conflict with their sex-based body could be sorted out, everything else will fall into place. In many ways, this promise of an ideal solution can drive the person to seek increasingly more active interventions in the hope that one of the interventions will indeed solve the problem, but the outcomes, as we are now learning, are very mixed, with the initially reported satisfactions gradually giving way to the underlying mental conflicts and difficulties (Bränström & Pachankis, 2019).

The organising force creates a black-and-white state of mind, as the natal body is seen as something patients do not want to be associated with, while the other idealised body is seen as the solution to all problems. Psychic pain is dealt with through projections into the unwanted aspects of the self, the body, while the desired gender is held in an idealised position in the individual. The splitting and projection required for this state of defence causes a degree of paranoia, as the person feels threatened by any sign of the return of projected aspects of the self. The extent of the projection required to maintain this position also means that the person is caught up in a concrete state of mind that makes any imaginative thinking very difficult. Words, thoughts, and actions are undifferentiated and consequently "thinking and feeling" can be experienced as a dangerous activity. For these reasons, we can understand why it feels so imperative for the trans person to seek concrete solutions to their concretely perceived problem through medication and surgery, and why their defence of their view of themselves and their "autonomy" is so important for them.

When individuals in disturbed states of mind powerfully project aspects of their mind either into their body or into another, be that a person, a group, or an ideology, they can lose their capacity to think symbolically. Hence a conflict in the mind is projected into the body where it is identified as a problem which needs concrete actions in order for it to be solved—a concrete physical solution to a psychic problem. This concrete form of thinking is also often attached to names and words.

Symbolisation and concrete thinking

Segal (1957) built on Klein's ideas by describing the difference between symbolic representation and a symbolic equation. In the case of symbolic representation, there is an acknowledgement of the difference between the symbol and the object being symbolised. Thus, in saying, "I've got butterflies in my stomach," we are describing a fluttering sensation in the stomach caused by the physiological effect of adrenaline. We do not actually mean we have butterflies in our stomach. However, in the case of a symbolic equation, there is no differentiation between the symbol and the object. This gives rise to what we mean by concrete thinking. This is when words (symbols) are treated as if they are the thing (object) itself. Patients in psychotic states of mind often think concretely and thus you might hear a person say, "There are butterflies living in my stomach," a statement of fact rather than a symbolic communication. In a symbolic equation, the statement "Give me a minute" is interpreted as allowing somebody exactly sixty seconds rather than the symbolic meaning of the idea, which is, "Give me some time." To develop an understanding of the difference between a symbolic equation and symbolic representation, the subject needs to be supported in establishing a psychic separation from the concrete object.

The psychotic and non-psychotic parts of the mind

Bion (1957) described the way a split can develop between a psychotic and non-psychotic part of the mind. The psychotic part hates any knowledge of psychological pain, vulnerability, damage, or weakness and tries to solve complex emotional problems through concrete physical actions. The psychotic part of the mind also attacks the part of the mind that can experience psychological pain and conflict; thus, the ego's perceptual and thinking apparatus is attacked, fragmented, and projected into the external world. The person feels that the external world contains a fragmented element of their mind that threatens to re-enter the personality violently. Bion called these objects in the external world, which contain elements of the unwanted mind, "bizarre objects". Patients in a psychotic state of mind may project their capacity to see into an external object such as a clock, for example. Then they believe the clock, which now contains an element of their capacity to see, is looking at them. These external objects have a threatening and persecutory quality as they threaten to push themselves back into the patient's mind. The clock, which symbolises awareness and observation of the passage of time, threatens to force its way back into the mind of the patient who unconsciously wants to remain unaware of the way time passes. The vacuum left by the fragmentation and projection out into the external world of parts of the patient's ego is then filled with an all-powerful and all-knowing delusional system. "I know the clock is watching me."

The delusional system is an attempt by the individual to repair a fragmented ego to provide coherence and continuity. Propaganda emanating from the psychotic part of the personality is used to deny the reality of the damage it has done to the ego. The non-psychotic part of the mind is left with the difficulty of dealing with emotional problems while being undermined and attacked by the psychotic part of the personality. The psychotic and non-psychotic parts of the patient's mind are in a dynamic relationship and wrestle for control. Sometimes the psychotic patient will project the non-psychotic part of the ego, to free themselves from the pain of the conflict between the two opposing parts of their mind.

In many ways, trans-identified states of mind can appear to be a fixed belief system that lacks room for ordinary doubts, anxieties, and questions. At times these states of mind can appear to have delusional intensity in their convictions. We think it is helpful to think of the person fluctuating between different states of mind, largely dominated by the psychotic part, which denies and projects all conflicts, doubts, and anxieties, while the non-psychotic part is located in others who are then felt to be looking on in a judgemental or persecutory way. It is helpful to support the non-psychotic part of the patient's thinking by finding a way to talk with them about the unbearable aspects that they have needed to project into the authority figures around them. This might include pointing out to the patient that they shift between these states of mind and the influences each has. This can be very disturbing, but also necessary and helpful. Certainly, the therapist needs to be aware that there might be different parts of the personality operating at the same time and to tune in to which part of the patient they are with at any moment in the work.

Transference and the countertransference

Freud (1895d) described transference phenomena in his early work with hysteric patients. He noticed the way patients unconsciously transferred repressed feelings and desires from childhood onto the therapist in the here-and-now. Initially, Freud thought that the transference was an obstacle to therapy; however, he later realised the transference could throw light on deep-seated, repressed (therefore unconscious) childhood conflicts. Patients develop powerful, transferential feelings towards the professionals who care for them. Professionals need to be sensitive to the meaning these roles carry for patients. They need to try to tune in to the patients' unconscious transference feelings towards them because this can convey meaningful insight into the nature of their early relationships: the "there-and-then" which underlies their difficulties in relating to others in the here-and-now.

Freud (1910d) first described the term "countertransference" to denote a patient's impact upon the therapist's unconscious mind. This idea was developed by Heimann (1950) to explain and make use of the therapist's feelings towards the patient. Her idea was that the patient generated feelings in the therapist that were responses to the patient's own transference feelings. If attended to, these could prove illuminating about the patient's unconscious attitudes towards the therapist and therefore shed light on how they experienced the attention of the early attachment figures in their lives.

A patient started a session by making a provocative statement about the therapist being a control freak and mean-spirited. Feeling irritated, the therapist replied by commenting on the patient's lack of gratitude for the help he had received. The patient triumphantly commented that this was exactly the sort of response she was talking about. Thus, the therapist enacted the countertransference by playing the role prescribed to them in the patient's transference (i.e. that they are mean and controlling).

Money-Kyrle (1956) developed the theory of countertransference by differentiating between normal and abnormal countertransference. In normal countertransference, the therapist takes in the patient's experience and subjectively identifies with them. The therapist then separates from the patient's subjective experience, objectively examining the interaction before deciding on an interpretation. In many ways, it is true to say that the therapist is having a conversation with themselves before talking to the patient. In the abnormal countertransference scenario, the therapist may have difficulty separating themselves from identification with the patient and reacts to the patient as if they were an aspect of themselves, rather than a separate other as in the example above. I believe this phenomenon applies in all mental health work.

In supervision, a therapist presents the case of Bryony, a fifteen-year-old girl who wants to transition. The therapist says that the girl is completely convinced that she wants to start taking hormone blockers and gets angry at the therapist's suggestion that they spend some time thinking about this. Bryony says that she is upset by her hormonal changes and she wants them stopped. After the session, the therapist notes that when she is with this patient, she is unable to function in her usual professional way. The therapist could not think of anything to say to the girl and believed if she questioned her it would cause upset with Bryony. The therapist also worried about provoking a threat of suicide.

This sort of presentation is very common in gender dysphoric young people. What is noticeable is the complete lack of any doubt or anxiety in their thinking. It is often argued that the young person is certain they know what they want, as if the absence of anxieties and doubts were evidence of a reliable assessment. The reality is that doubts and anxieties about transitioning would be completely appropriate. The rigid conviction that transition must be supported at all costs leaves no room for thoughtful examination. This state of mind is transferred to the therapist who temporarily identifies with Bryony's belief that any examination of her thinking could be damaging to her mental state. The supervisor was able to help the therapist see that they had been taken over by the patient's state of mind in the countertransference, in believing that anxieties, confusions, and doubts were unhealthy states of mind that should be avoided at all costs, rather than a healthy part of mental life. Bryony needed the therapist to recognise that the absence of doubts and anxieties about her wish to transition was part of the defensive state of mind trying to flatten the ordinary concerns and was helped when the therapist took this up with her.

Normal and pathological projection

Everybody uses what Bion (1959) would describe as "normal projective identification" to manage their emotional life, as it is a form of communication to the other/object, for example the crying infant to the mother. This will also occur between the patient and therapist and is helpful for the therapist to understand and empathise with the patient. It is important to make a distinction between this normal projective identification and "pathological projective identification" which is used to enviously attack the object. The therapist is likely to experience pathological projective identification as a psychic evacuation from the patient which is in phantasy pushed into the mind of the therapist, who can feel paralysed or taken over by it.

The value of a psychoanalytic model for psychodynamic work

In a blog entitled "How I Work with Gender-questioning Teens", Sasha Ayad (2018) outlines her exploratory approach:

> I've found that when I take the clients too literally, it can move us away from deeper exploration. I will try not to get wrapped up

in jargon, recycled narratives, and minute details in the client's gender story. It is tempting to dig deep into complex rationalisations, trying to unpack confounding ideas. Instead, I listen for something deeper, look for patterns, and stay present with the emotions.

The lack of a psychological model for thinking about gender dysphoria has hampered clinicians working with this group of patients. We believe that psychodynamic psychotherapy offers a model for thinking about fixed states of mind. It also offers a model for thinking about how individuals create split states of mind in which something can be acknowledged and accepted on the one hand, while being denied on the other. The theory of projection allows us to consider the ways in which unwanted aspects of the self are denied and split off into others, as well as the unconscious clues these provide when these issues are repeated in the transference and countertransference. Whatever the outcome of a person's wish to transition, they should be offered an extended assessment and exploratory therapeutic work before any medical treatment is commenced. Even when individuals go on to have medical treatment, this therapeutic work will help prepare them for life after the medical intervention. Gender transition is not an easy road to take and many members of the trans community have ongoing mental health problems, with many experiencing continuing symptoms of gender dysphoria despite medication and surgery.

TWELVE

Assessment and challenges of therapeutic engagement

All of us have a perceived self and an ideal self; the perceived self is how we view ourselves and the ideal self is how we wish we were. When these overlap, congruence occurs. It is impossible for these selves to overlap fully—we all have something about ourselves that we wish were different—but for most of us, the overlap is sufficient. When the distance is too great, it is called incongruence, a humanistic psychology concept developed by Carl Rogers (1951). This can lead to discomfort, anxiety, stress, and frustration. Indeed, it's worth noting that gender dysphoria has now changed to gender incongruence in the *International Classification of Diagnosis 11*.

Gender incongruence between mind and body

When a person states they are trans or complains of gender dysphoria, it is important to listen and investigate what is occurring for the individual. The presentation and message from a patient can be very fixed and one-dimensional. Rather than the patient presenting a distressing psychological symptom, they more usually talk of feelings of detachment from the body they were born in that is felt to contain unwanted aspects of the self. For instance, the patient might act almost as if they are a customer who has been sold the wrong suit and is outraged at the reluctance of the shop to give them a new one. In this way, a complex psychological configuration in the mind is treated as if it were a concrete problem located in the body.

The unaddressed problem is, however, that although medical interventions may interfere with the body and block its sexual development or functioning, they cannot completely eradicate the patient's natal gender. This can lead to a sense of persecution, as the body is a constant reminder of the continued existence of the unwanted aspects of the self. This persecution is often projected into others whose position of neutrality and/or curiosity is experienced as forcing doubt into them and thus undermining their belief in transition as the solution to their psychological problems. This is also apparent in extreme reactions to "mispronouning" or "deadnaming" or other external reminders of their natal body such as a member of the public incorrectly recognising their chosen gender.

Individuals need help and support in coming to terms with who they are, including their natal sex, as part of the maturational process. However, patients often put enormous pressure on family, schools, and clinical services to join with them in the belief that to transition to the "ideal" body, which they hope will eradicate unwanted aspects of who they are, is the only solution to their problems. When the family or clinical service accept, without sufficient question, the individual's assessment of the problem as being their natal sex, they are supporting the belief that psychic problems can be dealt with by interfering with the body's functioning. The patient acts as if they are convinced that a problem of self-representation in the mind can be cured by concretely treating the body. The cost is that the individual is dissociated from their own body, treating it like a mannequin rather than a part of the self with anxieties, feelings, and confusions. Incongruence is the psychological challenge we all face—we cannot be ideally perfect and must come to terms with our faults and limitations. However, transition is often sold to the mind as the solution to the individual's problems, a way of triumphing over faults and limitations.

Clinicians need considerable experience and clinical maturity to be able to carry out thorough assessments. One needs to be able to empathise deeply with the individual's confusion, distress, and mental pain, yet maintain adequate separation in order to be able to resist the pressure to join the patient in their view that an active, medical (rather than psychological) intervention is the only solution. Part of the developmental struggle of adolescence is to come to terms with our personality and our strengths, weaknesses, and limitations, including our natal sex and the different roles demanded of us in reproduction.

There are all sorts of anxieties attached to these activities and functions of the body. However, as described in the chapter on adolescence, these biological realities seem to be largely ignored in transgender services. The majority of young people prescribed puberty blockers go on to take cross-sex hormones, which ultimately have serious consequences for their adult life. Young people need an independent clinical service that has the long-term interests of the patient at heart. To some extent, this requires a capacity to stand up to pressure coming from various sources: from the young person, their family, peer groups, from online/social networking pressures, and of course from highly politicised pro-trans groups.

Comorbidity and complex problems in young people

A patient presenting with rapid-onset gender dysphoria in adolescence may be masking other mental health issues. There is a growing body of research which connects the development of gender dysphoria with psychological factors (Bonfatto & Crasnow, 2018; Chew et al., 2018; Dhejne et al., 2011; Donym, 2018; Patterson, 2018; Rustin, 2018; Withers, 2015, 2018). A group of parents whose children were treated at the GIDS wrote to the Tavistock Foundation Trust Board (Doward, 2018) to report that although their children had no long history of gender dysphoria, they had been on the autistic spectrum or suffered from social anxiety adjustment disorders. Their concerns were that the GID service in the United Kingdom was taking a superficial approach which was in danger of colluding with these young people's beliefs that all their problems would be solved if only they could change gender. Parents also expressed concern that their young people were being indoctrinated by online advice aimed to help them evade a proper psychological examination.

Disturbed states of mind often rely on primitive defences of the paranoid–schizoid position. This state of mind is particularly prone to ideas of magical solutions that involve the idea that you can eradicate an unwanted part of yourself through action. Clinicians need to be aware that the personality is dynamic, with all aspects of the individual operating in a dynamic relation to one another. So, for example, something called sexuality or identity should not be viewed as something completely separate to mental structure involved in autistic states of mind, or depression, or an eating disorder. The role of the assessment is to develop a holistic picture of the individual with the aim of understanding how different parts of the personality interact.

John—a seven-year-old boy

John was referred to the clinical service for assessment. When the therapist went to pick up the family from the waiting room, she could hear a child running amok. Opening the waiting room door, she saw John running around in a manic state. The mother was asking John to calm down while the father sat motionless in his chair, uninvolved in what was happening around him.

The therapist introduced herself and said they would be meeting in a room upstairs. The boy immediately shot out of the waiting room and up the stairs as if he knew where he was going. The mother shouted after him to wait for everybody else. He ignored her. The boy started trying to open various therapy room doors, prompting the therapist to direct him to her room. John rushed into the room and started picking objects up from the desk, asking "What's this?" and then rushing on to the next object without waiting for the answer.

The therapist gestured to the parents where to sit and the mother tried to get her son to sit next to her between her and her husband. John appeared to ignore his mother while continuing to move around the room. The therapist asked John if he could sit down and talk with them for a while. However, this seemed to have no discernible effect. All the while, he was continuously talking and saying things that were difficult to follow as he seemed to have a flight of ideas.

The therapist then directed her attention to the parents. The mother spoke at some length about John and the fact that he would never leave her side and that he dressed up in her clothes and put on her make-up. Then he would quickly take it all off and repeat with another outfit. The mother said that most of the time John said he was a girl but every so often he would revert to being a boy. Meanwhile, John was travelling the room in a swivel chair, bashing into the furniture. John's mother asked him in a resigned tone to stop but seemed unconcerned about the erratic behaviour of her son. John's father hardly said a word or moved during the whole meeting and appeared to be depressed.

At one stage, John started to wheel himself on the therapist's chair towards a partially open window and the therapist had to ask John quite forcibly to stay away from the window. The therapist was struck by the parents' lack of control over their child. They seemed to accept his behaviour as normal.

The mother mentioned that she and John had slept in the same bed since his birth while the father slept in the spare room. The father made no indication of how he felt about this. The mother then told the therapist that John had been school-refusing and social services were trying to help her get him to school. The therapist noted that the parents did not seem to be very concerned about John's school refusal. The therapist concluded the meeting by saying she would be meeting with the clinical team and then she would come back to the family with a care plan.

Discussion of John's presentation

We can see from this account that John is manic. He had a flight of ideas and cannot take anything in and is clearly in a disturbed state. It is important to assess the mental state of any young person as part of the assessment process. In the clinical team case discussion, the team decided that a child psychiatrist should see him as a next stage to try to assess, then treat his mania as a priority.

The next most striking aspect was the mother's description of the problem of separating from John. She seemed to have no capacity to control his behaviour as he is everywhere and into everything: opening doors, looking into rooms, opening drawers, touching objects on the desk. It was as if he could not be excluded from anything and yet could not stay in one place for any length of time. The therapist observed a child who had to get into every space at every moment, but once John was in something, he immediately wanted to get out.

Glasser (1979) described the "core complex" as a state where the child wants to be inside the mother because he finds the problems of separation difficult to manage, but once inside he feels their separate identity is threatened. This is a restless state as the individual feels uncomfortable outside the object but then claustrophobic and trapped once inside the object.

John's behaviour in the consultation seemed to fit this pattern, continually looking inside things, then continually moving on, as if he felt trapped. You could also argue that by getting dressed up in his mother's clothes, he was getting right inside the mother but then quickly had to take them off again. It was as if he could not settle anywhere or with anything. It was also evident that the mother seemed to encourage John's dependence upon her. She did not seem to think that John sleeping in her bed was a problem, and she did not seem to show any concern about the father's exclusion or John's school refusal. It was clear that the authorities had raised this with the parents as a problem. Indeed, the mother seemed unconcerned about what her husband thought or his apparent low mood.

Was John avoiding separation anxiety by getting completely inside her identity? By becoming her, in phantasy, he could completely dominate her. The fact that he still slept in her bed while the father slept in the spare bedroom showed the degree to which the mother was dominated by John. The father seemed wholly ostracised and appeared depressed. To this extent, he seemed unwilling or unable to intervene in helping John and his mother to separate. However, once John was inside his mother in fantasy, he would then feel trapped and declare that he was a boy as if to announce his separate identity from his mother.

The team took the view that in addition to John seeing the psychiatrist they would also suggest that the family start in family therapy to address the issue of helping John and his mother separate so that he could develop a mind and life of his own. The therapy might also try to address the issue of the father's absent profile as he seemed to accept his position of being pushed to the margin of the family, while John's mania and separation anxiety dominated the family environment in an unhelpful way. The mother's inability to separate from her son could also be addressed. All of this would need to be done before any work on understanding the nature of John's presentation as a "girl" if it persisted. The team thought John's mother was involved in a folie à deux as she did nothing to encourage his ability to separate from her and at times seemed to enjoy aspects of his attachment to her when they were "girls together".

The wish to remove pain

Families and services may feel that they are being humane by trying to alleviate the individual's distressing symptoms of gender dysphoria. But there is evidence that supporting the individual's wishes to transition can exacerbate rather than alleviate psychic distress. Dagny (2019) wrote:

> Ultimately, the opportunity to transition made my teenage dysphoria worse. This narrative told me that my hatred for my female body was justified—positive, even. It told me that the only way to feel better was to destroy my body—my female parts.

Staff working with children who are suffering from gender dysphoria obviously want to protect them from unnecessary pain and anxiety. However, pain and anxiety often provide an indication of an underlying problem that needs attention, and we believe this is the case with gender dysphoria. It's important to help children to assess their level of distress or discomfort. Children need to develop a capacity to notice pain and be helped to understand and process the experience as part of their learning about themselves. Children also need help differentiating the type, degree, and cause of pain and to be given some confidence that psychic pain can be both tolerated and understood. Parents and professionals are key in assisting any child with this process. Long-term problems arise when clinical staff feel forced into providing a quick solution to the patient's distress before the underlying causes of the presenting symptom have been examined. For example, the over-prescription of opioids for the treatment of pain is recognised to cause long-term harm to patients because they become addicted to medication leading to death by overdose, as the opioid epidemic in the USA over the last decade or so has revealed. The current transgender treatment has physical and mental long-term costs in terms of loss of sexual functioning and a lifelong need for medical interventions. Therefore, a thorough assessment of the underlying issues is critical, particularly in relation to young people.

Medicine also gets into trouble when its motive and raison d'être shifts from treating illness into providing ideal solutions to the problems of life. These promised solutions often come with hidden, unseen costs based on a belief that the facts of life can be overcome or ignored when they need to be accepted and faced.

James was a twenty-five-year-old detransitioner who referred himself for therapy describing himself as "autogynephilic", meaning he had a propensity to be sexually aroused by the thought of himself as a female (Blanchard, 1989). He complained that he had failed to establish any life of his own. He was born James, but transitioned in his late teens, living as a trans woman called Janet for six years. However, his dysphoria continued after gender reassignment surgery (GRS). He also felt that he never really passed as a woman and consequently he decided to detransition and reclaim his original name. He diagnosed himself as suffering from autogynephilia after reading about the condition. (We believe that in some cases, this male-to-female identification may have its roots in the unconscious desire to enter and possess the mother's body, in phantasy taking control of the woman's sexual organs.)

James was brought up by his mother, who was a single parent. He went on to say that he had never known his father and that he remembered resenting any male partner his mother introduced. James laughed as he said that he believes he frightened any male partner off and that his mother gave up dating men on account of his jealous reaction. He was seen by a CAMHS (child and adolescent mental health service in the NHS) when he was eight or nine on account of his separation anxiety and ongoing school refusal. He had failed to sustain any long-term relationships with men or women and still lived with his mother. He said that he realised he was autogynephilic when he noticed becoming sexually excited whenever he wore women's clothes and occupied women's spaces. James described his mother as an insecure woman who was rather over-involved with him.

We can see how James and his mother lived in a folie à deux whereby separation from one another was hard to bear. Any individual who came between them threatened their interdependency. I think James believed that neither party could bear any form of separation, fearing that it would lead to some sort of mental collapse or fragmentation. Autogynephilia is an attempt to solve the psychic problem he has in establishing a separate identity from his mother. James believes he is only safe, and his mother is only safe, when in fantasy he is right inside his mother. This ability to get inside his mother is concretely represented by wearing women's clothes and entering female spaces; in doing either, he feels he can access them whenever he needs.

The sexualisation of the enactment gives him a powerful feeling of triumphing over his separation anxiety. He is no longer a little boy that can't survive without relying upon a powerful mother figure. Instead, he is a powerful man who can get inside women whenever he wants. This is perhaps a different manner of entering a woman, which his father with an erect, potent penis, would have done to impregnate his mother, perhaps a phallic symbol James feels he could never compete with. Thus, the oedipal situation is avoided as James occupies his mother and vice versa. The cost is that neither party is allowed to be separate and live their own lives.

Technical problems when words are experienced as action

The "misuse" of pronouns can feel traumatising to some trans-identified people as can deadnaming (i.e. using a person's birth name rather than their new chosen name) and can produce extreme responses in both the individual who has been deadnamed but also from their "supporters" who often then vilify the person responsible. Of course, sometimes the deadnaming has been intentionally hurtful, but often it is a genuine mistake or slip.

Simone

Simone (previously known as Simon) was a twenty-six-year-old trans-identified woman who was being seen in a psychotherapy service. She was referred to the service for treatment of her depression and was pushing the service to agree her request for further surgery on mental health grounds. Simone also had a history of arguments with people in positions of authority and threatening them with complaints when they failed to comply with her wishes. She had previously had surgical operations to improve her feminine looks as she was preoccupied with passing as a woman. The service called a special meeting to discuss Simone's case on account of the fact that she had verbally abused the receptionist, who had subsequently complained to the management that she wanted action taken against the patient. Simone accused the receptionist of deadnaming her by calling her "Simon" and wanted to take out a formal complaint against the service for her treatment.

The descriptions of events by the two participants were very different. The receptionist said:

> I called Simone to the reception desk and she completely lost the plot, saying that she was transgender and that I had deadnamed her and wished death on all transgenders. She was in a blind rage. She looked at me in disgust saying that I was a worthless temp and she was going to get me sacked. She went on to say that I was a terrorist and that I should go back to the country I came from.

In her meeting with the manager, Simone insisted that the receptionist had called her by her previous name and had done so because "This woman hates transgenders and wishes me dead." Simone went on to tell the manager that the receptionist always looked down on her whenever she visited the clinical service. "That receptionist hates me and she deserved what she got." When the manager mentioned that they had an anti-bullying policy, Simone became extremely angry and said she was going to write to the manager's superior and complain about him too.

Case discussion

Simone is working very hard to maintain a picture of herself as being a female, evidenced in part through the many feminising surgeries. The team have no way of knowing what went on between the receptionist and Simone as there were no witnesses, and no way of knowing whether this is an accurate assessment of the way the receptionist looks at her or to what extent it is influenced by Simone's sensitivity which has a paranoid quality with her fear that people "see through" her appearance to the biological male. What is evident is that she believes the receptionist called her "Simon", and on hearing that, she felt immediately assaulted and accused the receptionist of "hating all transgender people and wanting them dead". This issue of deadnaming or mispronouncing touches on the fundamental issue of identity. Most of us construct our view of ourselves from a combination of how we experience ourselves to be, with how we are seen by others. "I always think of myself in this way, but my partner always tells me I'm like that." In other words, identity is a dynamic construct which describes us in relation to others. This sort of reflection demonstrates a capacity to tolerate the fact that we acknowledge we have a certain view, but that others may see things somewhat differently. We don't control the way we are seen; others come to their own conclusions. We may not always like the way we are seen or agree with it, but in a reflective state of mind it's just a difference of opinion. In this account, Simone feels concretely threatened by the receptionist's view of her, as if deadnaming literally threatens her existence. She then retaliates by attacking the receptionist's identity: "You are a terrorist." The other issue that comes across is the hierarchical structure of the relationship. Simone feels she is being demeaned and looked down on. In retaliation, she claims she could get the receptionist sacked and refers to the receptionist at one point as a "useless temp" as if Simone is the one with all the authority and power.

The belief that you can change sex and control the way you are seen is possibly related to powerful defences of denial and control. The unwanted self is viewed as the lowly temp who has no value, while at the same time Simone occupies the powerful position of someone who can get the lowly receptionist sacked. In this way Simone tries to evacuate unwanted and humiliating parts of herself into the receptionist, while creating a view of herself as being powerful and able to control people. Simone is dealing with the threat of the return of these unwanted projected parts of herself. We might understand how she wishes to project and triumph over these vulnerable feelings, but also that she is living in a world where she continually tries to convince herself and others that she is a natal woman. This is a persecuted state of mind that is always threatening to break down as you can't control the way you are seen. Simone may go into a paranoid state where she experiences the attacks through doubts in her own mind as coming from the outside world, hence her feeling that the receptionist is a terrorist threatening her life.

When words/names become an issue in the clinical setting it is helpful to explore and understand this with each individual, rather than unquestioningly affirming in order to avoid any disturbance of thought. Psychotherapeutic exploration provides an opportunity for the individual to understand what drives and motivates them. This can be difficult when words are no longer differentiated from actions as the patient can feel physically attacked by the therapist's thinking and words. Due to the importance of their mental defences, the patient may also put intense pressure on the therapist to accede to concrete solutions and requests. The therapist needs to anticipate the way their words will be heard and to demonstrate an empathetic understanding of the patient's subjective experience, before offering another view of the patient's unconscious communication at a symbolic level.

A psychotherapist presented the case of an eighteen-year-old girl called Denise, who was transitioning and wanted to be known as Greg. She started the session by angrily stating that her mother had dead-named her by calling her Denise. "She knows what she is doing, and it just makes me furious."

At this point, only a few seconds into the appointment, the clinician has a dilemma which needs to be attended to. When names and words become concrete, it makes the process of exploration in consultations difficult, as words can be experienced as dangerous actions that threaten the individual, rather than an exchange of ideas. This is evident in some of the terms used to describe things in the trans community. For example, deadnaming may be experienced as an aggressive act. In the example above, Greg (formerly known as Denise) believes that her mother is deliberately assaulting her identity by using her given name. The therapist is now in a position of taking sides—the patient or her mother, Greg or Denise?

In many settings the professional may be faced with a forceful demand to call the transitioning young person by their new name, in place of their given/birth name. The patient may become extremely upset if the therapist refuses to comply or accidently uses the birth name, although alternatively, any immediate agreement to use the preferred name may mean the therapist has colluded with an attack on an aspect of the individual's personality. While we would not advocate getting into an upsetting conflict with the patient, we also do not believe that it is helpful for the person to eradicate their natal self or unwanted aspects of their personality. It is important in the clinical example above that the therapist is able to "keep alive" the little girl Denise and learn more about her life and feelings as well as how "Greg" feels now and views things differently. We believe it is a mistake to go along with the idea that you can eradicate a hated part of the self. We believe the therapist's stance is neither to agree nor to disagree if possible, but rather to investigate what the patient believes is wrong with "Denise", and why becoming "Greg" will solve their problem.

Managing the countertransference

The therapist has the task of trying to understand the young person's psychic structure, accepting that many of the doubts, confusion, and anxieties may be projected into them with considerable effort put into ensuring that they stay there. A therapist can look for ways to comment on the absence of the person's own doubts, anxieties, or conflicts. Also, it can be helpful, if the patient is felt ready for it, to sensitively comment on the way projections seem to be residing in others. It is also important to understand the drives that keep the young person's psychic equilibrium in place and the huge anxieties that they are defending against. The therapist must understand that the individual may often think and experience interpretations in concrete ways. It is essential to try to understand the way the young person sees the therapist in the first instance, because this sort of "analyst-focused interpretation" might help support the young person's view which in turn might slowly increase their capacity to reflect on their mental state. This is painstaking work, and the therapist is looking to contact the parts of the young person's mind that are outside the psychic retreat. Perhaps there are parts of the young person that may be concerned about the direction of travel or remember something from their pre-solution state of mind.

Concrete solutions to psychic problems

An assessment should include a full discussion about the losses and risks involved in any active intervention that could interfere with biological functioning. The question of how in touch the individual is with the implications of this medical intervention should be a crucial dimension of the assessment. For example, if the individual has no concern at all about the prospect and outcomes of medical intervention, this lack of concern should be thought of as a symptom that needs to be investigated, rather than simply a positive indication of the patient's motivation.

The concrete nature of communications is evident in the young person who wishes to cure their mental distress through medical treatment of the body. The young person's psychological problem has been concretely projected into the body. Then there is a demand for the body to be medically altered, as if the change to the body can miraculously resolve a problem that exists in the mind.

A fourteen-year-old girl called Samantha is referred to the gender identity service. The family doctor explains in the referral letter that she wants to start socially transitioning. Samantha arrives at the consultation with a short haircut, dressed in jeans and wearing Doc Martin boots. She also appears clinically obese.

At the start of the consultation, Samantha says that she wants to change her name to Justin and move from her girls' school to a boys' school. After several consultations, it becomes apparent that Samantha associates her sensitivity with being female and sees objectivity with being male. The therapist's dynamic formulation is that Samantha's "ideal" self is a hard, masculine figure that always seemed to be objective and that she despises emotional "sensitivity" and female figures.

The family therapist reported that in response to Samantha's request to transition, her father appeared to be calm and rational, but her mother was extremely upset. It also became clear that Samantha rather admired her father but seemed to despise her mother. Indeed, the family therapist commented on the way Samantha would pull away from her mother whenever she tried to make emotional contact with her daughter. Samantha's mother had become upset when talking about how Samantha used to play with dolls and seemed to be happy being a girl. She said that she felt as if she had lost her daughter. At this point in the session, Samantha looked daggers at her mother as if she hated to be reminded of the way her mother saw her as a little girl.

Over time in the individual therapy, it became evident that Samantha associated her given name with a weak little girl who became upset when she was teased by other girls for being overweight. She saw Justin as a strong, powerful man who was unaffected by feelings.

Social stereotypes of the oversensitive, emotional woman and the calm, rational man are reflected in Samantha's psychic structure. She idealises her father's "rational" objective thinking while despising and pushing away her mother's "emotionality". Thus, a rigid stereotype of masculine objectivity is something she powerfully wishes to identify with, while distancing herself from any unwanted emotions which she identifies with femininity. The wish to change her name is a way of adding external support to the existing internal split.

In the case of Samantha, we can see that she distances herself from her feelings of sensitivity at being teased or being overweight. She cannot bear her feelings of upset associated with the idea that she is overweight, as they threaten to overwhelm her ego with depressive feelings associated with the loss of the ideal view of herself. To defend the ego, she detaches herself from her body which she blames for "letting her down" and locates all her unwanted feelings of hurt in her "weak" feminine body. At the same time, she retreats into a "masculine" objective mind. In this way, she retreats from the depressive position where psychological suffering involves facing the pain of the loss of the ideal, into a split between an idealised logical mind and a hated emotional body. This split is evidence of paranoid–schizoid functioning. (N.B. Paranoid–schizoid thinking is a transient state of mind which is primitive but normal and not to be confused with a psychiatric diagnosis of paranoid schizophrenia.) You could postulate that the physical frame of a hard man represents a body armour that is seen as protecting a fragile internal state.

The role of the defensive structure

The therapist needs to understand the role that the defensive structures play in supporting the ego and managing anxiety, before pointing out the cost of the defences. The fact is that human beings are complicated, and our problems are usually multidimensional. The solutions to our problems usually involve separating things and looking at an issue from different points of view, encouraging an open mind, displaying curiosity and a desire to explore things. However, this exploratory stance can be experienced as very disturbing or offensive to gender dysphoric patients. This is because it threatens to undermine their internal defences and belief system, which they rely upon to protect them from overwhelming feelings of anxiety and guilt.

Fixed states of mind

Two of the current diagnostic criteria for gender dysphoria are the demonstration of persistence and consistence in the patient's gender identity, but we strongly question the value of these diagnostic symptoms when forming a care plan for a young person. Many young people who present at gender clinics appear to be frozen in their current preoccupations, with any natural doubts and anxieties about their wishes for transition absent and projected into those around them. This conviction is often used as part of the diagnostic criteria for proceeding with concrete medical interventions, rather simplistically accepting that the absence of anxiety or doubt in the young person's mind is clear evidence of the need to transition. Anxiety and doubt about decisions which have far-reaching consequences would be very appropriate emotional responses as part of a decision-making process, especially when it could set someone on a path to permanently altering their physical body and adversely affecting their sexual life, their potential fertility, and their general medical health.

After unconsciously projecting their doubts and confusions into the "grown-ups" or professionals, the young person often watches to see what impact their presentation has upon those around them. This is in order to ensure that the concealed confusion, doubt, or anxiety has been identified in the listener and that the projection has successfully got through. When the therapist prematurely projects back into the young person, it can produce an explosive reaction, as the young person feels that what they projected into the therapist for safekeeping is re-projected, in a way that seriously disturbs the young person's psychic equilibrium. The therapist needs to be supported in thinking about this mode of communication better to understand their reactions. It is not that the therapist should be a model of calm and tranquillity, for example when the patient is demanding a mastectomy or penectomy, but more about understanding that reacting to a concerning psychic provocation with equal force and re-projecting this is unlikely to produce the required therapeutic results. This is because everyone needs to have their defensive structures respected. The therapist needs to check their own impatience for change and wait for the appropriate moment to test the patient's readiness for an attempt to pierce their psychic defences.

Splitting off sexuality

Children and adolescents have all sorts of phantasies and anxieties about the mechanics of sex and sexual roles. These desires and conflicts touch on infantile fears of being invaded or invading, being overpowered or being powerful. We have heard from staff, ex-patients, and parents who have been recently involved with gender specialist services that the assessment process with gender dysphoric young people does not pay much attention to the importance of sex and reproduction. Transitioning involves placing a block on the development of sexuality. It is odd, then, to think that sexual phantasies and preoccupations are not discussed as part of the assessment process. Of course, when working with younger age groups, this has to be carefully managed and age-appropriate, but it is essential to explore the person's fears and phantasies about sex and sexual orientation. Understanding the areas of difficulty might avoid altogether the need for medical treatments such as hormone blockers, which are designed to prevent the development of sexual characteristics. It is easy to understand why a young person who is in tremendous conflict regarding their sexual development might report "improvement" in their feelings of distress or dysphoria, because any sexual development literally gets blocked. But people need to come to terms with their sexual selves and therefore, rather than joining the anxious adolescent in a belief that the whole area should be avoided or stopped, using hormone blockers, it helps if a therapist can support the person to begin to think about their fears and anxieties.

In our experience it is not possible to assess a young person's capacity to make an informed consent to medical treatments that will seriously affect their future adult lives. A young person cannot be expected fully to understand or consider the way their current thinking may be affected by family dynamics, their developmental anxieties, and experiences and traumas from the past, as well as other complexities around mental health and cognitive functioning. This work can certainly not be achieved in a few assessment meetings and requires the professional to work sensitively with the young person over a long period of time. (Furthermore, at the time of writing, it is true to say that the field of gender identity medicine has insufficient gold standard research or evidence base of outcomes to afford any clinician to request or expect the child to give an informed consent to medical interventions. The professionals are inadequately informed themselves and cannot provide the patients and their parents with sufficient prediction of risk—but that is for another book.)

Split states of mind

Double bookkeeping is another important issue when trying to understand the psychic organisation. Although the young person may maintain a belief that they need to transition, this may not have been thought about in relation to the losses or cost of transitioning. The therapist is attempting to bring in different aspects of the patient's personality. This can often be represented through the patient's wish to change names or change schools. While conflicts with the young person over what they are called may be unproductive, the therapist must keep in mind the natal sex and identity of the individual. For example, if the young person wants to change their name from Joanne to John, the therapist should try to keep in mind what Joanne represents and why she is felt to be so unwanted or disliked. The little girl Joanne has existed thus far and is important, so her body and identity need to be considered and kept in mind. Attempts to eradicate unwanted aspects of the self are universally employed by all humans, but it is not really possible as discarded parts of the self tend to re-emerge, particularly when the ego is under pressure.

Mental health is based on an ability to integrate various aspects of the self, while differentiating between psychotic and non-psychotic forms of thought. We may not be able entirely to eradicate our omnipotent phantasies, but it is helpful if one can recognise the difference between reality-based thought and wishful thinking. Many detransitioners report that at some (more hidden) level of their mind, they knew they had doubts that might contradict their beliefs and ideas about transition, but they reflect that they needed an adult to address this split-off aspect of their mind and to point out their double bookkeeping in order to allow that part of themselves to be given permission to emerge. This is the therapeutic task as the therapist identifies and supports silent and hidden aspects of the self that are anxious about the implications of transition.

The movement between fluid and rigid states of mind

In our clinical experience, the young person goes through often long phases of maintaining their fixed belief (that they need to transition) while occasionally opening up and exploring their feelings in the therapy, but this is usually followed by a retreat into a fixed state of mind. At these times, the therapist must try to respect the defences and wait for the patient to re-emerge. The grievances in relation to parental figures will emerge in the transference relationship, and the therapist will be asked to tolerate quite a bit of provocation, as their work with the individual is continually attacked and undermined by parts of the patient's mind determined to keep a grip on the current defensive solutions. It is helpful if the therapist can see the hatred or anger involved in these attacks as a developmental step. We need to appreciate them as evidence of the young person's desperate wish to keep their defensive psychic structure.

Many young people develop gender dysphoria as a symptom, in response to an emotional crisis or breakdown. This crisis usually occurs, as we have suggested, on the cusp of the depressive position, as the young person starts to integrate their experience, and fears of depressive guilt or collapse confront them. In many of the clinical cases presented in this book, there is an inability to fully attack the parents for their failings due to perceived fragilities in the parents, or due to the extent of the rage in the young person. The idea of transitioning may take the place of other sorts of psychological transition as a young person moves from the paranoid–schizoid into the depressive position, or from childhood to adulthood, or from pre-oedipal stages into the oedipal conflict. The role these developmental challenges pose to the person need to be explored and understood.

It should be remembered that any movement or interest in development in the therapy can provoke a negative therapeutic reaction as the patient believes their development threatens their need for support and treatment (Riviere, 1936). A negative therapeutic reaction can sometimes lead to a disruption or even a premature end of the therapy. However, accounts from detransitioners sometimes evidence that it can be that in these dramatic or angry episodes "a seed is sown" and this allows an ongoing positive therapeutic effect, where the person takes up the thinking they have started with the therapist, even after the therapy has ended apparently badly. This can actually be an after-effect of any psychological therapy where change continues after the ending.

Grievances towards parents

Most of us harbour grievances towards our parents for failing to provide us with the ideal mind, body, and/or environment. These grievances are often based on the belief that we would have been in a much better position to deal with life if only our parents had not, for example, favoured our younger sibling or given us large ears. Grievances towards parents who bequeathed their genetic inheritance and so failed to provide their child with the ideal self that could master painful psychic states need to be explored and understood. John Steiner, in a paper entitled "Time and the Garden of Eden Illusion" (2018), describes a phantasy of the individual returning to an illusory ideal relationship with the mother. This is often connected with an ideal time, place, or relationship in the patient's life before things went wrong. The grievance with trans patients is often expressed through the demand to change their given name as well as their given gender. Indeed, there are often conflicts over the use of names and extreme sensitivities to deadnaming and mispronouning. Changing the name chosen by the parents represents an unconscious complaint against them. They not only gave their child the "wrong body" but also gave them the wrong name. This represents a wish to kill off the individual created by the parents, creating instead someone who has chosen their own name and their own gender. This might be an expression of an underlying grievance against the parents for failing to give them the ideal self they believed they are entitled to.

This issue often becomes a sensitive one during the assessment as the young person insists on being called by their new name while the parents, or just one of the parents, may desist from this. The therapist is immediately under pressure to endorse the new identity. If they choose to resist, they are believed to be difficult and antagonistic; if they go along with the demand, they are thought to be endorsing the idea that the young person can change their identity and succeed in getting rid of their old self which is imbued with all their faultiness and damage.

In many ways, the therapist must find a means of relating that avoids unhelpful confrontations without colluding in an unhelpful manner. Indeed, we take the view that people can change their name, but they cannot get rid of the person they were. You can do surgery on the body, but it is mistaken to try to surgically remove a part of the personality. Psychological maturity and mental health are based on an ability to tolerate different aspects of the personality and intolerance does not help psychic integration. As part of the assessment consultation, it is helpful to try to understand what problems the patient had with their given name and what aspects of their personality they were wanting to try to get rid of by transitioning and what ideas they have of whom they are going to become. For example, what do they associate with their natal name and sex, and what do they hope will be achieved by acquiring the new name and gender?

We suspect that in many cases, thoughts of transitioning relate to these powerful phantasies of returning to an ideal state where the individual believes they will be protected from unmanageable feelings such as humiliation and shame. When the medical intervention fails to provide the ideal state the individual is seeking, it will inevitably bring disillusionment, self-hatred, and despair. The transition is viewed as an antidepressant, whereas detransitioners say in hindsight that they were using the idea of transitioning in order to get away from something in themselves or in their lives.

The importance of supervision

The power of the projective process is likely to have a noticeable impact on the professionals working with gender dysphoric people, since they can expect to have confusion and doubts projected into them which will then be dismissed by the patient as being irrelevant. Psychoanalytic supervision is an essential support for any clinical work, as the resistances are likely to provoke unhelpful, and at times, toxic reactions between the patient and the therapist. Supervision can turn a dyadic situation of projective gridlock into a triadic one where the supervisor offers a third perspective, thus throwing light on the misunderstandings and inevitable enactments taking place between therapist and patient. This can be particularly important when the therapist's thinking is captured by the patient's narrative and there is a collusion between the patient's wish to deny their own doubts and anxieties and the therapist's fear of disrupting a positive therapeutic relationship.

Conclusion

A thorough general assessment should aim to establish a picture of the young person's personality, family dynamics, cognitive deficits, and possible psychiatric disorders. Then an extended psychotherapeutic approach should assess and attempt to understand the meaning of the patient's presentation. Importantly, this includes an understanding of the family and social context in which the gender incongruence has emerged.

It involves an appreciation for the less conscious factors that underlie gender identity. This difficult psychological work can feel threatening, as it challenges the individual's often strongly held conviction that only a change in sexual identity can bring them the relief they need. Much later, the assessment should examine the issue of informed consent.

The fantasy that the body can be changed and sculpted as a way of being rid of profound psychological problems needs to come under much closer scrutiny. There is a great reluctance even to consider that the difficulties can be understood, at least sometimes, through the lens of body dysmorphia, where the individual becomes obsessed with a perceived physical flaw. Many children who are drawn to the idea of transition have a fragile ego structure that threatens to fragment if overwhelmed by psychic pain. And, like other individuals, they can experience daydreams in the vein of "If only I were …" to help manage the emotional struggles of day-to-day life. A trans-identifying child can become more fixated and invested in the daydream idea, and it becomes a belief that *if only* they could transition, all their problems would be resolved. Plastic surgeons are very familiar with patients who seek surgeries in order to erase or manage a psychological difficulty, and the ethical among them refer these patients to psychiatrists. Rapid medical and surgical interventions in those with gender dysphoria will leave any underlying problems completely unaddressed. Surgical interventions cannot remove all evidence of natal sex—which remains as a constant, and often persecutory, reminder of the continued existence of any unwanted aspect of the self.

Young people need help and support in coming to terms with who they are, as part of the maturational process. However, gender dysphoric patients often put enormous pressure on family, schools, and clinical services to join with them in the belief that to transition to the "ideal" body is the only solution to their problems. When the family or clinical service accepts this, often without sufficient exploration, the patient receives confirmation that their mind's problem of self-representation can be cured by concretely treating the body. The cost is that the individual is dissociated from their own body, treating it like a mannequin rather than a part of the whole self. Arguments made about encouraging the young person to discover their "authentic self" and demanding "the human rights of the young person" deny the dynamic and changing nature of human development. Children and young people's identity and their sexual attractions have the potential to change as they mature.

Whatever decisions are made regarding medical treatment, a thorough psychotherapeutic and psychiatric assessment is essential to be able to help vulnerable young people, their families, and their clinical teams make informed decisions. It is a process of opening a dialogue with the individual about their motive, beliefs, the issues they are struggling with—and, crucially, trying to understand the complex role of gender identity in their more global functioning. A clinician has a duty to protect, and this cannot be honoured without a thorough understanding of who the young person is and how they arrived at the place where they are.

Young people who present with gender dysphoria are looking for a powerful intervention because they have encountered a developmental hurdle or trauma that threatens to cause a psychic catastrophe. They want to be free from this and become convinced that transition will provide a solution to the problems associated with life. We all struggle to manage loss, jealousy, feelings of sadness, anger, depression, feeling inadequate, anxiety about aggression, and envy. We all need psychic defences that protect us from these feelings when they threaten to overwhelm us. In the end, all of us make compromises in terms of the way we try to deal with the facts of life and the problems they bring. However, these psychic compromises have unseen, long-term costs when individuals present with very fixed ideas about the "problem" and the "solution".

Therapists also need to support the part of the patients that may be denied or projected into others who voice concerns and doubts about the wish to transition. They need to see behind fixed states of mind to underlying conflicts, doubts, and anxieties. The therapeutic process involves bringing these concerns into the picture so that they can be thought about and the different aspects of the patient's personality understood.

Throughout our careers in mental health care we have been familiar with this type of clinical presentation; depressed patients feel worthless and suicidal; anorexics feel too fat and starve themselves; obsessional patients perform their rituals repetitively before other interactions. We need to show both empathy and understanding of the mental defences while also making objective assessments of the patient's difficulties. In our opinion this must also apply to patients seeking gender transition.

Patients with gender dysphoria need services that are protected from political activism; the professionals involved need to be able to work in an environment that is protected from political intrusion. A rigid "one size fits all" affirmative approach is unhelpful and potentially harmful. The rapidly expanding and poorly understood area of gender dysphoria in young people requires new approaches and a model to ensure a more clinically rigorous, balanced, and ethical treatment for this complex area. The enquiry also needs to be widened to include societal and political factors and this should be holistic and multidimensional.

We have not attempted to address all of this here and we hope that more expertise will develop in these other areas.

We are not saying our model is the only one to consider and we are sure we have not covered everything. What we reiterate is that treatments for people experiencing gender dysphoria need to be evidence-based on long-term, high-standard research studies and provide an independent and thorough examination of all treatment outcomes. The ordinary ethical standards of good practice need to be restored to this clinical area because our duty is first and foremost to "do no harm". We hope that, in time, some aspects of this book, connected with the current trends of the unquestioning affirmation model and the push towards medicalised treatments, will become outdated. We sincerely hope the ideas that we have offered might continue to be a helpful addition as a model for thoughtfulness and understanding for a person who expresses gender incongruence.

Afterword

We commenced writing this book just over a year ago. In this short time the clinical landscape of gender dysphoria, along with the political and social environments, has rapidly been changing.

As previously stated, we believe there is much yet unknown in the area and we do not think that ours is the only way to explain or understand things. Our aim is for this book to be a contribution to the treatment, support, and care of people who do not feel comfortable in their own bodies. As in all areas of life, the fashions of language change. This is particularly true in the area of gender identity, so if/when our language becomes outdated or politically incorrect, we hope that many of our ideas will still provide a model for clinical understanding.

Susan Evans and Marcus Evans
23 February 2020

Addendum

Useful psychoanalytic and clinical terms used in the book

The id, ego, and superego—Freud's structural theory of the mind

Freud (1923b) described three areas of the mind that work in dynamic relation to one another: Freud thought of the ego as the charioteer who must make the two horses which pull the chariot—the id and the superego—do what he wants. The id is the part of the mind that contains drives and unconscious phantasies associated with those drives; in contrast, the superego represents internalised rules and regulations which, Freud believed, were based on an identification with parental values. The instinctual forces emanating from the id demand satisfaction, but the satisfaction needs to be achieved in the context of an internalised social environment represented by the superego. The ego integrates perceptions and is aware of the nature of the individual's relationship with the internal and external world. In this way, the ego must deal with conflict and tolerate frustrations associated with the task of balancing the instinctual desires in a social context.

The ego needs to be able to bear a certain amount of psychic pain in order to tolerate the inherent anxiety and conflicts involved in being in relationship to others. It is important to stress that we all employ psychic defences in order to protect our egos from overwhelming psychological pain and anxiety. Indeed, these psychic defences are essential for healthy functioning. However, there are problems when overwhelming psychological turmoil or conflict drives the individual to employ primitive defences in a rigid way. Rigid defences protect the ego but interfere with its capacity to perceive and respond to the demands of reality. When the ego is exposed to too much pain altogether, it either collapses and cannot function, or it fragments. These concepts are fundamental to our way of understanding gender dysphoria, seeing it as a symptom of a fragile ego that feels threatened by conflicts and psychological pain.

Internal object

The internal object is a psychoanalytic term used to describe the internal representations of an early, significant person in an individual's life. When you find yourself talking to someone in your imagination, you are talking to an internal object (Freud, 1917e).

Unconscious phantasy and conscious fantasy

Psychoanalysis differentiates between phantasy which is used to describe an unconscious set of beliefs, whereas fantasy is used to describe conscious thoughts and daydreams (Freud, 1915e). Unconscious phantasy describes the mental activity lying behind conscious thought that structures the individual's relationships with his or her internal objects. The influence and consequences of unconscious phantasies are evident when the individual is emotionally upset or disturbed. Phantasies and fantasies can be in operation at the same time at different levels of the mind. Conscious fantasies are often underpinned by unconscious phantasies. A person can be aware of their own fantasies, but unaware of any unconscious phantasies behind this.

Mental defence mechanisms

Conflict is painful and it is often assuaged by various defence mechanisms which are used by the mind to try to eradicate a whole variety of unpleasant states of mind. Initially, infants rely on primitive defence mechanisms to protect themselves from unbearable states or feelings. However, during normal development, there is a tendency for individuals to rely less on primitive defence mechanisms as they develop more subtle and complex ways of protecting themselves from anxiety. The earliest and most primitive defence mechanisms include denial, splitting, projection, and rationalisation. Defence mechanisms only become pathological when they are used too much and/or become embedded in the personality. Mature defence mechanisms include repression, sublimation, and reaction formation (Freud, 1926d).

The type and strength of defences used by an individual may vary according to the amount of anxiety the individual has to deal with at any one time. For example, at times of high anxiety, the individual is more likely to resort to the use of primitive defence mechanisms. To some extent, a fluctuation between the use of primitive and more mature defence mechanisms is normal. In situations where an infant or young person must cope with high anxiety over a long period of time, his capacity to develop more mature ways of functioning may be inhibited.

The foundations of the individual's mind and the capacity to understand themselves in relation to others begins in utero and is built in infancy—the relationship between the infant and the maternal object or other primary carer providing the basis for this. The infant communicates to the parent through eye movements, sounds, and bodily movements. When the infant is distressed, he starts to cry and his movements become irregular, as the baby looks to communicate pain and discomfort. This is a communication to the parent to do something about a threatening pain. The infant is crying out and pushing the pain and anxiety out of his body and mind and into the primary caregiver, often the mother or father. The infantile ego can only cope with limited amounts of psychic pain and develops defence mechanisms to protect the ego from being overwhelmed.

Secondary sex characteristics

Features that appear during puberty in humans including pubic hair, widened hips, and enlarged breasts of females, with facial hair and Adam's apple of males, and change of pitch of voice.

References

Ard, K. L., & Keuroghlian, A. S. (2018). Training in sexual and gender health—expanding education to reach all clinicians. *New England Journal of Medicine*, *379*(25): 2388–2391.

Asch, S. E. (1951). Effects of group pressure upon the modification and distortion of judgment. In: H. Guetzkow (Ed.), *Groups, Leadership and Men* (pp. 177–190). Pittsburgh, PA: Carnegie.

Ayad, S. (2018). How I work with gender-questioning teens. Paediatric and Adolescent Gender Dysphoria Working Group. An International Discussion Space for Clinicians and Researchers. http://gdworkinggroup.org/2018/11/12/how-i-work-with-rogd-teens/ (last accessed December 11, 2020).

Bell, D. (2001). Who is killing what or whom? Some notes on the internal phenomenology of suicide. *Psychoanalytic Psychotherapy*, *15*: 21–37.

Bilek, J. (2018). Who are the rich, white men institutionalizing transgender ideology? *The Federalist*, 20 February https://thefederalist.com/2018/02/20/rich-white-men-institutionalizing-transgender-ideology/ (last accessed March 28, 2021).

Bion, W. R. (1957). Differentiation of the psychotic from the non-psychotic personalities. *International Journal of Psychoanalysis, 38*: 266–275. Republished in: *Second Thoughts* (1967). New York: Jason Aronson.

Bion, W. R. (1958). On arrogance. *International Journal of Psychoanalysis, 39*: 341–346. Republished in: *Second Thoughts* (1967). New York: Jason Aronson.

Bion, W. R. (1959). Attacks on linking. *International Journal of Psychoanalysis, 40*: 308–315.

Bion, W. R. (1963). *Elements of Psycho-analysis.* London: Heinemann.

Birksted-Breen, D. (1996). Phallus, penis and mental space. *International Journal of Psychoanalysis, 77*(4): 649–657.

Blanchard, R. (1989). The concept of autogynephilia and typology of male gender dysphoria. *Journal of Nervous and Mental Disease, 177*(10): 616–623.

Bonfatto, M., & Crasnow, E. (2018). Gender/ed identities: an overview of our current work as child psychotherapists in the Gender Identity Development Service. *Journal of Child Psychotherapy, 44*: 29–46.

Bränström, R., & Pachankis, J. E. (2019). Reduction in mental health treatment utilization among transgender individuals after gender-affirming surgeries. *American Journal of Psychiatry, 4*: doi: 10.1176/Appi.Ajp.2019.19010080.

Britton, R. (1999). Getting in on the act: The hysterical solution. *International Journal of Psychoanalysis, 80*(1): 1–14.

Britton, R. (2004). Subjectivity, objectivity, and triangular space. *Psychoanalytic Quarterly, 73*(1): 47–61.

Britton, R. S. (1989). The missing link: parental sexuality and the Oedipus complex. In: J. Steiner (Ed.), *The Oedipus Complex Today: Clinical Implications* (pp. 83–101). London: Karnac.

Campbell, D. (1995). The role of the father in a pre-suicidal state. *International Journal of Psychoanalysis, 76*: 315–323.

Campbell, D., & Hale, R. (2017). The core complex. In: *Working in the Dark: Understanding the Pre-suicidal State of Mind* (pp. 30–41). London: Routledge.

Cantor, J. M. (2018). American Academy of Pediatrics policy and trans-kids: fact-checking. *Sexology Today!* http://sexologytoday.org/2018/10/american-academy-of-pediatrics-policy.html (last accessed December 11, 2020).

Cantor, J. M. (2020). Transgender and gender diverse young people and adolescents: Fact-checking of AAP policy. *Journal of Sex & Marital Therapy, 46*(4): 307–313. doi: 10.1080/0092623X.2019.1698481.

Chew, D., Anderson, J., Williams, K., May, T., & Pang, K. (2018). Pediatrics. Hormonal treatment of young people in gender dysphoria: a systematic review. *Official Journal of the American Academy of Pediatrics, 141*(4): e20173742; doi: https://doi.org/10.1542/peds.2017-3742; https://pediatrics.aappublications.org/ (last accessed December 11, 2020).

Coleman, E., Adler, R., Bockting, W., Botzer, M. A., Brown, G., Cohen-Kettenis, P. T., & Zucker, K. J. (2011). *Standards of Care for the Health of Transsexual, Transgender, and Gender Nonconforming People* (7th edn.). Retrieved from the website of the World Professional Association for Transgender Health: www.wpath.org (last accessed December 11, 2020).

Costa R., Dunsford, M., Skageberg, E., Holt, V., Carmichael, P., & Colizzi, M. (2015). Psychological support, puberty suppression, and psychosocial functioning in adolescents with gender dysphoria. *Journal of Sexual Medicine, 12*: 2206–2214.

D'Angelo, R. (2019). Psychiatry and the ethical limits of gender affirming care. In: M. Moore & H. Brunskell-Evans (Eds.), *Inventing Transgender Children and Young People* (pp. 73–92). Newcastle upon Tyne, UK: Cambridge Scholars.

Dagny. (2019). Dagny on social media, gender dysphoria, "trans youth", and detransitioning. *Feminist Current*, June 4. https://feministcurrent.com/2019/06/04/dagny-on-social-media-gender-dysphoria-trans-youth-and-detransitioning/ (last accessed December 11, 2020).

Davies-Arai, S. & Young, T. (2019). Transgender children: A discussion. *Civitas*. http://civitas.org.uk/content/files/2399-B-Transgender-Children-WEB.pdf (last accessed December 11, 2020).

Dhejne, C., Lichtenstein, P., Boman, M., Johansson, A., Langstrom, N., & Landon, M. (2011). Long-term follow-up of transsexual persons undergoing sex reassignment surgery: cohort study in Sweden. *PLoS One, 6*(2): e16885.

Dhejne, C., Van Vlerken, R., Heylens, G., & Arcelus, J. (2016). Mental health and gender dysphoria: A review of the literature. *International Review of Psychiatry, 28*(1): 44–57.doi.org/10.3109/09540261.2015.1115753.

Donym, S. (2018). The new homophobic bridge to nowhere: child transition. *Medium*. https://medium.com/@sue.donym1984/the-new-homophobic-bridge-to-nowhere-child-transition-c621d6188d6e (last accessed December 11, 2020).

Doward, J. (2018, November 3). Gender identity clinic accused of fast-tracking young adults. *The Guardian*.

Freud, S., with Breuer, J. (1895d). The psychotherapy of hysteria. In: *Studies on Hysteria. S. E., 2*. London: Hogarth.

Freud, S. (1897). Letter 71. Extracts from the Fliess Papers. *S. E., 1*: 163–175. London: Hogarth.

Freud, S. (1910d). The future prospects of psycho-analytic therapy. *S. E., 11*. London: Hogarth.

Freud, S. (1911c). Psycho-analytic notes on an autobiographical account of a case of paranoia (Dementia paranoides). *S. E., 12*: 3–79. London: Hogarth.

Freud, S. (1915e). The unconscious. *S. E., 14*: 159–215. London: Hogarth.

Freud, S. (1917e). Mourning and melancholia. *S. E., 14*: 237–258. London: Hogarth.

Freud, S. (1920g). *Beyond the Pleasure Principle. S. E., 18*. London: Hogarth.

Freud, S. (1923b). *The Ego and the Id. S. E., 19*: 3–66. London: Hogarth.

Freud, S (1926d). *Inhibitions, Symptoms and Anxiety. S. E., 20*: 75 174. London: Hogarth.

Glasser, M. (1979). Some aspects of the role of aggression in the perversions. In: I. Rosen (Ed.), *Sexual Deviation* (2nd edn.) (pp. 279–300). Oxford: Oxford University Press.

Hakeem, A. (2018). Parallel processes: Observations from psychotherapeutic work with gender dysphoria. In: A. Hakeem (Ed.), *TRANS: Exploring Gender Identity and Gender Dysphoria* (pp. 70–79). London: Trigger.

Heimann, P. (1950). On counter-transference. *International Journal of Psychoanalysis, 31*: 81–84.

Helena. (2020). At what cost? Trans healthcare, manipulated data, and self-appointed saviors. *Medium*. https://medium.com/@helenakerschner/at-what-cost-trans-healthcare-manipulated-data-and-self-appointed-saviors-dc81c4be7ae2 (last accessed December 11, 2020).

Hogland, P. (2018). Insight into insight psychotherapy [editorial]. *American Journal of Psychiatry, 175*(10): 923–924.

Kalin, N. H. (2020). Reassessing mental health treatment utilization reduction in transgender individuals after gender affirming surgeries: A comment by the editor on the process. *American Journal of Psychiatry, 177*(8): 764.

Kernberg, O. F. (1975). *Borderline Conditions and Pathological Narcissism*. New York: Jason Aronson.

Kirkup, J. (2019, March 3). Is Britain FINALLY coming to its senses over transgender madness? *Mail on Sunday*. https://dailymail.co.uk/news/article-6765249/JAMES-KIRKUP-Britain-FINALLY-coming-senses-transgender-madness.html (last accessed December 11, 2020).

Klein, M. (1935). A contribution to the psychogenesis of manic-depressive states. *International Journal of Psychoanalysis, 16*: 145–174. Republished in: *Love, Guilt and Reparation and Other Works 1921–1945*. London: Hogarth, 1985.

Klein, M. (1946). Notes on some schizoid mechanisms. *International Journal of Psychoanalysis, 27*: 99–110. Republished in: *Envy and Gratitude and Other Works 1946–1963*. London: Hogarth, 1975.

Laufer, M., & Laufer, M. E. (1984). *Adolescence and Developmental Breakdown: A Psychoanalytic View*. New Haven, CT: Yale University Press.

Lemma, A. (2013). The body one has and the body one is: The transsexual's need to be seen. *International Journal of Psychoanalysis, 94*(2): 277–292.

Lemma, A. (2018). Trans-itory identities: some psychoanalytic reflections on transgender identities. *International Journal of Psychoanalysis, 99*(5): 1089–1106.

Levine, S. B. (2016). *Barriers to Loving: A Clinician's Perspective*. London: Routledge.

Levine, S. B. (2020). The gender revolution. In: *Psychotherapeutic Approaches to Sexual Problems: An Essential Guide for Mental Health Professionals* (pp. 81–98). Washington, DC: American Psychiatric Association Publications.

Littman, L. (2018). Rapid-onset gender dysphoria in adolescents and young adults. Available at https://journals.plos.org>plosone>articles (last accessed December 11, 2020).

Lucas, R. (2009). *Differentiating psychotic processes from psychotic disorders*. In: *The Psychotic Wavelength, A Psychoanalytic Perspective for Psychiatry* (pp. 125–141). London: Routledge.

Malone, W., Wright, C., & Robertson, J. (2019). No one is born in the wrong body. *Quillette*. https://quillette.com/author/william-j-malone-colin-m-wright-and-julia-d-robert/ (last accessed December 11, 2020).

Marchiano, L. (2019). Transgender children: the making of a modern hysteria. In: M. Moore & H. Brunskell-Evans (Eds., *Inventing Transgender Children and Young People* (pp. 56–73). Newcastle upon Tyne, UK: Cambridge Scholars.

McNeil, J., Ellis, S. J., & Eccles, F. J. R. (2017). Suicide in trans populations: A systematic review of prevalence and correlates. *Psychological Sexual Orientation and Gender Diversity, 4*(3): 341–353.

Memorandum of Understanding on Conversion Therapy in the UK (2019). London: British Psychological Society. https://google.com/url?sa=t&rct=j&q= &esrc=s&source=web&cd=2&cad=rja&uact=8&ved=2ahUKEwjGv6_x4c 3lAhWXTxUIHbjjAAkQFjABegQIChAE&url=https%3A%2F%2Fwww.

cosrt.org.uk%2Fmembers-and-professionals%2Fmemorandum-of-understanding-on-conversion-therapy-in-the-uk%2F&usg=AOvVaw0ZjHj2qq5ZgWppvs23ZZa3 (last accessed December 11, 2020).

Milgram, S. (1963). Behavioural study of obedience. *Journal of Abnormal and Social Psychology*, 67(4): 371–378. https://doi.org/10.1037/h0040525.

Money-Kyrle, R. (1956). Normal counter transference and some of its deviations. *International Journal of Psychoanalysis*, 37: 360–366.

Money-Kyrle, R. (1971). The aim of psychoanalysis. *International Journal Psychoanalysis*, 52: 103–106.

Moore, M., & Brunskell-Evans, H. (2019). *Inventing Transgender Children and Young People*. Newcastle upon Tyne, UK: Cambridge Scholars.

Oppenheimer, A. (1985). La sexualité masculine, ou comment s'en débarrasser. In: *Les Sexes de l'Homme* (pp. 125–138). Paris: Seuil.

Oppenheimer, A. (1991). The wish for a sex change: a challenge to psychoanalysis? *International Journal of Psychoanalysis*, 72: 221–231.

Patterson, T. (2018). Unconscious homophobia and the rise of the transgender movement. *Psychodynamic Practice*, 24(1): 56–59.

Perelberg, R. (2019). *Sexuality: Configurations of Excess*. London: Routledge.

Pilgrim, D., & Entwistle, K. (2020). GnRHa ("puberty blockers") and cross sex hormones for children and adolescents: informed consent, personhood and freedom of expression. *The New Bioethics*, 26: 3, 224–237. doi: 10.1080/20502877.2020.1796257.

Quinodoz, D. (1998). Termination of a fe/male transsexual patient's analysis: An example of general validity. *International Journal of Psychoanalysis*, 83: 783–798.

Rey, H. (1994). *Universals of Psychoanalysis in the Treatment of Psychotic and Borderline States*. London: Free Association.

Riviere, J. (1936). A contribution to the analysis of negative therapeutic reaction. *International Journal of Psychoanalysis*, 17: 304–320.

Rogers, C. R. (1951). *Client Centred Therapy*. Boston, MA: Houghton Mifflin.

Rosenfeld, H. (1971). A clinical approach to the psychoanalytic theory of the life and the death instincts: an investigation of the aggressive aspects of narcissism. *International Journal of Psychoanalysis*, 52: 169–178.

Rustin, M. (2018). Clinical commentary by Margaret Rustin, child and adolescent psychotherapist. *Journal of Child Psychotherapy*, 44: 132–135.

Scull, A. (2015). *Madness in Civilisation*. London: Thames & Hudson.

Segal, H. (1957). Notes on symbol formation. *International Journal of Psychoanalysis*, 38: 391–397.

Simonsen, R. K., Giraldi, A., Kristensen, E., & Hald, G. M. (2016). Long-term follow-up of individuals undergoing sex reassignment surgery: Psychiatric morbidity and mortality. *Nordic Journal of Psychiatry, 70*(4): 241–247.

Steensma, T. D., Biemond, R., de Boer, F., & Cohen-Kettenis, P. T. (2011). Desisting and persisting gender dysphoria after childhood: A qualitative follow-up study. *Clinical Child Psychology and Psychiatry, 16*: 499–516.

Steiner, J. (1982). Perverse relationships between parts of the self: a clinical illustration. *International Journal of Psychoanalysis, 63*: 241–251.

Steiner, J. (1993a). *Psychic Retreats: Pathological Organisations of the Personality in Psychotic, Neurotic and Borderline Patients*. London: Routledge.

Steiner, J. (1993b). Problems of psychoanalytic technique: Patient-centred and analyst-centred interpretations. In: *Psychic Retreats: Pathological Organisations of the Personality in Psychotic, Neurotic and Borderline Patients* (pp. 116–130). London: Routledge.

Steiner, J. (2018). Time and the Garden of Eden illusion. *International Journal of Psychoanalysis, 99*: 1274–1287.

Stekel, W. (1910). Symposium on suicide. In: P. Friedma (Ed.), *On Suicide* (pp. 33–141). New York: International Universities Press, 1977.

Swedish National Board of Health and Welfare and Evolution of the Diagnosis of Gender Dysphoria (February 2020). Prevalence, psychiatric comorbidity and suicide.

Van Der Miesen, A. I. R., Hurley, H., & De Vries, A. L. C. (2016). Gender dysphoria and autism spectrum disorder: A narrative review. *International Review of Psychiatry, 28*: 1, 70–80. doi: 10.3109/09540261.2015.1111199.

Winnicott, D. W. (1956). Primary maternal preoccupation. In: *Through Paediatrics to Psychoanalysis: Collected Papers* (pp. 300–305). London: Tavistock.

Withers, R. (2015). The seventh penis: towards effective psychoanalytic work with pre-surgical transsexuals. *Journal of Analytical Psychology, 60*(3): 390–412.

Withers, R. (2018). Be careful what you wish for: trans-identification and the evasion of psychological distress. In: M. Moore & H. Brunskell-Evans (Eds.), *Inventing Transgender Children and Young People* (pp. 121–134). Newcastle upon Tyne, UK: Cambridge Scholars.

World Health Organization (2004). *The ICD-10 Classification of Mental and Behavioural Disorders: Clinical Descriptions and Diagnostic Guidelines—Tenth revision (2nd ed.)*. Geneva: World Health Organization.

Zucker, K. J. (2008). Therapists with gender identity disorder: Is there a best practice? *Neuropsychiatrie de l'Enfance et l'Adolescence, 56*(6): 358–364.

Index

AAP *see* American Academy of Paediatrics'
adolescence, 97, 115–116
 affirmative model of treatment, 116
 anxiety, 103–104, 115
 childhood to adulthood, 97
 desire to transition, 57, 115, 133
 development, 99–100
 discussion, 115
 disdain towards authority, 100–101
 fantasies of, 103
 fear of adulthood, 99
 gender exploration, 101–103
 hatred of sexed body, 103–104
 identity control by enactment, 104–105
 immature ego, 101
 peer groups, 98–99
 powerful defences, 101
 psychic defences, 101
 ROGD teenagers, 102
 separation and rebellion, 98
 social media influence, 104–105
 split in family, 105–115
 trans-identified children, 113
affirmative approach, 6, 15–17, 116
 see also adolescence
amenorrhoea, 73
American Academy of Paediatrics' (AAP), 16
analyst-focused interpretation, 223
 see also therapeutic engagement
Anderson, J., 213
anxiety, 181, 183, 189, 223, 225–227, 241 *see also* adolescence; early development in context of family: psychic retreat
 absence of, 31, 208–209
 infant, 196, 199, 201
 parental, 61–62
 and puberty, 73–74, 75, 116, 118, 193, 203
Asch, S. E., 23
autogynephilia, 218–219 *see also* therapeutic engagement
Ayad, S., 209

belief-confirmation model *see* affirmative approach
Bell, D., 143
and Tavistock, 3–4
Bell, K., 5
Biemond, R., 16, 37, 203
Bilek, J., 33
biological *see also* psychoanalytic model; therapeutic engagement
realities, 212–213
sexes, 201–202
Bion, W. R., 66, 160
bizarre objects, 206
container and contained, 195–197
normal projective identification, 209
"On Arrogance", 160–161
split, 181, 206
Birksted-Breen, D., 179
bizarre objects, 206 *see also* psychoanalytic model
black-and-white thinking, 84, 85, 151, 165 *see also* emotionally unstable personality disorder; separation–individuation
Blanchard, R., 218
Boman, M., 213
Bonfatto, M., 213
borderline personality disorder, 151–152, 165–167 *see also* emotionally unstable personality disorder
Bränström, R., 204
Britton, R. S., 128, 165, 198

CAMHS *see* child and adolescent mental health service
Campbell, D., 139, 144
Cantor, J. M., 16
Chew, D., 213
child and adolescent mental health service (CAMHS), 194, 218
clinical pressures, 34–35
Cohen-Kettenis, P. T., 16, 37, 203

collapse of ideal, 152–156 *see also* emotionally unstable personality disorder
comorbidity and complex problems, 213–214 *see also* therapeutic engagement
comorbid mental health conditions, 169, 184–185
case study, 170–180
clinical discussion, 178–180
countertransference, 183
dealing with frustrations, 183
delusional system, 180–181
fixed states of mind and belief systems, 180
general discussion, 180–184
grudge towards parents' sexual relationship, 179
hated phallic identification, 179
initial consultation, 170–172
narcissistic castration, 177
overarching rationalization, 180
paranoid schizophrenia, 170–180
phantasy underpinning sex change, 182
psychotic patients' oscillation, 174
removing sanity or psychosis, 182
separation from mother, 171
sessions, 172–177
split, 181
third session, 177–178
withdrawal to depressed state, 178
concrete thinking, 204–205, 205–206 *see also* psychoanalytic model
conflict, 240
confusion of registers, 88 *see also* separation–individuation
conscious fantasy, 240
consent, informed, 5, 6, 27, 232
contagious social forces, 21–22
container and contained, 195–197 *see also* psychoanalytic model
control of identity, 104–105 *see also* adolescence
core complex, 216 *see also* therapeutic engagement

countertransference, 155, 158, 183, 207–209, 223 *see also* psychoanalytic model; therapeutic engagement; transference
Crasnow, E., 213

Dagny, 40, 104, 217, 241
D'Angelo, R., 75, 147
Davies-Arai, S., 4, 22
deadnaming, 148–149, 219
de Boer, F., 16, 37, 203
defensive structure, 96, 225 *see also* separation–individuation; therapeutic engagement
delusional system, 180–181, 206 *see also* psychoanalytic model
dependence on maternal object, 201 *see also* psychoanalytic model
depressed state, withdrawal to, 178
depressive position, 190–194 *see also* psychoanalytic model
desire to transition, 57, 115, 133 *see also* adolescence
desisters *see* detransitioners
detransitioners, 22, 39, 57–58
    case discussion, 55–56
    case presentation, 40, 52
    confidence and relationship with primary giver, 55
    euphemisms and intervention, 50
    first consultation, 41–49
    second consultation, 50–52
De Vries, A. L. C., 32
Dhejne, C., 213
diagnostic criteria, 31
disdain towards authority, 100–101 *see also* adolescence
dissociation from body, 86–88 *see also* separation–individuation
disturbed states of mind, 214 *see also* therapeutic engagement
doctor–patient dynamic, 33–34
Donym, S., 213
double bookkeeping, 227–228 *see also* therapeutic engagement

Doward, J., 213
dyadic relationship, 117, 166 *see also* excitement as psychic defence
and supervision, 116, 165, 231
dysphoria, 87

early development in context of family, 61, 75–76
    anxieties, 62
    case presentation, 63–72
    eating disorders and gender dysphoria, 72–74
    "helicopter" parenting, 62
    need for multidisciplinary team, 74–75
    "paranoid–schizoid" thinking, 75
    sense of self, 62–63
    sexual development, 62, 75
    "snowplough" parenting, 62
    triangulation, 70
    unempathetic parents, 62
eating disorders, 72–74
ego, 239–240 *see also* adolescence; emotionally unstable personality disorder; psychoanalytic model
    destructive superego, 161, 167
    immature, 101
    security and infant's, 189–190
emotionally unstable personality disorder, 151, 168
    black-and white thinking, 151, 165
    borderline personality disorder, 151
    collapse of ideal, 152–156
    ego destructive superego, 161, 167
    general discussion, 163–165
    hysterical defence, 159–163
    marsupial pouch, 166
    role of supervision, 165–167
    self-harm, 156–159
    split, 161
    therapeutic relationship elements, 167
    triangular space, 165–166
Entwistle, K., 33

excitement as psychic defence, 117, 130–131
  addiction to "dressing up", 118
  case study, 118
  clinical discussion, 127–130
  dyadic relationship, 117
  family consultation, 119–121
  hysteric patient in therapeutic relationships, 129
  individual consultation, 121–127
  phantasies of penetration, 118
  transexual ideal, 127–128
exploratory therapy, 18

facts of life, 200–201 *see also* psychoanalytic model
family dynamics, 93 *see also* separation–individuation
fantasy, 34 *see also* phantasy; unconscious phantasy
  conscious, 240
  of different self, 63
  idealised, 149
  of transitioning, 148
father/partner role, 199–200 *see also* psychoanalytic model
fear of adulthood, 99 *see also* adolescence
feminism, 24–26
fixed states of mind, 180, 210, 225–226 *see also* separation–individuation; therapeutic engagement
fluid and rigid states of mind, 228–229 *see also* therapeutic engagement
Freud, S., 147, 241
  countertransference, 207
  delusional system, 180
  The Ego and the Id, 192
  Oedipus complex, 198
  repetition compulsion, 147
  structural theory of mind, 239–240
  transference, 207

GD *see* gender-diverse
gender
  exploration of, 101–103 *see also* adolescence
  specialism, 32–33

gender-diverse (GD), 16
gender dysphoria, 29, 87
  affirmation model for care, 6
  in borderline states of mind, 164
  comorbid problems, 11, 75, 133, 151
  development and, 59
  DSM-5, 30
  eating disorders and, 72–74
  females with, 25
  informed consent and under age, 5
  medical categorisations, 29–32
  psychoanalytic model, 8
  psychological traumas, 7
  rapid-onset, 7–8, 213
  rise of, 13–14
  transition, 7
  treatment, 184
gender identity *see also* therapeutic engagement
  disorder, 29–30
  incongruence, 20, 211–213
  work, 10–11
gender identity services (GIDS), 3, 4, 5, 16, 29, 213
gender reassignment surgery (GRS), 218
GIDS *see* gender identity services
Glasser, M., 216
"good enough" mother, 190 *see also* psychoanalytic model
grievances *see also* separation–individuation; therapeutic engagement
  towards parental figures, 84–85
  towards parents, 229–231
group thinking, 23–24
growth development and anxiety, 189 *see also* psychoanalytic model
GRS *see* gender reassignment surgery

Hakeem, A., 85
Hale, R., 139
hatred of sexed body, 103–104 *see also* adolescence
Heimann, P., 207
Helena, 13
"helicopter" parenting, 62 *see also* early development in context of family

homosexuality, 24–26
hormone blockers, 36, 227
hormone treatments, 36–37
Hurley, H., 32
hysterical defence, 159–163 *see also* emotionally unstable personality disorder
hysteric patient, 129 *see also* excitement as psychic defence

ICD 10, 30
id, 239–240
idealised fantasy, 149
ideal self, 146, 211 *see also* therapeutic engagement
    mourning the loss of, 197–198
identity control, 104–105 *see also* adolescence
immature ego, 101 *see also* adolescence
incongruence, 211 *see also* therapeutic engagement
infant's ego and sense of security, 189–190 *see also* psychoanalytic model
informed consent, 5, 6, 27, 232
internalised
    function, 195 *see also* psychoanalytic model
    homophobia, 24
internal object, 240
International Statistical Classification of Diseases and Related Health Problems see *ICD 10*

Johansson, A., 213

Kernberg, O. F., 151
Kirkup, J., 14
Klein, M., 55, 164, 189
    infant's ego and sense of security, 189–190
    projective identification, 194
    symbolic representation and equation, 205

Landon, M., 213
Langstrom, N., 213
Laufer, M. E., 115

Lemma, A., 182, 184
Levine, S. B., 26
Lichtenstein, P., 213
Littman, L., 24, 202
Lucas, R., 167

Malone, W., 18
mania, 215–216 *see also* therapeutic engagement
Marchiano, L., 21
marsupial pouch, 166
mastectomy, 50
maternal preoccupation, 194 *see also* psychoanalytic model
May, T., 213
Memorandum of Understanding on Conversion Therapy (MoU), 17–19
mental
    defence mechanisms, 240–241
    health, 228, 230
    illnesses, 30–31
mental health professional (MHP), 156–158
MHP *see* mental health professional
Milgram, S., 36
mind
    disturbed states of, 214 *see also* therapeutic engagement
    fixed states of, 180, 210, 225–226
    fluid and rigid states of, 228–229
    schisms in, 86
misogyny, 24–26
"misuse" of pronouns and deadnaming, 219–222 *see also* therapeutic engagement
Money-Kyrle, R., 200
    countertransference theory, 208
    facts of life, 115
MoU *see Memorandum of Understanding on Conversion Therapy*

narcissistic castration, 177
negative therapeutic reaction, 229 *see also* therapeutic engagement
normal and pathological projection, 209 *see also* psychoanalytic model

INDEX

normal maternal preoccupation, 199
  see also psychoanalytic model
oedipal triangle, 127, 198 *see also*
  psychoanalytic model
Oppenheimer, A., 177, 179, 182

Pachankis, J. E., 204
Pang, K., 213
paranoid–schizoid *see also* black-
  and-white thinking; early
  development in context of
  family; psychoanalytic model;
  therapeutic engagement
  and depressive positions, 189–194
  position, 190
  thinking, 75, 225
paranoid schizophrenia, 170–180
parasuicide, 135
parental homophobia, 24
pathological projective identification,
  209
Patterson, T., 213
peer groups, 98–99 *see also* adolescence
penis envy, 26, 201 *see also*
  psychoanalytic model
perceived self, 211 *see also* therapeutic
  engagement
Perelberg, R., 88
phallic symbol, 179, 219
phantasy, 34 *see also* excitement as
  psychic defence; fantasy;
  unconscious phantasy
  of penetration, 118
Pilgrim, D., 33
political activism, 22–23
pressure, professional, 27–28, 34–35
primary maternal preoccupation, 194
  see also psychoanalytic model
primitive defence, 196 *see also*
  psychoanalytic model
  mechanism, 241
projection
  normal and pathological, 209
    see also psychoanalytic model
  of unwanted feelings, 87 *see also*
    separation–individuation

projective identification, 194 *see also*
  psychoanalytic model
  normal and pathological, 209
psychic *see also* adolescence; excitement
  as psychic defence;
  psychoanalytic model;
  separation–individuation
  defence, 101, 117, 190
  pain, 204
  retreat, 83, 95, 203–204
  states, 95
psychoanalytic model, 8, 11–12, 189
  attack on differences between
    generations, 202–203
  attitude of "non-questioning
    certainty", 194
  biological sexes, 201–202
  bizarre objects, 206
  concrete thinking, 204–205
  container and contained, 195–197
  delusional system, 206
  dependence on maternal object, 201
  depressive position, 190–194
  facts of life, 200–201
  "good enough" mother, 190
  growth development and anxiety,
    189
  infant's ego and sense of security,
    189–190
  internalised function, 195
  mourning the loss of ideal self,
    197–198
  normal and pathological projection,
    209
  normal maternal preoccupation,
    199
  oedipal triangle and thinking, 198
  paranoid–schizoid and depressive
    positions, 189–194
  paranoid–schizoid position, 190
  penis envy, 201
  primary maternal preoccupation,
    194
  primitive defences, 196
  projective identification, 194
  psychic pain, 204
  psychic retreats, 203–204

INDEX

psychotic and non-psychotic parts of mind, 206–207
puberty, 193
questions about sexual development, 193
role of father/partner, 199–200
separation from mother, 192
split, 190, 206
symbolisation and concrete thinking, 205–206
thinking, 193
third object, 198
transference and countertransference, 207–209
value for psychodynamic work, 209–210
psychobabble, 9
psychological traumas, 7
psychotic and non-psychotic mind, 206–207 *see also* psychoanalytic model
puberty, 193

Quinodoz, D., 178

rapid-onset gender dysphoria (ROGD), 7–8, 24, 102, 213 *see also* adolescence
teenagers, 102
reaction to rejection, 88 *see also* separation–individuation
discussion of assessment, 92–93
individual assessment, 90–91
reality-testing, 146 *see also* suicidal ideation
regretters *see* detransitioners
repetition compulsion, 147 *see also* suicidal ideation
Rey, H., 174
Riviere, J., 229
Robertson, J., 18
ROGD *see* rapid-onset gender dysphoria
Rogers, C. R., 211
Rosenfeld, H., 72, 143
Rustin, M., 213

schisms in mind, 86 *see also* separation–individuation
Scull, A., 30
secondary sex characteristics, 75, 241 *see also* early development in context of family
Segal, H., 205
self, 146 *see also* early development in context of family; emotionally unstable personality disorder classification of "trans identity", 20
harm, 156–159
perceived and ideal, 211
sense of, 62–63
separation *see also* adolescence; separation–individuation; therapeutic engagement
anxiety, 216
from mother, 95, 171, 192
and rebellion, 98
separation–individuation, 77, 94–96
assessing comorbid factors, 94
"black-and-white" thinking, 84, 85
confusion of registers, 88
defensive structure, 96
dissociation from body, 86–88
family dynamics in assessment process, 93
grievances towards parental figures, 84–85
projection of unwanted feelings, 87
psychic retreat, 78–86, 95
reaction to rejection, 88–93
schisms in mind, 86
separation from mother, 95
sexual development, 25, 62 *see also* early development in context of family; psychoanalytic model
questions, 193
"snowplough" parenting, 62 *see also* early development in context of family
social *see also* adolescence; therapeutic engagement
contagion, 21
media influence, 19–21, 104–105
stereotypes, 224

257

societal, cultural, and political trends and clinical environment, 13
AAP policy statement on affirmation, 16
affirmative approach, 15–17
anxiety-provoking challenge, 25
clinical environment, 26–27
clinical pressures, 34–35
contagious social forces, 21–22
doctor–patient dynamic, 33–34
fear of accusation of "transphobia", 15
financial and ethical conflicts, 35–36
gender identity incongruence, 20
gender specialism, 32–33
goal of exploratory therapy, 18
homosexuality, misogyny, and feminism, 24–26
hormone treatments, 36–37
ICD 10, 30
internalised homophobia, 24
Memorandum of Understanding on Conversion Therapy, 17–19
medical categorisations, 29–32
learning the script, 28–29
parental homophobia, 24
political activism, 22–23
power of transgender identifying groups, 22
pressure on professional, 27–28, 34–35
psychological forces in group thinking, 23–24
psychological influence of transgender websites, 21
rivalry, envy, and difference between sexes, 26
satisfaction surveys, 33
self-classification of "trans identity", 20
social media influence, 19–21
trans medicine, 34
treatment models, 28
workload pressure, 35–36
specialist gender services, 10–11

Stekel, W., 135
suicidal ideation, 135, 149–150
 assessing patients with, 147
 case discussion, 146–148
 case study, 136–148
 fantasy of transitioning, 148
 idealised fantasy, 149
 ideal self, 146
 managing harsher superego, 146
 reality-testing, 146
 repetition compulsion, 147
 sessions, 136–144
 symbolic meaning of "deadnaming", 148–149
 third session, 144–146
 threats of suicide, 149–150
 unconscious suicide phantasy, 144
 suicide, 135, 144, 147, 149
 superego, 146, 147, 161, 167, 239–240
 supervision, 116, 128, 131, 168, 208–209
 see also emotionally unstable personality disorder; therapeutic engagement
 groups, 156–160, 162–163
 importance of, 231
 role of, 165–167
 symbolisation and concrete thinking, 205–206 see also psychoanalytic model

Tanner stage, 2, 36
Tavistock Clinic

split, 161, 181, 206 see also adolescence; emotionally unstable personality disorder; psychoanalytic model; therapeutic engagement
in family, 105–115
between ideal and bad mother, 190
off sexuality, 226–227
states of mind, 227–228
Steensma, T. D., 16, 37, 203
Steiner, J., 73, 166, 167, 178, 183
psychic retreat, 203
"Time and the Garden of Eden Illusion", 230